The New Populist Reader

The New
Populist Reader

Edited by
Karl G. Trautman

Westport, Connecticut
London

Library of Congress Cataloging-in-Publication Data

The new populist reader / edited by Karl G. Trautman.
    p. cm.
    Includes bibliographical references and index.
    ISBN 0–275–96023–4 (alk. paper).—ISBN 0–275–96024–2 (pbk. :
alk. paper)
    1. Political planning—United States. 2. Populism—United States.
3. Elite (Social sciences)—United States. 4. United States—
Politics and government—1993– 5. United States—Economic
policy—1993– 6. United States—Social policy—1993– I. Trautman,
Karl G., 1960– .
    JK468.P64N49   1997
    320.973—dc21   97–11072

British Library Cataloguing in Publication Data is available.

Library of Congress Catalog Card Number: 97–11072
ISBN: 0–275–96023–4
    0–275–96024–2 (pbk.)

First published in 1997

Praeger Publishers, 88 Post Road West, Westport, CT 06881
An imprint of Greenwood Publishing Group, Inc.

Printed in the United States of America

The paper used in this book complies with the
Permanent Paper Standard issued by the National
Information Standards Organization (Z39.48–1984).

10 9 8 7 6 5 4 3 2 1

Contents

Acknowledgments   xi
Introduction   xiii

Chapter 1   Contemporary Economic Populism   1

Chapter 2   Questioning Free Trade: Potential Implications of
             GATT   3

             ''Free Trade and Federalism'' by William T. Waren,
             State Legislatures, May 1996

Chapter 3   Supply and Demand Skewed: The Market Dynamic
             Misrepresented   12

             ''How Copper Came a Cropper'' by Paul R.
             Krugman, *Slate*, July 26, 1996

             ''Gambling on Agriculture's Future'' by A. V. Krebs,
             The Progressive Populist, July 1996

Chapter 4   The 1996 Telecommunications Bill: What Forces
             Shaped the Law   21

             ''The Tele-Barons: Media Moguls Rewrite the Law
             and Rewire the Country'' by Jonathan Tasini, *The
             Washington Post*, February 4, 1996

Chapter 5   Legal Reform, Small Business, and the ADA   27

            "Unreasonable Accommodation: The Case Against
            the Americans with Disabilities Act" by Brian
            Doherty, *REASON*, August/September 1995

Chapter 6   Opening Up the Fed: Democratization of National
            Economic Policy—Economic Élites versus the Public
            Right to Know   39

            "Statement of Ralph Nader on the Nomination of
            Alan Greenspan as Chairman of the Federal Reserve
            Board before the U.S. Senate Committee on Banking,
            Housing and Urban Affairs," March 26, 1996

Chapter 7   Corporate Welfare   52

            "Business' Clout Keeps the Government Breaks
            Coming" by Aaron Zitner and Charles M. Sennott,
            The Boston Globe, July 9, 1996

Chapter 8   Health Care   60

            "Wall Street in Hospital Scrubs: Managed Care and
            American Health" by Julia Raiskin, *Perspectives*,
            June 1996

            "Health Insurance Reform Act," Senators Joe Biden,
            John Kerry, and Howell Heflin, *Congressional
            Record*, April 23, 1996

            "In Praise of Unlikely Capitalists" by Joan Retsinas,
            The Progressive Populist, August 1996

Chapter 9   A Concluding Speech from a True Believer   71

            "Populism" by Senator Byron Dorgan,
            Congressional Record, February 23, 1996

Chapter 10   Postscript   80

Chapter 11   Contemporary Cultural Populism   84

Chapter 12   The Mass Media, Sex, and Violence   86

            "Remarks by Senator Bob Dole on Hollywood and
            American Values," May 31, 1995

"Remarks by Bob Dole, Republican Candidate for President of the United States, on Hollywood and American Values," July 30, 1996

"When TV Talk Shows Were Merely Tasteless" by Suzanne Fields, *The Washington Times National Weekly Edition*, June 2, 1996

"Willie D: A Gangsta Rapper Goes Straight Up on the Radio" by Cynthia Thomas, *The Houston Chronicle*, December 2, 1996

Chapter 13　The University Élite and Political Correctness: The Proposed University of Massachusetts Speech Code　　　100

"A New Speech Code Proposed at the University of Massachusetts" by Robert M. Costrell, November 6, 1995

Chapter 14　The Growth of Legalized Gambling: Unkept Promises at What Cost?　　　106

"The Diceman Cometh: Will Gambling Be a Bad Bet for your Town?" by Ronald A. Reno, *Policy Review*, March/April 1996

Chapter 15　Professional Football, Loyalty, and the Power of the Average Fan: The Betrayal of Cleveland—The "Browns" Move to Baltimore　　　114

"Fans Rights Act of 1995" Senator Mike DeWine, *Congressional Record*, November 30, 1995

"The Fan Freedom and Community Protection Act of 1995" testimony by Representative Martin R. Hoke on H.R. 2740, May 16, 1996

Chapter 16　Protecting Community from the Power of Unrestrained Economic Freedom　　　122

"American Capitalism Is Dangerous" by Michael Gray, *The Herald* (Western Michigan University), October 23, 1995

"Bucking the Establishment: Greenfield, Massachusetts" by Constance E. Beaumont, *How Superstore Sprawl Can Harm Communities*, 1994

Chapter 17   Reconceptualizing Work for the Twenty-first Century   134

             "Work: A Blueprint for Social Harmony in a World
             Without Jobs." *The End of Work* by Jeremy Rifkin,
             The Putnam Publishing Group, 1995

             "Career Seen as a Calling, with more Satisfaction in
             Work and Life" by James Ricci, *The Detroit Free
             Press*, September 16, 1996

Chapter 18   A Concluding Speech from a True Believer   150

             "The Conservatism of the Heart" speech by Patrick
             J. Buchanan, August 11, 1996

Chapter 19   Postscript   159

Chapter 20   Contemporary Governmental Populism   162

Chapter 21   How Money Corrupts Democracy: The Need for
             Campaign Finance Reform   164

             "Campaign Finance Reform" Senators Russ Feingold
             and Paul Wellstone, June 24, 1996, and Senators
             Robert Byrd and Fred Thompson, June 25, 1996,
             Congressional Record

Chapter 22   Power to the People: Instigating Congressional Term
             Limits from the States   177

             "Whose Government Is It, Anyway?" by Paul Jacob,
             University of West Los Angeles Law Review, 1996

Chapter 23   Opening Up the Two-Party System: Reforming Ballot-
             Access Laws and the Presidential Debates   185

             "The Importance of Ballot Access to Our Political
             System" by Richard Winger, *The Long Term View*,
             Spring 1994

             "Let Perot Debate" by Anthony Corrado, January
             1997

Chapter 24   Empowering Jurists: Democratizing the Judicial System   196

             "Unlocking the Jury Box" by Akhil Reed Amar and
             Vikram David Amar, *Policy Review*, May/June 1996

Chapter 25   Welfare Reform: The Importance of Responsibility,
              Work, and States' Rights   207

              "Conference Report on H.R. 3734, Personal
              Responsibility and Work Opportunity Reconciliation
              Act of 1996" Representatives Dave Weldon, Marge
              Roukema, Steny Hoyer, and John Kasich,
              Congressional Record, July 31, 1996

Chapter 26   Environmental Protection and Religion   215

              "Leading America Closer to the Promise of God's
              Covenant" Keynote Address by U.S. Secretary of the
              Interior Bruce Babbitt, April 11, 1996

Chapter 27   A Concluding Speech from a True Believer   221

              "The New Agenda" speech by Richard D. Lamm,
              June 1, 1996

Chapter 28   Postscript   229

              Selected Bibliography   233
              Index   235
              About the Editor and Contributors   241

Acknowledgments

This book would not have been possible without the help of many kind people. First and foremost, I would like to thank my family. Over the years, my mother was a constant source of good advice, encouragement, and political energy. My father helped give me the background that sparked my interest in politics and the personal discipline which helped me finish this book. My brother and I have always debated over politics and economics. Our discussions have helped me analyze my thoughts with more precision. My interest in law, and in particular how politics interacts with it, was sparked by discussions with my stepfather.

I would like to thank several special teachers: Joy Adler, Jo Beth Wolf, Jean Elshtain, and Mike Shapiro. By encouraging my creativity, they helped me explore a wide range of thoughts and ideas. Their willingness to allow me to follow my own path of imagination was a great gift.

I did most of my research for the book at Baker University. The university's generosity helped make my book possible. In particular, I would like to thank Harold Cordry, Barbara Chinander, John English, and Joe Fossati. Their friendship and advice were invaluable. Dawn Bennett helped me research topics in the early part of the project. Sally Gronniger did an excellent job typing the manuscript. I thank them both. My students provided a great outlet for my ideas on populism. Their enthusiasm helped sustain my energy.

Most important, I would like to thank my wife, Deb. She has brought me the love and support that made this book a reality. Moreover, the best image for my role in this book was provided by her. She said, ''Compare the book to cable TV; and you get to do the programming!'' I like that image.

Introduction

If you have bought this book for a political science class, you may be wondering what a "new" populist is. One cannot answer that inquiry without first understanding what populism is. At its most basic notion, populism is symbolized by political movements, sometimes represented by charismatic individuals, interest groups, political parties, and politicians. They claim that there is illegitimate power operating against the American political creed, and this power is exercised by self-serving, out-of-touch élites that apply it against the will of the majority of the people.

This definition presupposes that there is an American political creed that is easily understood and concisely defined. That is hardly the case. The American political creed is loose and ambiguous; it is defined by ideals that logically contradict each other if they are taken to the extreme. Individualism and egalitarianism and minority rights and majority rule are two examples. The Constitution was designed to keep these competing ideals in balance by separating power institutionally and by level of government.

Yet on another level our national political creed is simple and clear: Americans distrust power, particularly power that is visibly exercised.[1] The origins of this skepticism date back to the political atmosphere of mid-eighteenth century colonial America. When the British began to overtly exercise their political sovereignty, a sentiment began to develop that the British power, although legal, was somehow illegitimate.

Populism is expressed uniquely in different historical eras. Sometimes populist energy is directed at economic forces. At other times populists criticize cultural trends. Governmental power can also be the aim of populist reforms. Because populism manifests itself through different discourses, it is awkward to categorize. Wherever people see illegitimate power unchallenged, the potential for populism is present.

Political rhetoric is the usual way populists voice their discontent. Action is passionately demanded to stand up to élitist power. Because emotions drive both the leaders and followers, populism is difficult to systematically analyze. Consequently, reason and logic are not the most effective methods to understand populism's appeal. Instead, it is necessary to try to understand the political hurt of citizens, where the people feel America has gone wrong.

Before a concept can be researched and analyzed, there must be a certain level of agreement as to its intellectual premises: What exactly are we studying? One's ideology tends to distort the study of populism from the very beginning. As Joseph Schumpeter states: "Analytic work begins with material provided by our vision of things, and this vision is ideological almost by definition."[2]

Thus populism is used to describe both conservative and liberal political movements in the United States. In his 1996 book, *The Populist Persuasion*,[3] Michael Kazin chronicles the various by-products of both species of populism: from the anticorporate and agrarian Populist movements of the late nineteenth century to the anti-Eastern Establishment views of Richard Nixon and the "silent majority." Within the last several years, this tendency has revealed itself again. In the 1996 book *Storming The Gates*,[4] Dan Balz and Ronald Brownstein describe the antitax, progun, and right-wing Christian forces that elected a Republican Congress in 1994 as "populist conservatives." In the same year, Harry C. Boyle and Nancy N. Kari criticized Pat Buchanan's self-described populism in an article titled "Populists: Stand Up and Fight: The Era Of Phony Populists" in *The Progressive Populist* (April 1996).

Without a widely accepted premise, and thus a stable definition, populism has been largely ignored in the teaching of political science.[5] That is tragic because the forces of populism are intimately tied to the energy of democracy. If people are concerned enough to cry out against what they see as the illegitimate use of power, then they implicitly care deeply about the quality of their democracy.

THE STRUCTURE AND INTENT OF THE BOOK

This book divides populism into three types (economic, cultural, and governmental) so that the reader can understand how the forces of populism define the majority will and the élites who are thwarting it *differently*, depending on how particular parts of the American political creed are interpreted.

As part of its premise, *The New Populist Reader* questions the legitimacy of how power is exercised. Economic, cultural, and governmental power is examined directly, sometimes without the mediating context of conventional structures and widely accepted premises. For example, Chapters 1 through 10 analyze economic power from a point of view critical of dominant economic theories, such as free-market liberalism. Chapters 11 through 19 analyze cultural power separately from the constitutional protection of freedom of speech. Chapters 20 through 28 critically analyze the current state of our government, minimizing what government does right.

Economic populists question the actual, not just the theoretical, power of individual citizens in a world-capitalist economy. Economic élites are perceived as using money and power to shape public policies. Cultural populists see knowledge élites using their power to shape media symbols, images, ideas, and words. They also are skeptical of the power of individuals, families, and communities to resist images that they believe are potentially harmful to their well-being. Governmental populists question the ability of politicians to resist iniquity. For example, the movement for term limits recognizes the corrupting nature of public power while the crusade for campaign finance reform recognizes the corrupting nature of money.

A society structured on progress puts power into the hands of experts and professionals. The shrinking middle class, declining moral standards, and the constant partisan bickering are seen as examples of the failure of the professional class. Consequently, the financial wizard on Wall Street, the creative director in Hollywood, and the ambitious politician in Washington are blamed for these downfalls. More significantly, the institutions that they represent are seen as deficient. Progress has simply not lived up to its promise. Power is too often denied to ordinary people.

The book purposefully minimizes the positive aspects of economic freedom, artistic freedom, and political stability. The readings suggest that élites are hijacking these concepts and using them for their selfish interests. In particular, these concepts are brought up in political discourse to chill debate and stop political change, not necessarily to defend their historical truth.

The concept of the book assumes that the United States operates within a class system, where economic, cultural, and political mobility is severely limited. This goes against the widely accepted truth (or hope) that all Americans are free to rise up to their natural ability, no matter where they start in life. This concept is purposefully overstated in order to force the reader to confront the issues of mobility and class. Too often mainstream political science ignores these crucial issues and our political dialogue suffers.

It will be very difficult for populism to succeed as a unified political movement. There are simply too many interpretations of it. For example, an organization, started in 1995, called The Alliance, is devoted to strengthening American democracy by organizing and challenging corporate power. A headline given to a speech at its founding convention read, ''Populists Distrust Corporations even more than Government.'' Well, some populists do. Other types, like the populist-conservative leaders of the Republican House class of 1994, would strongly disagree with that statement.

The intent of the book is to understand how contemporary populist ideas correlate with citizen demands for democratic renewal in the United States. Understanding how citizens and politicians *perceive* the relationship between the wishes of the majority and governmental policies allows us to analyze the current state of American democracy with a fresh perspective. Freed from the limitations that traditional ideological categories put on American politics, *The New Populist Reader* allows you to

• Observe links between populist ideas which a strict adherence to ideology would tend to conceal.

• Apply discourse analysis to political controversies. Recognizing how problems are understood differently (through the language of economics, culture, and government) allows you to distinguish the commonalities and differences which make up the controversy.

• Detect the distorted power relationships that help explain why some feel that our government habitually disillusions its citizens.

By analyzing these different critiques of power, you will be able to apply your own judgment as to which critiques are more accurate and why. In the process, you will be implicitly discovering which parts of the American political creed *you* believe are most threatened and why. This brings alive the ideas of American democracy in a personal way, revitalizing the power and responsibility of citizenship to each reader. As Jeffrey Bell states, "Populism is optimism about people's ability to make decisions about their lives."[6] This book is structured on that optimistic assumption.

NOTES

1. Samuel Huntington, *American Politics: The Promise of Disharmony* (Cambridge, MA: Belknap Press, 1981): 75.

2. Joseph Schumpeter, *History of Economic Analysis* (New York: Oxford University Press, 1954): 42–43.

3. Michael Kazin, *The Populist Persuasion* (New York: Basic Books, 1995).

4. Dan Balz and Ronald Brownstein, *Storming the Gates* (Boston: Little, Brown, 1996).

5. The books which come closest to analyzing American politics in a populist mode are *The Irony of Democracy*, tenth edition, by Thomas R. Dye and Harmon Zeigler (Belmont, CA: Wadsworth, Dye and Zeigler, 1996) and *Democracy for the Few*, sixth edition, by Michael Parenti (New York: St. Martin's Press, 1995). Even though they do not explicitly analyze populism, they critically examine political power, thus allowing the reader a nonpluralistic interpretation of American politics.

6. Jeffrey Bell, *Populism and Elitism* (Washington, D.C.: Regnery, 1992).

The New Populist Reader

CHAPTER 1

Contemporary Economic Populism

The merchant has no country.

—Thomas Jefferson

The struggle between private wealth and public good is an age-old conflict in American politics. The nineteenth-century populists made this battle their primary focus for political change. Today, economic populists continue this fight. However, the circumstances are vastly different today than they were in 1890.

The most significant change is that the participants in the struggle are larger and better organized. Powerful corporations and governmental policy makers vie over who can better serve the interests of the majority. Big businesses use free-market ideology as justification for their place in society. Government tries to actualize the ideal of equality by consciously taking the side of the less powerful in its struggle with the forces of big money.

Ideologically, the contest is straightforward. Conservatives embrace business because they trust the market more than government. Liberals embrace government because they trust government more than the market. But ideological conflicts can mask underlying disputes. An open-minded conservative might recognize that select government action is needed to curb the excesses of the market. A liberal with an open mind might recognize that sometimes majority interests are served by opposing certain government policies and defending business interests.

However fundamentally, economic populists take the side of government. They do not accept how modern capitalism is evolving. The gap between the rich and poor, and the shrinking middle class, justifies their skepticism. Additionally, they see how the influence of money in politics helps determine who can enter, set the rules, and compete in the market. This undermines their faith in equality.

When American society looks to economic discourse to justify policy choices or distributional outcomes, the space for political action begins to shrink. Politics becomes associated with prohibited behavior and treated as illegitimate interference in the market. The movement for "free trade" symbolizes the triumph of this way of thinking: objective/rational economics conquers subjective/emotional politics. What price are we willing to pay for this? Chapter 2 analyzes some of the "fine print" that proponents of free trade usually do not emphasize: the threat to our federal system of government. Chapter 3 details how large amounts of money can manipulate free markets, either by institutional design or deliberate corporate action. The results often favor big business over small business.

Big money can also unjustly limit the amount and scope of information that we receive from the media. Chapter 4 describes how the 1996 Telecommunications Act, touted as a free-market reform, could potentially increase economic concentration in emerging communications industries.

Chapter 5 focuses on how the good intentions of legislation can unfairly discriminate against small business and local governments. In particular, the Americans with Disabilities Act is portrayed as an open-ended law that will eventually force many small businesses and local governments to spend unreasonable amounts of money to comply with.

According to economic populists, the heart of illegitimate power is the Federal Reserve Board. Chapter 6 describes why Ralph Nader feels that the board needs reforms. All the characteristics which threaten American democracy—secrecy, unaccountability, élitism, and separatism—are discussed.

Defenders of big business point to independence and fierce competition as positive characteristics that the marketplace rewards. However, certain corporations get special favors from government, effectively shielding them from the free market. Subsidies and special tax legislation give them advantages over less well connected companies and individuals. Chapter 7 takes a look at corporate welfare, and the difficulty Congress has in cutting it.

Populists strongly believe in individual responsibility. However, they also feel that there are basic societal responsibilities that should not be avoided if the market fails. Chapter 8 deals with parts of the fast-changing health care industry and the challenges government and charities face to meet citizen needs.

Chapter 9 focuses on reconnecting the historical legacy of populism with the current wave of economic anxiety that many American workers feel. While corporations have benefited enormously in recent years from governmental policies that have prioritized fighting inflation, and expanding international trade, other parts of American society have not. Modern populists, like Byron Dorgan, believe that government should include more consideration about how their policy choices affect the domestic workforce. Should increased business profits come at the expense of laying off productive American workers?

CHAPTER 2

Questioning Free Trade: Potential Implications of GATT

Since the beginning of the 1990s, there has been a growing worldwide movement towards liberalizing trade between nations. Described as "free trade," the movement gathered global strength as Soviet communism collapsed. "Free trade" has become institutionalized with the passage of the latest version of the General Agreement on Trade and Tariffs (GATT). GATT is designed to reduce obstacles to international trade. The latest negotiating session (the Uruguay Round) ended up establishing the World Trade Organization (WTO), designed to enforce GATT trade rules. A lame-duck Congress passed the implementing act after the 1994 election.

"Free trade" has been opposed for many different reasons. A fundamental objection is that it threatens political sovereignty; economic decisions are given de facto preference over political decisions. The reading analyzes how the WTO could infringe upon American federalism. Populists feel that shifting basic policy responsibilities away from markets and governments towards international organizations and agreements implies a lack of faith in democracy.

FREE TRADE AND FEDERALISM

WILLIAM T. WAREN

The World Trade Organization is intended to open up new markets for profitable exports, but is it a threat to state sovereignty?

Consider the following hypothetical: Auto manufacturers in Michigan, encouraged by the state and federal governments, develop a cheap high performance electric vehicle. No foreign manufacturer can match it. U.S. manufacturers begin to export their electric cars and trucks to Japan and Europe in large numbers.

As the United States begins to dominate the world market, European and Japanese governments suddenly impose a variety of new tax and regulatory measures. Britain slaps a 50 percent sales tax on electric vehicles. Japan, citing safety concerns unique to electric vehicles, imposes new regulations that would require the complete redesign of American-built electric cars and trucks. Germany bans the sale of most American electrics altogether on human rights grounds, alleging that some of their parts are manufactured in Mexico using child labor.

The United States brings a complaint to the World Trade Organization (WTO) in Geneva, Switzerland, charging that the new taxes and regulations are trade barriers inconsistent with the General Agreement on Tariffs and Trade (GATT) and is sustained on appeal. Under threat of trade sanctions, authorized by the WTO, the Japanese and Europeans drop their barriers. The U.S. auto industry booms. Thousands of high-paying jobs are created for American workers.

Far-fetched? Maybe. Maybe not.

This is the way the new GATT is intended to work. This so-called Uruguay Round agreement substantially strengthens GATT, providing for a World Trade Organization and new tools to knock down barriers to international commerce. Many state legislators believe the agreement is essential to boosting employment and economic growth in their districts. States are counting on export industries to revive local economies, and they are counting on the WTO to open foreign markets for those industries.

Imagine another hypothetical example. Say the Oregon legislature in response to environmental advocates passes a law reducing state regulations and sales taxes on electric cars and trucks to encourage citizens to buy the new vehicles. Only Ford, GM, and Chrysler manufacture electric vehicles.

From *State Legislatures*, May 1996
Reprinted with permission.

Germany, Britain, and Japan respond by filing a complaint with the World Trade Organization in Geneva, alleging that Oregon's policy discriminates against their manufacturers who export traditional gasoline-powered vehicles into Oregon. A WTO dispute resolution panel rules against the Oregon statute. When the United States balks at suing Oregon to preempt its statute, the WTO authorizes Germany, Britain, and Japan to impose heavy tariffs on a variety of Oregon goods, principally timber products. Oregonians employed in the forestry and wood products industry descend on the legislature.

Again, far-fetched? Maybe. Maybe not.

GATT CUTS BOTH WAYS

The new GATT is a two-edged sword. Just as the United States can use it to attack foreign laws and policies that create problems for U.S. exporters, so foreign governments can challenge U.S. laws at both the federal and state levels. The WTO will have the power to review state statutes and regulations and enforce trade sanctions if state law is found to be a trade barrier in violation of the agreement.

The agreement therefore raises a number of questions related to state sovereignty. Will the WTO frequently seek the preemption or coerced repeal of important state laws? Will foreign trade experts sitting on WTO panels have any understanding of how American federalism works or why state sovereignty is important? Will state laws be a convenient target of retaliation by foreign countries whose practices are being challenged by the United States?

State legislators have many grievances with the national government and the federal courts. Decisions often do not reflect local conditions and local public opinion. So does the new GATT exacerbate this problem? Does it lodge significant power over states even farther away in Geneva?

State legislators will have to answer those questions for themselves. And they will have to answer in light of the intended economic benefits of expanded trade and the imperative of avoiding a disastrous trade war.

Expanding Trade

The General Agreement on Tariffs and Trade, a multilateral agreement among 123 nations, sets the basic rules for international trade. The goal is to encourage free trade by reducing or eliminating barriers to international commerce such as tariffs, government regulations, taxes, and subsidies.

When GATT was established in 1948, merchandise exports by the United States amounted to 0.5 percent of gross domestic product, reports Joe Cobb of the Heritage Foundation. By 1993, such exports accounted for 11.6 percent of GDP in the United States. The American economy is no longer self-contained. According to Cobb, one in six American manufacturing jobs is, directly or indirectly, related to exports.

This growth in trade was one of the original goals of GATT. The architects of the agreement believed that the trade wars and protectionism of the 1920s and 1930s were underlying causes of the Great Depression and ultimately World War II. They theorized that GATT would lay the foundation for an expanding world economy and an increasing economic interdependence and unity among nations.

Since the war, GATT has been extremely helpful in reducing tariff barriers, says Cobb, from an average 40 percent in 1948 to 4.7 percent today. Even more important, GATT established a system of international law and arbitration to resolve trade disputes. A repetition of the disastrous trade wars of the 1920s and 1930s has been avoided.

Two Principles of Fair Trade

The GATT system of trade law seeks to reduce barriers to international commerce based on two principles: "most favored nation" and "national treatment." The principle of "most favored nation" forbids favoring the producers of one nation over those of another. For example, it forbids applying a 10 percent tariff of German wine and a 20 percent tariff on French wine, or applying a 10 percent tax on profits by Dutch firms and a 50 percent tax on Danish and Italian ones. The principle of "national treatment" forbids a government favoring its own citizens and enterprises over foreigners, such as requiring emission controls only on foreign-made automobiles.

The principles of "most favored nation" and "national treatment," of course, are riddled with exceptions and qualifiers. International trade law is often a morass of contradictory formulas. A major exception, for example, allows customs unions and free trade areas such as those established by NAFTA (North American Free Trade Agreement) and the European Union to set their own internal rules.

THE NEW GATT

The Uruguay Round is the eighth GATT round. ("Round" is GATT jargon for a periodic renegotiation of GATT rules.) Congress approved the new GATT by passing implementing legislation in 1994. The Uruguay Round agreement is the most ambitious attempt, to date, at international trade liberalization. It provides new tools to attack nontariff barriers to trade. It extends trade rules to important areas, including services, agricultural products, and textiles. Rules are tightened in such key areas as government procurement and subsidies. Most important of all, it establishes a World Trade Organization (WTO) with real power to enforce its rulings with trade sanctions.

State Impact

The Uruguay Round agreement focuses as never before on nontariff barriers to trade, such as economic regulations, taxes, and subsidies. Moreover the agreement extends for the first time to services. State legislatures are very much in the business of regulating and taxing economic activity, particularly in the services arena. And states are very much in the business of promoting local economic development with tax incentives, grants, regulatory waivers, and infrastructure investments that might be characterized as subsidies. A wide range of state activities and state laws might be subject to challenge if other nations regard them as discriminatory. Indeed, the European Union already has compiled a long list of state laws and practices to which it objects.

The second reason why states are vitally affected is that the WTO has enforcement power. Unlike the old GATT, the new agreement does not depend on the good faith of the parties. The United States has no ''veto'' over WTO decisions or its authority to apply sanctions. The WTO can authorize trade sanctions targeting industries in a particular state if the United States fails to comply with one of its rulings. The Uruguay Round explicitly requires national governments to bring ''subnational units'' (as states would be called in Geneva) into compliance. Each member-nation of the WTO is fully responsible under GATT to ensure compliance by regional and local governments. If, for example, a WTO panel rules against an American state law and is sustained on appeal, then the United States has only three options:

- To comply with the ruling

- To negotiate compensation in the form of trade advantages for the injured nation

- To accept GATT-authorized retaliation such as higher tariffs or other trade barriers directed at U.S. exports (and perhaps singling out the exports of a particular state)

Another reason for concern is that GATT standards of nondiscrimination are broad and subject to interpretation by WTO panels (composed of foreign nationals unlikely to be familiar with federalism concerns generally or the U.S. constitutional law of federalism in particular). Beyond basic standards of ''most favored nation'' and ''national treatment,'' GATT requires that each member of the WTO ensure that measures (such as taxes or regulations) are not more trade restrictive than required.

The GATT standards for nondiscrimination contrast with the traditional U.S. constitutional standards. The Commerce Clause and Foreign Commerce Clause bar states from discriminating against out-of-state and foreign commerce. But the Constitution also establishes a system of federalism. U.S. constitutional law has developed, through 200 years of Supreme Court decisions, a careful balance of federalism and free trade values.

Experts disagree about the degree to which the GATT standards will vary from U.S. constitutional standards. Professor Robert Stumberg of Georgetown Law School says GATT standards of nondiscrimination, although providing some weight to other valid public purposes, will tilt the balance more toward trade values. They are, he says, in effect a "Commerce Clause on steroids." Cobb at the Heritage Foundation takes a more sanguine view. He regards GATT standards as a good incentive for states to consider the economic efficiency of current and proposed public policies.

The Beer Case

The best example of the potential unpredictability of GATT nondiscrimination standards and how they may differ from U.S. constitutional law is presented by the *Beer II* decision (rendered by a GATT panel before the adoption of the Uruguay Round accord). In February 1992, a GATT panel issued its report on Canada's challenge to U.S. federal and state laws providing for the regulation and taxation of the beer industry. Many, perhaps most, of the challenged state laws clearly discriminated against out-of-state or foreign commerce and would have been quickly struck down in a U.S. court under the Commerce Clause or Foreign Commerce Clause. But not all of the state laws found to be discriminatory under GATT would have been regarded as discriminatory under U.S. constitutional law.

For example, the GATT panel found a Minnesota statute offering favorable excise tax treatment for microbrewery production to be discriminatory. Favorable tax treatment was conditioned solely on the size of the brewery. Minnesota's statute was absolutely neutral with respect to whether the microbrewery was located in Minnesota, another state, Canada, or anywhere else. Yet the dispute resolution panel in Geneva found the Minnesota tax preference discriminated against large Canadian producers. It is unlikely that a U.S. court would have reached a similar finding.

What the GATT panel did, in effect, was view Minnesota's law in terms of the economic competition between microbrewers, primarily in the United States, and large Canadian breweries, both of whom target the same market of upscale beer drinkers. Needless to say, *Beer II* alerted state officials to the possible effect of trade agreements on state sovereignty and American federalism.

States Alerted

When the Clinton administration prepared implementing legislation for the Uruguay Round agreement in 1994, the National Conference of State Legislatures (NCSL) and other state groups including the National Association of Attorneys General, the Multistate Tax Commission and the Federation of Tax Administrators expressed the states' concerns to the White House and Capitol Hill. NCSL told President Clinton and key members of Congress that efforts to expand U.S. exports through international trade agreements, particularly the Uruguay Round accord, can and must proceed in ways that are consistent with traditional American values of constitutional federalism.

In other words, NCSL was saying that we can have free trade and federalism—if we work at it. NCSL took the middle ground between those who urged opposition to GATT based on the threat to state sovereignty and those who regarded the potential preemption as an acceptable price to pay for concessions wrested from our trading partners in the course of Uruguay Round negotiations. NCSL argued that many, if not all, federalism problems could be corrected in the GATT implementing legislation and through the process by which the United States files "reservations" or exceptions to the agreement for certain categories of law and policy.

Protecting the States

Lengthy negotiating sessions between the office of the U.S. Trade Representative (USTR) and the states resulted in a compromise. It provides three basic federalism protections:

- Broad "national treatment reservations" or exceptions to the GATT provisions on trade in services that help protect state tax law from preemption
- Provisions in the GATT implementing legislation to ensure that GATT and WTO panel rulings are not directly binding on the states as a matter of U.S. law
- Procedural protections to ensure consultation with the states and a vigorous defense of state law

A high priority for state negotiators was the protection of state tax laws. A worst-case scenario is the prospect of WTO panels subjecting state tax laws to preemption, resulting in major losses of revenue or the need to fundamentally reconfigure state revenue systems. Relatively broad "reservations" to GATT, filed in Geneva at the request of NCSL and others, provide substantial protection for state revenue measures, at least with respect to trade in services.

An equally high negotiating priority for the states was to bar private enforcement of the GATT. This goal was largely achieved with new provisions in the GATT implementing legislation and its accompanying statement of administrative action. It bars private lawsuits to preempt state laws based on GATT. WTO panel rulings are not to be regarded as the foreign policy of the United States binding the states under the Supremacy Clause. Absent these protections, states would undoubtedly face thousands of private lawsuits challenging any and every state law, regulation, or tax as allegedly inconsistent with GATT. They also help ensure that GATT standards of nondiscrimination are not bootstrapped onto the many Commerce Clause challenges to state law that are filed every year.

The United States is allowed to sue a state alleging preemption, but the federal government is constrained by a series of rules related to legal procedures, evidence, and remedies. For example, the federal government must bear the burden of proof in court showing that a state law is inconsistent with GATT, regardless of the findings of a WTO panel. USTR is required, at least thirty days before the federal government sues a state, to file a report with Congress justifying its proposed action. (Presumably, few presidents will be eager to take political responsibility for suing a state to enforce a judgment on behalf of a foreign country.) Even in the event of an unfavorable judgment, states are protected from retroactive liability, a particularly important protection in tax cases where hundreds of millions in retroactive damages might otherwise be awarded to foreign firms.

The third category of protection involves guarantees that states are to be consulted and their interests protected when another country challenges state laws in the WTO or when a U.S. challenge could prompt retaliatory action against state laws. Among other provisions, definite time tables are established for notice to states of potential disputes that may affect them. Counsel for the state has an opportunity to advise and assist the U.S. trade representative in defending state law. USTR is required to consult with states on all matters related to state law.

So, has the problem been resolved? Maybe. Maybe not.

Clearly, the federalism safeguards in the compromise agreement will be helpful to states, assuming that they organize themselves to defend their sovereignty. Nonetheless, states still might face political and economic pressure to curb economic development programs and to reduce taxation and regulation of foreign businesses. The threat of trade sanctions against North Dakota's sugar beet farmers or Wisconsin's machine tool industry would get the attention of legislators in Bismarck and Madison. In such circumstances, it may not be necessary to haul the state into federal court and preempt a state statute by process of law.

TIME WILL TELL

Legislators, over a period of many years, will have to wait and see how sensitive the WTO is to the sovereignty of American states. At least for the next few years, our trading partners may be reluctant to directly challenge states. The prudent course would be to wait until the WTO is well established and more assured of its legitimacy. If they are smart, foreign firms that have problems with state subsidies, taxes, and regulations will seek quietly and discreetly to resolve them by meeting with governors and legislative leaders. They will find considerable sympathy for legitimate business concerns and for measures that improve economic efficiency. They will find very little sympathy, however, for proposals that would appear to place home-state firms at a disadvantage.

The United States is a great trading nation, committed at least for now to competing internationally. Unquestionably, the World Trade Organization can help break down barriers to U.S. exports. At the same time, the United States is a federal republic, one of only a handful in the world. The American people like to keep political power close to home—where they can keep an eye on it. The WTO is not going to work for the United States unless our federalism is preserved. Continued public support for trade liberalization will in part depend on preserving local control. In theory, the values of free trade and federalism can be balanced and harmonized. The question is whether they will be.

CHAPTER 3

Supply and Demand Skewed: The Market Dynamic Misrepresented

Supply and demand for a product or service is a basic concept studied in economics and marketing classes. How this concept is played out in today's business world is much more complicated.

The first reading describes how the Sumitomo Corporation manipulated the price level of copper by cornering the market. The reading investigates how huge sums of money were made when massive amounts of copper were bought and held off the market until the shortage increased demand, and then sold at a high level of profit.

The second reading describes how the international agricultural market operates by analyzing the Chicago Board of Trade. In particular, "futures" contracts (promises to deliver specified amounts of commodities on a particular date) are criticized as unfairly favoring large, corporate interests at the expense of individual ranchers and farmers.

Populists are skeptical that market outcomes are always legitimate. Do these readings bring out this skepticism? How can government regulations ensure fair market operations?

HOW COPPER CAME A CROPPER

PAUL R. KRUGMAN

SUMITOMO'S ROBBER-BARON TACTICS MAKE THE CASE FOR REGULATION

Last year, the world was astonished to hear that a young employee of the ancient British firm Barings had lost more than a billion dollars in speculative trading, quite literally breaking the bank. But when an even bigger financial disaster was revealed last month—the loss of at least $1.8 billion (the true number is rumored to be $4 billion or more) in the copper market by an employee of Sumitomo Corporation—the story quickly faded from the front pages. "Oh well, just another rogue trader," was the general reaction.

Thanks largely to investigative reporting by the *Financial Times*, however, it has become clear that Yasuo Hamanaka, unlike Nick Leeson of Barings, was not a poorly supervised employee using his company's money to gamble on unpredictable markets. On the contrary, there is little question that he was, in fact, implementing a deliberate corporate strategy of "cornering" the world copper market—a strategy that worked, yielding huge profits, for a number of years. Hubris brought him down in the end; but it is his initial success, not his eventual failure, that is the really disturbing part of the tale. To understand what Sumitomo was up to, you don't need to know many details about the copper market. The essential facts about copper (and many other commodities) are (1) It is subject to wide fluctuations in the balance between supply and demand and (2) It can be stored, so that production need not be consumed at once. These two facts mean that a certain amount of speculation is a normal and necessary part of the way the market works: It is inevitable and desirable that people should try to buy low and sell high, building up inventories when the price is perceived to be unusually low and running those inventories down when the price seems to be especially high.

So far so good. But a long time ago somebody—I wouldn't be surprised if it were a Phoenician tin merchant in the first millennium B.C.—realized that a clever man with sufficiently deep pockets could basically hold such a market up for ransom. The details are often mind-numbingly complex, but the principle is simple. Buy up a large part of the supply of whatever commodity you are trying to corner—it doesn't really matter whether you actually take claim to the stuff itself or buy up "futures," which are nothing but promises to deliver the

From *Slate*, July 26, 1996. Reprinted with permission.

stuff on a specified date—then deliberately keep some—not all—of what you have bought off the market, to sell later. What you have now done, if you have pulled it off, is created an artificial shortage that sends prices soaring, allowing you to make big profits on the stuff you do sell. You may be obliged to take some loss on the supplies you have withheld from the market, selling them later at lower prices, but if you do it right, this loss will be far smaller than your gain from higher current prices.

It's nice work if you can get it; there are only three important hitches. First, you must be able to operate on a sufficiently large scale. Second, the strategy only works if not too many people realize what is going on—otherwise nobody will sell to you in the first place unless you offer a price so high that the game no longer pays. Third, this kind of thing is, for obvious reasons, quite illegal. (The first Phoenician who tried it probably got very rich; the second got sacrificed to Moloch.)

The amazing thing is that Sumitomo managed to overcome all these hitches. The world copper market is immense; nonetheless, a single trader, apparently, was able and willing to dominate that market. You might have thought that the kind of secrecy required for such a massive market manipulation was impossible in the modern information age—but Hamanaka pulled it off, partly by working through British intermediaries, but mainly through a covert alliance with Chinese firms (some of them state owned). And as for the regulators . . . well, what about the regulators?

For that is the disturbing part of the Sumitomo story. If Hamanaka had really been nothing more than an employee run wild, one could not really fault regulators for failing to rein him in; that would have been his employer's job. But he wasn't; he was, in effect, engaged in a price-fixing conspiracy on his employer's behalf. And while it may not have been obvious what Sumitomo was up to early in the game, the role of "Mr. Copper" and his company in manipulating prices has apparently been common knowledge for years among everyone familiar with the copper market. Indeed, copper futures have been the object of massive speculative selling by the likes of George Soros, precisely because informed players believed that Hamanaka was keeping the price at artificially high levels, and that it would eventually plunge. (Soros, however, gave up a few months too soon, apparently intimidated by Sumitomo's seemingly limitless resources.) So why was Hamanaka allowed to continue?

The answer may in part be that the global nature of his activities made it unclear who had responsibility. Should it have been Japan, because Sumitomo is based there? Should it have been Britain, home of the London Metal Exchange? Should it have been the United States, where much of the copper Sumitomo ended up owning is warehoused? Beyond this confusion over responsibility, however, one suspects that regulators were inhibited by the uncritically pro-market ideology of our times. Many people nowadays take it as an article of faith that free markets always take care of themselves—that there is no need to police people like Hamanaka, because the market will automatically punish their presumption.

And Sumitomo's strategy did indeed eventually come to grief—but only because Hamanaka apparently could not bring himself to face the fact that even the most successful market manipulator must accept an occasional down along with the ups. Rather than sell some of his copper at a loss, he chose to play double or nothing, trying to repeat his initial success by driving prices ever higher; since a market corner is necessarily a sometime thing, his unwillingness to let go led to disaster. But had Hamanaka been a bit more flexible and realistic, Sumitomo could have walked away from the copper market with modest losses offset by enormous, ill-gotten gains.

The funny thing about the Sumitomo affair is that if you ignore the exotic trimmings—the Japanese names, the Chinese connection—it's a story right out of the robber-baron era, the days of Jay Gould and Jim Fisk. There has been a worldwide rush to deregulate financial markets, to bring back the good old days of the nineteenth century when investors were free to make money however they saw fit. Maybe the Sumitomo affair will remind us that not all the profitable things unfettered investors can do with their money are socially productive; maybe it will even remind us why we regulated financial markets in the first place.

GAMBLING ON AGRICULTURE'S FUTURE

A. V. KREBS

It has been called the nation's largest legalized gambling casino. With the statue of Ceres, the Greek goddess of agriculture, overlooking its Art Deco building in the heart of Chicago's financial district, the Chicago Board of Trade, along with its neighbor, the Chicago Mercantile Exchange, is at the hub of the world's hedging and speculation in agriculture commodities.

For the majority of the nation's family farmers, however, the Board of Trade and the futures market are the objects of scorn. "Want to know how you can make a small fortune investing in the commodity futures market?" one farmer asks. "Yes," another answers. "Start with a large one!"

In 1996 our nation's family farmers find themselves increasingly subjected to a commodity market driven by flawed government policy, speculators, and corporate greed rather than the free-market ideal of "supply and demand." Consumers also are paying higher prices for the food they consume each day, although those costs may be hidden.

To many, the locomotive engine driving this long train of economic injustices is fueled in the commodity trading pits of the nation's futures exchanges. In the trading pits of the Board of Trade and the Merc, contracts are traded on raw materials from wheat, corn, and soybeans to cattle, pork, plywood, and gold, among others, as well as stocks and bonds. These transactions are supposed to prevent violent price gyrations or sellouts in the nation's grain supplies, for example, which could result in famine and "economic anarchy."

Rather than insurance agents, however, the pits are full of high-stakes gamblers who place bets on what the price of raw materials will be at some point in tomorrowland. These traders employ whatever information and "ingenuity" that are available to them in an attempt to cover their bet.

The futures contract itself is simply a binding agreement to deliver or take delivery of a given quality and quantity of a commodity at an agreed-upon price at a specific date and place. A futures option gives a buyer the right to buy or sell a specific quantity of a commodity at a specified price within a specified period of time regardless of the market price of that commodity.

The purpose of buying and selling futures contracts is not to actually obtain or rid oneself of the commodity. Rather it "hedges" or "speculates" on future

From *The Progressive Populist*, July 1996.
Reprinted with permission.

price changes in that particular commodity. Of all the commodities traded in the various exchanges throughout the world, it is estimated that less than 5 percent of contracted commodities are ever actually delivered.

Hedging is most often used by commodity dealers, food processors, warehouse operators, and a select few farmers who seek to protect against potential losses from fluctuations in the value of a commodity that must be held in inventory or which must be purchased or sold at a later date.

This global trade in raw material commodities has become well over a $60-billion-a-year business, which confirms Karl Marx's observation that the trade in commodities is the "head waters of capitalism."

Ten years ago, while traveling with the Reverend Jesse Jackson through a number of southern African nations, the president-emeritus of the North American Farm Alliance, Merle Hansen, visited with many of those nations' agricultural ministers. He recalls:

"Sitting across the table from the Minister of Agriculture in Dar es Salaam, Tanzania, facing the Indian Ocean, almost halfway around the world, I asked the Minister how he went about determining how prices were set for their farmers. His answer was simple and direct: the Chicago Board of Trade!"

Two years ago the headlines and stories documenting the curious trading ventures of Hillary Rodham Clinton in the futures market gave the public a rare and fleeting glimpse into the élite insider manipulations, cunning and often unsavory workings of a multibillion-dollar industry that remains to many an enigma.

The publicity caused some members of the public to ask the perennial questions: In corporate agribusiness who wins? Who loses? Who profits? Who pays?

In sorting out the various "insider" schemes at work in the cattle futures market at the time the future First Lady was in the market, it becomes clearer and clearer that those who reaped hundreds of thousands or millions of dollars in a very short period of time were not the thousands of producers of cattle and the millions of consumers of meat.

For example, Mrs. Clinton's ability to miraculously turn $1000 into nearly $100,000 in ten months of futures trading did not obviously come about from, as she would later explain, following market events in the *Wall Street Journal*. Rather, her "success" coincided with a period when a select group of executives from meat-packing houses, grain companies, feed lot operators, and commodity brokers garnered tens of millions of dollars in an "insider" trading scheme in the cattle futures market.

Although there is no direct evidence that Mrs. Clinton herself knew of the scheme in 1978–79, it is apparent that she benefited from it. Meanwhile, it is estimated that between 75 and 95 percent of those individual investors who buy and sell in the commodity futures markets lose money.

Neal Smith, former Iowa Democratic congressman and onetime chairman of the House Small Business Committee, which in the late 1970s made the last really thorough investigation of the futures market industry, points out, "There are no rewards for honesty. This system leaves opportunities for manipulation and interplay with the futures market by those who have the information earlier than the farmer or rancher does."

Despite claims to the contrary by such corporate agribusiness giants as the American Farm Bureau Federation, actual farmer participation in the Board of Trade is limited to a select few, since most family farmers have come to have little faith in the system.

Missouri soybean farmer Wayne Cyrts believes the Board of Trade has failed to acknowledge farmer concern over those recurring complaints of unfair trading practices of speculative sellers, as opposed to those who have ownership of the actual commodity.

"As farmers we have no problem with speculators in the market," he points out, "as long as they have taken a position of production costs similar to that of the farmer, which means they must buy, or be able to produce, commodities before they can sell them—period!"

The fallacy of corporate agribusiness's so-called "supply and demand" argument in the futures market can be seen, for example, in figures obtained from the Futures Industry Association and the U.S. Department of Agriculture's Crop Production Summaries that show the effects of speculation in commodities.

Between 1989–1993 the yearly average shows that for each bushel of wheat produced by the farmer 11.2 bushels were traded in the nation's commodity trading pits. For corn the ratio was 7.1 trades for every bushel produced and for oats the ratio was 7.5 to 1.

For soybeans a staggering 26.1 bushels were traded for every bushel actually produced.

A long-time critic of this so-called agricultural "paper blizzard harvest," still called by some the "free-market" system, is David Senter, a former Texas farmer and American Agriculture Movement director who now serves as a family farm legislative consultant in Washington, D.C. He believes, as do most other family farm organizations, that immediate steps are needed to curb the manipulation and speculation which affect day-to-day commodity prices.

All that trading and speculation on paper can only lead to giving false "supply-and-demand" signals in the agricultural commodities market, critics say. That in turn pegs foodstuffs at prices that really have no relationship to the raw materials from which they are produced (and allows the food producers to set prices based more on their own relative position in the marketplace and their own profitability considerations than on the so-called—and mythical—free market).

"[Board of Trade] speculators depress the price of commodities by selling unlimited numbers of futures contracts, regardless of what we can produce or what's in storage. These paper contracts with nothing to back them up should be barred," Senter said.

In 1996, with one of the worst droughts of the twentieth century stretching from South Texas to the wheat fields of Kansas, U.S. corn stocks are at a forty eight-year low in the face of increasing demand for corn overseas. Futures contracts have helped to drive grain prices to record highs in a market that has been extremely volatile most of the year. Currently, the United States produces about half of the world's corn and controls about 85 percent of its corn trade.

Five-dollar corn and seven-dollar wheat are considerably less of a bonanza for farmers than Americans are led to believe. Farmers who signed contracts at last year's low prices to deliver corn and wheat to the market now must buy from dwindling high-priced stocks to fulfill their agreements.

Ranchers also must buy grain to feed their cattle and poultry while prices paid to cattle ranchers, the largest single user of grain, are at a ten-year low. "Prices are lower than costs of production of 95 percent of our cow-calf producers, estimates Chuck Lambert, an economist for the National Cattlemen's Beef Association. Meanwhile, Iowa Beef Processors (IBP), the world's largest meat packer, reports company profits have nearly tripled since 1993.

In the wheeling-and-dealing futures markets, "it's chaos," one Board of Trade broker admits. "This is really straining our relationships with customers who don't understand what's going on here."

Another trader aptly described the situation to a *Wall Street Journal* reporter: "You don't really know where you are from one minute to the next," Paul Georgy, president of Allendale Inc., a McHenry, Illinois, commodity brokerage declared. "And we have no recourse when a broker decides to take the big orders and ignore the little ones. We try to explain it to our customers, who are mostly the smaller guys."

The "big orders," like the big hogs at feeding time, are what most family farmers see as the major impediment to stability in the commodity futures. In many cases those "big orders" come from the giant grain companies—like Cargill and Continental Grain—and the mammoth commodity and food processors—like IBP, Archer Daniels Midland, and ConAgra.

In 1981 testimony before a House Agricultural Subcommittee reviewing agricultural export issues, author Frances Moore Lappe quoted one Board of Trade official telling a group of agribusiness executives, "Stability, gentlemen, is the one thing we can't deal with."

Both farmers and consumers want food security with fair and relatively stable prices, but grain traders and the brokers take their profits from market instability. It matters little to the commodity traders whether prices rise or fall. The profit lies in the price spread!

To ensure an environment of this "controlled instability," researcher Oscar Billey Martinson told *The Des Moines Register*, grain traders seek as much control as possible over networks of professional and trade organizations, links between individual employees and government agencies and interlocks with the boards of banks and railroads. They also make every effort to ensure they have corporate representatives on government regulatory boards.

For farmers the key to a stable futures market lies in limiting paper trades. From the general public's point of view, based on recent scandals in the industry, it is time to seriously question the many false perceptions that have been held for so long, fostered by the agricultural community and by their friends in the U.S. Congress.

It is precisely the lack of a proper public perception of the futures market that allows the industry to continue rhapsodizing about the so-called "invisible hand" that is supposed to stabilize prices. As a starting point in reforming the futures industry to help rebuild economic and political democracy, it is vital that the public have a true understanding of both the role the futures market serves in the nation's economy and the consequences of its abuses.

CHAPTER 4

The 1996 Telecommunications Bill: What Forces Shaped the Law

Recent technological developments have revolutionized global communications. The growth of satellite and cable television, the Internet, and cellular telephones are making communication potentially more diverse, quick, and portable for millions of people. The movement towards deregulating the emerging industries culminated with the passage of the 1996 Telecommunications Act.

Its purpose was to unleash market forces, which were needlessly hampered by outdated governmental regulations. In theory, the ''brave new world'' of telecommunications would produce products and services that would meet the demand of almost every consumer.

This reading challenges this claim by suggesting that the legislation was framed with a pro-corporate bias. The large communication corporations are equated with the ''robber barons'' of the nineteenth century, who essentially bought off legislators in order to write new laws which would protect their economic interests.

What affect does economic concentration in the media have on our politics? Do the corporate interests of ''big media'' more reflect, or direct, consumer wants and preferences?

THE TELE-BARONS: MEDIA MOGULS REWRITE THE LAW AND REWIRE THE COUNTRY

JONATHAN TASINI

An unprecedented string of megamergers sweeps through the media industry. AT&T puts 40,000 workers on the street. Major publishing companies demand that creators sign away rights to their works in perpetuity. Lawmakers put forth a radical overhaul of the nation's telecommunications laws. These events are all connected to the rise of a modern-day business élite that is casting a great shadow across the globe.

They are signs that, after nearly a century's absence, the robber barons are back. Not the same families that dominated the American economy at the beginning of the Industrial Revolution—the Mellons in finance, the Carnegies in steel, the Rockefellers in oil. These are new robber barons, but in several key respects they are much like their predecessors: accumulating tremendous profits, dominating their markets, and influencing the lives of millions of workers. The new pantheon of robber barons includes the Sony and Bertelsmann chieftains, Rupert Murdoch, Disney's Michael Eisner, Microsoft's Bill Gates, TCI's John Malone, Ted Turner, the Dream Works' titans (run by the trio Jeffrey Katzenberg, David Geffen, and Steven Spielberg) and Time Warner's Gerald Levin. With almost lightning speed they are consolidating in their hands a breathtaking amount of power.

According to *Broadcast and Cable* magazine, the top ten telecommunications players—Disney, Time Warner, Viacom, Murdoch's News Corp., Sony, TCI, Seagram (which owns MCA), Westinghouse/CBS, Gannett, and GE (NBC's corporate parent) alone control more than $80 billion in revenues in that industry. In most cases, they dominate at least a controlling share of their market, and in their grasp are the technological and economic tools to control where we work, what we do, how we get our information, and how we interact with the people we know. In effect, they are creating a new industry, combining cable, telephone, entertainment, computing, and publishing into a single, vertically integrated business that *Business Week* recently estimated could generate a trillion dollars in revenue by the time they're through.

The fast pace of change and the vast reshaping of these industries makes the

From *The Washington Post*, February 4, 1996.
Reprinted with permission.

long-term future still unclear. But there is compelling evidence that we should be more worried than we seem to be.

At first glance, for example, a casual observer might think the arena is more competitive than in the old days when three networks controlled television and AT&T was the only name in telephone service. But any current comparison must look at the panorama and scope of the new single industry that is being created.

Now, in an era of less regulation than there was before, we are molding a new, powerful oligopoly. After its $19 billion purchase of Capital Cities/ABC, Walt Disney doesn't just give us Mickey Mouse. Its Magic Kingdom sprawls across television stations; it controls a large share of cable programming, not just through the Disney Channel but also with its majority ownership of ESPN as well as its stake in the Arts and Entertainment Network; it owns half of the Lifetime cable network as well as cable operations in Germany, Japan and Scandinavia; it owns radio stations, newspapers and magazines all over the country; Disney has major joint ventures with Dream Works and two of the Baby Bells, Ameritech and Bell South; and it still owns its theme parks.

Besides the megamergers—Westinghouse's $5.4 billion bid for CBS last summer and Time Warner's $7.5 billion purchase of Turner Broadcasting—there are innumerable other ventures creating a vast web of interconnecting interests among the major powerhouses. Just last week, Microsoft and MCI allied to enhance their fortunes on the Internet, and Rupert Murdoch has now added cable news to his global empire. Murdoch, who once boasted that new technology would undermine authoritarian regimes, is forging an alliance with the same Chinese government that now censors all foreign broadcasts coming into the country. In the unfolding future, the new robber barons could control every sound we hear and piece of information we receive—whether television news, on-line data, feature-length films or prime-time action series.

Like the personal wealth of the robber barons of old, the riches of the emerging group are also staggering. Starting with Gates's $15 billion personal fortune (which *Forbes* magazine says is growing at a rate of $450 million per month), the ranks of the richest people also include Viacom's Sumner Redstone (with an estimated net worth of $4.8 billion); Murdoch ($3.3 billion); S. I. Newhouse ($4.3 billion); and Turner ($2.5 billion). In addition, many of the top brass in these companies take home multimillion-dollar salary and bonus packages that are many times what their workers bring home.

Like the Goulds, Morgans, and Vanderbilts, the modern-day robber barons are aided by governments that have so far failed to protect the public interest forcefully. The most recent and potentially damaging example is the sweeping overhaul of the nation's telecommunications law passed last week. To most of America, the bill has been portrayed as an important step toward unleashing the wonders of technology and freeing up companies to give us better service and more entertainment.

What few in the debate have been talking about, however, are consumers—

what the people who pay for this stuff might gain from this overhaul. Instead, what has been unleashed is a high-stakes scramble for control of an emerging industry, one that has generated what may be an unprecedented flurry of lobbying—including faxes, phone calls, dinners, and massive national advertising campaigns—by industries vying for a piece of the action.

Senator Bob Dole's opposition to the bill (over the issue of broadcast spectrum) obscured the broader picture: The conglomerates were squabbling among themselves over who would get what, but only a few elected officials challenged the legislation's basic premise—that by breaking down the current divisions the consumer will be better served.

"Despite the scope of its impact on their lives," argued Senator Bob Kerrey, hardly a radical, on the Senate floor last year when the issue was first heating up, "Americans neither asked for this bill nor do many of them even know we engaged in this debate. This one is being driven by corporations . . . successful communication companies treat technology as if its status were somewhere between King and God. . . . Rather than being a Contract with America, this legislation looks like a Contract with Corporations."

In a nod to their predecessors, the new robber barons have spent generously on influencing the legislative process to serve their ends—disparate though their interests may currently appear. Though there is no firm number, tens of millions have been spent on advertising and other indirect lobbying for the telecommunications bill. The Center for Responsive Politics says that of the $2 million major communications and entertainment companies gave to Democrats and Republicans in Congress during the first half of last year, one third went to members who sat on the conference committee dealing with the telecommunications bill. The two biggest beneficiaries were the two chairmen whose committees have greatest oversight of the bill: Senator Larry Pressler (R-S.D.) who got $103,165, and Rep. Jack Fields (R-Tex.), who received $97,500.

In essence, while the bill purports to increase competition and thus serve the consumer better, in fact it does little to limit economic concentration in media as a way of guaranteeing the flow of ideas and indeed will almost surely set off a new wave of mergers and alliances. Though in some pockets there may be more competition, a recent study by the Center for Media Education, a nonprofit center that has been critical of the changes taking place in the industry, shows that the new conglomerates will be given freer range to cross-own businesses in cable, broadcast, radio, print, and telecommunications; rates for all sorts of services are predicted to rise, according to the study. While some consumer safeguards are kept in place, the legislation significantly weakens or repeals many others. Under the new law, to take one example, if a company has a broadcast license up for renewal, it will face a far less stringent standard of proof that it is providing public interest programming.

Besides seeking to rid themselves of government restraints, the second pillar of the media mogul's strategy is to cut labor costs dramatically. By the end of the year, the telephone companies alone will have eliminated more than 200,000 jobs since 1992—while, in a familiar pattern, their executives continue to reap millions in pay and stock options. The irony is that these industries are being touted as the great job prospects of the future when, just as in other industries, these conglomerates are routinely engaging in widespread layoffs.

The move for dominance will also mean taking more and more control away from creators. In a sharp departure from past practice, writers, photographers, and artists are being forced to give up their rights forever to works that they create. It used to be that writers were paid a fee for a onetime print use. Today, an increasing number of newspapers and magazines (among them *The New York Times*, the Tribune Co., Times-Mirror, and others) are demanding all future rights to an article—and for no more money. The media giants could cash in on works for decades, without having to pay additional money to many of those who actually created the work.

The final piece of the new robber barons' strategy is that they, like the old robber barons, present themselves as only trying to do what's best for society, branding critics worried about the concentration of power as neo-Luddites trying to stand in the way of progress. Shaped by a broad, bipartisan intellectual and political élite including Alvin and Heidi Toffler, Al Gore, and Newt Gingrich, their mantra hums with words like "synergy" and "competitiveness." Indeed, most people are subtly seduced by the combination of the technology and its language. Think about it: the "information superhighway." But information is not like coal dust or toxic fumes; it comes only if you want to plug in and it imposes no physical danger. And, better yet, it's delivered to your doorstep by a highway, one of the enduring symbols of the freedom and expanse of this country. Just as any driver would cruise up the on-ramp leading to a highway, step on the accelerator and, with enough gasoline, go forever, everyone is being offered limitless travel on the electronic pathways.

But the easy access to the torrent of information on the Internet, a small slice of the electronic pathways of the future, has lulled us into a false sense that data will be free and accessible. Instead, the politics and economics of the Internet are not the model of the future. Rather than an open highway, the robber barons are building a series of "toll roads." Sure, we can count on getting directly through our TV sets video-on-demand, new shopping networks and other entertainment. But only those people with the proper skills, equipment and, most important, money may be able to plug in.

Obviously, someone has to pay for many useful commercial services. But the danger is that conglomerates will use their market power to drive out competitors and, like typical oligopolists, tacitly conspire to raise fees, limit service, and control supply. And we are not dealing with ballbearings or sneakers but with a future resource that will define economic survival and an informed citizenry.

I believe they are overreaching. When a tiny band of people seeks to hold the power to reach into every aspect of our lives, it suggests that we need a whole new approach to reining in capitalism in the global information age. So far, economic policy has been one-sided, skewed too much toward the multinational corporations.

Before it's too late, the public must snatch back the reins. Money flowing around the world at the command of a small group of financial wizards must be harnessed and reinvested in local communities. We need to demand action from political leaders to retool, update, and enforce antitrust laws whose genesis dates back to the abuses of the old robber barons. And no better reason exists for strict campaign finance laws, eliminating private money from the political system, than a quest to make sure our choices are not limited and controlled by a few information providers.

Obviously, arguing for more government action in today's political environment might strike some as odd. But it is possible that strong reaction to their avarice might reverse the move toward less government control. Given the choice, more Americans do not favor the concentration of power. They understand that we live in a profoundly unequal society, and that it's time we ask why.

CHAPTER 5

Legal Reform, Small Business, and the ADA

In 1990, the Americans with Disabilities Act (ADA) was passed into law with overwhelming bipartisan support. Designed to promote equality for the disabled, supporters claimed that another aspect of unfair discrimination was being legally prohibited. The reading contends that Congress did not anticipate some of the unintended consequences of the legislation. In particular, that ambiguous wording has allowed individuals to abuse the intent of the law by creatively "stretching" definitions of disabilities.

In addition, the imprecise wording has given federal bureaucrats de facto control over how the law is applied. Moreover, the sweeping scope of the law unfairly burdens businesses and local governments as they must financially comply with new regulations. Finally, the reading examines how the ADA, as it is now, is not necessarily the most reasonable method for society to help the disabled.

In what ways are the disabled similar to other groups (like racial minorities and women) who have been historically discriminated against? Does the ADA contribute to the "victimization" of our society? Why is it so difficult for politicians to address this issue in public?

UNREASONABLE ACCOMMODATION: THE CASE AGAINST THE AMERICANS WITH DISABILITIES ACT

BRIAN DOHERTY

... A kinder, gentler Republican president was in the White House, the Democrats controlled Congress, and Senator Edward Kennedy praised Senate Minority Leader Bob Dole for his key role in passing a new antidiscrimination law.

Any sweeping regulatory package in civil rights wrappings that wins the enthusiastic support of those two is bound to mean trouble. The law was the Americans with Disabilities Act (ADA), and it gives the feds veto rights over such issues as whether a prospective employer can ask a would-be truck driver if he has epilepsy; how far grab bars must be from the back walls of toilet stalls; what surfaces are permitted for subway platforms; how restaurant seating must be arranged; and dozens of other aspects of running businesses and city governments. The law has created an entire industry around interpreting it and, as the old cliché goes, provided plenty of work for lawyers, if not for the handicapped.

In theory, the ADA merely banned discrimination against the disabled in employment and public accommodations, and only forced employers and storekeepers to make "reasonable accommodations" that did not constitute an "undue burden." Unlike its predecessor law, the Rehabilitation Act of 1973 (which forbade discrimination against the disabled only in federally funded programs), the ADA gave individuals the right to sue over alleged violations.

No grassroots movement campaigned for the bill, but it was phenomenally popular in Congress, spearheaded by various congressmen with disabilities themselves or disabled friends or relatives. It passed the Senate 76–8, and the House 403–20. (Not even firebrand Newt Gingrich could bring himself to vote against it, though Dick Armey did.) Despite warnings about huge costs and runaway litigiousness, President Bush loved the feel-good law, especially as he prepared for campaign '92.

"The message from the Bush administration was not a subtle one: 'We're going to support this. You can try to block it, but good luck—you're not going to,' '' says business lobbyist John Tysse.

Facing such daunting odds, business groups settled for minor concessions, such as a limited right to do pre-employment physicals and the right not to hire current users of illegal drugs. But the greatest business victory in limiting the ADA was taken away in a civil rights bait-and-switch. The original ADA's remedies did not include punitive damages or jury trials, but the 1991 Civil Rights Act retroactively amended the law to include them.

Once the bill was in motion, a disabled person from every member's district was sent to lobby for the ADA. "You'd look out in the hall, and see fifty people in wheelchairs and people climbing out of wheelchairs trying to crawl up the Capitol steps, and logic and rationality go out the window," reminisces Lori Eisner, a staffer for Representative Tom DeLay (R-Tex.), one of the few congressmen to vote against the ADA. "The ADA is filled with lack of definition, everything's open-ended, but the attitude was, this is a feel-good thing, let the courts decide."

The "feel-good thing" is now reality, and it doesn't feel nearly as good as promised. The ADA has emerged as a prime example of congressional irresponsibility. While many of its specific results surely could not have been intended, the law's vague prescriptions and wide reach guaranteed it would become, and will remain, an expensive headache to millions without necessarily improving the lives of its supposed beneficiaries.

Many presumed benefits haven't yet blossomed, but the costs are all too real. Businesses as tiny as family-owned diners and corner dry cleaners are dodging regulators, in some cases paying tens of thousands in legal costs. Cash-strapped local governments are spending billions to comply with public-accommodation requirements. And the ADA's intended beneficiaries—blind, deaf, or wheelchair-bound Americans now on public assistance—are no more likely to be in the mainstream workplace now than in 1991. Most of the law's benefits have accrued to the already-employed, and then mostly to plaintiffs with back injuries or emotional problems, not to the sympathetic lobbyists who stormed Capitol Hill.

We've all heard ADA anecdotes that strike most people (except plaintiffs' lawyers and the judges who don't throw these suits out on their face) as patently absurd: the overweight fellow who sues for bigger seats in theaters, the guy who claims he brought a gun to work because of a psychiatric difficulty, the nightclub ordered to provide space for possible wheelchair-bound strippers, the woman who claims her offensive smell is a protected disability. Such cases aren't typical, however, and in most of them the plaintiff loses.

But they do suggest the opportunism the law has spawned, the potential scope of its definition of civil rights, and the difficulty of interpreting such vague terminology as "reasonable accommodation." Five years and two important elections after the ADA passed, it is finally possible to give it the sober scrutiny it deserved before it became law.

THE COSTS OF DOING GOOD

The ADA's total costs are impossible to estimate with certainty. All we can know about are individual cases, and even there most people don't want to talk. With a law that is usually triggered by activist complaints, says a restaurateur, "in a lot of cases someone is afraid that something they say is going to come back to them."

The law rewards "good faith" compliance, so it behooves any business owner or manager not to say anything publicly that might betray a lack of good faith toward the ADA or its application. Lawyers, pundits, consultants, city officials, trade group reps, even people forced to pay tens of thousands trying to obey the law, all emphasize they have no problem with the concept of the ADA, just the uncertainty and stringency of its application.

Richard Kubach Jr. is one of the very few victims of the law who are willing to talk about it. For the past twenty-two years, he has run Philadelphia's Melrose Diner. Opened by Kubach's father, the diner celebrated its sixtieth anniversary in March and attracts a clientele that ranges from bums to yuppies. It is a South Philadelphia landmark, with 100 full-time equivalent employees, doing about $5 million a year in business.

Kubach shows hints of Stockholm Syndrome when he talks about how helpful the local disabled activist group who challenged his diner's four front steps were in explaining to him what he would have to do to satisfy them. "Outside of the fact that it was through litigation, they've behaved in a favorable way," he says, sounding weary and beaten.

"It was difficult to get a real handle on what was required. I attended conferences in D.C. with top officials of Justice and different Departments responsible for overseeing the ADA, and in front of several hundred people they admitted they were unclear about the direction things would go," he says. The specific meaning of many ambiguous phrases in the law, such as "undue burden" and "reasonable accommodation," will have to be revealed through case law. But we don't have a lot of that yet—and it takes cases like Kubach's to establish it.

Compliance cost Kubach nearly a year and about $65,000. He was delayed by the harsh winter of 1993–94, which made the activists think Kubach was intentionally dragging his feet. But it was hard to build a ramp when the area in question is buried in ice, snow, and sleet.

The ultimate ADA goal of complete, unhindered access with no need for any assistance still isn't met at the Melrose Diner. Given the building's stainless steel exterior and sixty-year-old structure, a complete retrofit was impossible. There are still, for example, no barrier-free paths to the bathrooms inside.

And for all Kubach's expense and trouble, no hugely pressing social problem has been solved. Previously, says Kubach, "the problem of the disabled came up infrequently, but they were usually coming with people who could bring the wheelchair up the stairs, or we could send busboys out to get them who could lift them up. But it wasn't considered satisfactory to send people out to lift them, or bring them through the kitchen." Hence the lawsuit.

Restaurateur Blair Taylor isn't as sanguine about his experience with the ADA. He owns the Barolo Grill in Denver—"a very high profile, upscale, Jags-and-Rolls-Royces type of Italian restaurant in an expensive shopping district called Cherry Creek." As we talk the week before Valentine's Day, he is interrupted by nearly a dozen phone calls within an hour, seeking reservations for Valentine's Day. The Valentine's Day reservation book has been packed for a couple of weeks already.

Taylor is "a forty-year-old yuppieish kind of white guy. I'm a safe, wonderful target for these things." "These things" for Taylor mean nearly two years of legal conflicts with both the Justice Department and the city of Denver that ended up costing around $100,000 in construction and legal fees.

Taylor's troubles started in December 1992, just after opening the Grill, with a phone call from the DOJ (Department of Justice). "Apparently they had been peering in during construction, and noticed we hadn't done some work we should have done. They told me they were investigating complaints for non-compliance," he says. He wasn't immediately responsive: "The first week of running a new restaurant isn't when you have a lot of free time." Taylor insists that he could take a walk from his restaurant and find forty businesses in worse ADA shape than his was. He thinks he may have been under surveillance because of complaints against the former owner of a restaurant in the location, but "never can I get a specific answer from DOJ. They'll just say, 'No, Mr. Taylor was a horrible person.' "

Not exactly a horrible person, but DOJ civil rights lawyer Kate Nicholson, who worked on the Barolo case, does call Taylor "very difficult." She denies any malice or example-making, stressing that Taylor made continual promises to make changes by given dates and missed them all. DOJ isn't generally quick to sue, she says.

DOJ was unhappy with the four-inch step up to the door of the Barolo Grill, even though parking valets would always be available to help wheelchair users over the hump. Justice Department enforcers also didn't like the eleven-inch raised platform in the back of the Barolo, with nine tables in addition to the seventeen on the main floor.

A ramp to the platform was built, destroyed, and then rebuilt in response to Justice's complaints. The first time the ramp wasn't long enough for DOJ's very detailed building standards. The ramp is now the requisite eleven feet long and forty-one inches wide to navigate an eleven-inch rise, costing Taylor three tables worth of space in his usually sold-out restaurant.

The front ramp created a whole new set of problems, since it violated Denver city ordinances and required variances. "I said, 'I promised the federal government I'd do this ASAP, and city law won't let me do it?' '' says Taylor. "It was an eight-and-a-half month process through various city boards.

"The federal government at the same time are saying, 'Faster, faster.' They'll say Mr. Taylor went back on his word several times, but the city wouldn't let me keep my word." DOJ's Nicholson was uncertain of the details of Taylor's problems with the city. All she knew was, he was violating the law and wasn't quick enough to remedy things.

By February 1994 Taylor had city permits for his ramps, bathrooms, fire alarm, roof drainage, sanitary water waste management tests, new air systems, and strobe lighting—"a tremendous number of irrelevant things that were at bottom about putting in two ramps." The DOJ went ahead and sued anyway in April, since they still had some complaints.

"They're demanding a $50,000 fine, the maximum for a first-time offender. And the price tag to go into federal court is very expensive anyway. We're forced to go to a settlement conference. I say that I'm in complete compliance, and if I can just pay a fine I'd like to go home."

DOJ didn't agree. Its complaints included the handrails on the entrance ramp had two more inches between them and the restaurant's window than the law allows; the restroom grab bar was mounted two-and-a-half inches too far from the back wall; carpeting ended two inches before the patio door; and the wine storage room didn't have a ramp to its door (which was also not wide enough).

DOJ's biggest complaint was the back alley exit ramp, insisted on by Denver as a fire-safety precaution. Because delivery trucks use the alley, the handrails did not extend all the way to the bottom of the ramp, as the ADA demands; if they did, trucks would knock them down forthwith. The ramp was also steeper than the ADA allows. Since federal ADA regulations don't require this exit ramp, the feds decided Taylor should remove it. Disgusted, Taylor says, "You can't use common sense—would you rather use a ramp slightly too steep without handrails all the way to the end, or would you rather die in a fire?" The ramp is now gone.

The suit was settled with a $16,000 fine. Six thousand dollars of it went to protesters from Atlantis/ADAPT, a local handicapped-activist group that picketed the Barolo Grill.

"The federal government flew two attorneys for every meeting, gave them hotels, rental cars, meals. They came in from D.C. seven times," says Taylor. "We figure at least $250,000 was spent to force a restaurant in Denver to comply." He says the restaurant continues to average about one wheelchair-using patron a month—the same as before the case: "Nor have we ever once had a customer's wheels touch the ramp to the upper platform."

Mike Auberger thinks Taylor has an attitude problem. Auberger is a member of Atlantis/ADAPT, the local activist group who set up tables on the sidewalk in front of the Barolo, eating cans of Chef-Boy-R-Dee and drinking cheap wine with a sign displayed: "Accessible Seating."

"Taylor created his own problems," Auberger says. "It's real clear the contractor and owner violated city construction laws. You should expect them to come down hard. They could have made him take everything out.

"We don't appear to public opinion to be reasonable, but we are," Auberger says. He and Robin Stephens, and four of their ADAPT colleagues, met me in March in their offices. Despite the phony egalitarianism implicit in their wanting all to meet me together, Auberger, the only one with a conventionally clear voice, did most of the speaking. Stephens, whom Auberger credits as the main organizer of their twenty-three ADA lawsuits (so far) against Denver businesses, talked a little.

They aimed their first wave of suits at the Cherry Creek district where Barolo is located, "a real chi-chi area where all the watches cost $5,000," Auberger says. Their campaigns usually start by writing letters, followed by demonstrations. Only then do they resort to lawsuits.

"It's a hell of a lot easier to do it in a meeting. It takes a hell of a lot of energy to do the demonstrations, to do the lawsuits. We'll do that if that's what it takes. But my preference is, let's do it nice and resolve it as amicably as possible."

After Cherry Creek—where only the Barolo case garnered DOJ involvement—Atlantis/ADAPT has its eyes on lower downtown Denver, an area with mostly older buildings. Another wave of demonstrations and possible lawsuits is building up to hit Denver, and ADAPT has affiliate organizations in thirty-three other cities. With the ADA's provisions for private-party suits, these groups have a direct financial incentive—as well as ideological motivations—to launch such campaigns.

Private citizens aren't the only ones bedeviled by strict application of the ADA. The Washington (D.C.) Metropolitan Area Transit Authority has already spent almost $40 million on ADA reform, says spokeswoman Patricia Lambe. So it's not just a matter of money that made them rebel against a particular ADA requirement that they found irrelevant and completely unnecessary. "It's principle and science," Lambe insists, explaining D.C. Metro's refusal to change the platform edging in all their train stations to a raised surface of rubber bumps—allegedly to prevent blind riders from falling in front of trains.

The D.C. Metro system commissioned a study that found the current platform edging perfectly suitable to prevent that tragedy—which occurs far less frequently than sighted people falling. The rare falls by the blind that have occurred were caused by things other than the difference in surfacing between the edge and the main platform anyway, Lambe insists. "Where is the data saying this was ever a problem?"

Besides, she says, the ADA was meant to be a civil rights law, not a safety regulation. The D.C. Metro system told the Federal Transit Administration (FTA) it intends to keep its current platform edging. Instead, under an agreement with the FTA, the Metro will intensify the flashing lights at the platform edge.

For many individuals and municipal authorities, though, cost is the issue. The National Association of Counties estimates the ADA will cost counties $2.8

billion to comply from 1994–98. The U.S. Conference of Mayors sees cities spending $2.2 billion over the same period.

Consider sidewalk curb cuts, which provide miniramps for wheelchair users on city sidewalks. Various municipalities estimate the cost of installing the cuts at $500 to $4,000 each—and most cities have a lot of curbs. The ADA's curb-cut requirement kicks in any time work is done on roads or sidewalks. Philadelphia recently lost a suit in which it argued that merely resurfacing the street in front of the sidewalk shouldn't mean having to replace the curbs. Now just filling potholes can trigger ADA-related sidewalk overhauls.

Many cities, like many businesses, are simply flouting the law. The official deadline for ADA compliance for local governments was January 26, 1995 and no one is pretending this means anyone is actually in compliance. Every town and county in the nation is a lawsuit away from serious trouble.

Still, ADA experts at municipal government associations emphasize that good-faith efforts with the disabled community can insulate cities from suits. Governments can avoid expensive structural retrofitting by emphasizing "program compliance" instead of "structural compliance": holding meetings downstairs instead of upstairs, for instance. . . .

The estimates of the ADA's costs are almost certainly skewed downward, perhaps unintentionally, by advocates. The Job Accommodation Network, a government-funded disability consulting service at West Virginia University, is often cited for its figures emphasizing the very low costs of accommodating the disabled in the workplace. Their data, based on surveys (with a 45 percent response rate) of people who call them seeking advice, indicate that 68 percent of ADA accommodations cost less than $500, and that only 22 percent cost more than $1,000. The median cost, calculates the network, is $200 per accommodation; the average, $992.

Some lawyers guess that those figures are in the ballpark. But Wendy Lechner of the National Federation of Independent Businesses calls them "complete hooey." She says, "There is no meaningful average. We know that small-business owners are not being surveyed to find out their costs. It's all anecdotal evidence from a small amount of respondents."

One reason the ADA might not be showing its eventual full costs is simple, yet not one a business owner would generally admit out loud. The ADA costs nothing if you do nothing about it, merely crossing your fingers and hoping not to get sued.

Hamilton Brown, an ADA consultant for the National Association of Towns and Townships, estimates that only about half of his clients have done anything at all about the ADA. And even though his clients include only small, mostly rural governments, they still probably have more money to play with than the Texas small-business men with whom David Pinkus of Texas Small Business United works.

"The typical small businessman won't read any of these hundreds of pages of federal regulations," Pinkus says. "They just want a small checklist that everyone can agree on: If you do this, we won't sue you. But the government doesn't want to give anyone the impression they won't ever be sued. So businessmen think, I might as well wait to get sued and then do what they ask me to do." . . .

Certainly the most difficult requirements of the ADA involve the wheelchair-bound, even though they represent a minuscule portion of the "49 million disabled" figure bandied about by activists. Fewer than 2 percent of the disabled are wheelchair-bound, about 529,000 people between the ages of fifteen and sixty-four. Yet it is the requirements for the proper width of "handicapped" bathrooms (though the wheelchair-bound are the only handicapped who need them) that stymie the introduction of clean, modern public toilets in cities like New York and San Francisco. And it is these requirements that are causing one Los Angeles plumber to be denied payment for his work on a municipal convention center, because some of the toilets are an eighth of an inch too close to the wall.

As the members of Atlantis/ADAPT in Denver made clear to me, life can be painful and difficult for the wheelchair-bound when no one allows for their problems in navigating streets, public transit, or the insides of stores. That's what the ADA is all about, they say, not the petty complaints of business owners.

But the wheelchair-bound aren't the biggest users of the ADA. Of the nearly 40,000 complaints the Equal Employment Opportunity Commission (*EEOC*) (which handles employment complaints under the law) received by the end of 1994, only 7.3 percent had to do with people disabled in their extremities, which would cover wheelchair users, as well as people with orthopedic problems, missing digits, and the like. The blind and the deaf together accounted for only 6 percent of complaints. A plurality fell into categories for which the meaning and seriousness of the "disability" are far more nebulous—and thus ripe for more complicated legal contentiousness—such as back impairments (19.5 percent), neurological impairments (12.1 percent), and emotional/psychiatric impairments (11.4 percent).

"The ones that go to court are usually not the good cases, the ones involving obvious disabilities," says Nancy Noall, an Ohio ADA lawyer. "Legal problems start when the claimed disability is not something an employer or typical person considers a handicap. . . . Sometimes there are just ones who are faking it. Back injuries with no medical evidence, where they won't accept any accommodation except getting a helper to do the entire job."

The heaviest burden isn't making reasonable physical accommodations, says Austin, Texas, attorney Dewey Poteet. It's handling employees with kid gloves: "Like if an employee has missed on average a hundred days a year over the last three years, for nothing specific, but much of it for various doctor visits. That should be a straightforward issue—attendance—but there are medical issues involved, and therefore ADA implications."

Questions of mental illness can turn open-and-shut cases into insoluble dilemmas. Labor attorney Frank Cronin of Los Angeles tells of a secretary who couldn't remember assignments she had been given. Because of her memory problems, she was getting frustrated and in disputes with her boss, who needed a secretary who could handle a fast-paced, high-pressure office environment.

She asserted that her memory loss came from taking antidepressants. If she took too much, she suffered memory loss; too little, depression, which manifested itself in weeping and fights around the office. Her boss was ADA-savvy enough to know that depression equals disability. So rather than fire her, he took away many of her tasks but kept her at the same pay. Hiring someone else to do the jobs she used to do cost the employer $40,000.

She then claimed that this discrimination in job assignments caused her to become more depressed and to start missing too many days. She was eventually fired, and fighting off her lawyer cost another $20,000. "This is a typical pattern in psychological injury cases," says Cronin. "It's impossible to accommodate it."

Another Cronin case involves a part-time insurance clerk. Very bouncy, colorful dresser, always telling interesting stories, married twenty years, Cronin relates. Then she had recovered memory therapy that "discovered" sexual abuse from her father as a child. After this therapy, she became miserable, depressed, and cut off from her family. She became obsessed, started wearing black, and her depression led to absenteeism. After six to eight months of that, she was fired. And she sued.

"The lawsuit is still pending. Because the legal standards are so unclear, we won't know until the jury tells us, How do you reasonably accommodate someone who is so depressed they are always thinking about their problems at work? Is her depression enough to be qualified as a disability? None of these questions can be answered without very expensive legal proceedings with tons of expert witnesses," says Cronin. "I'm getting depressed just thinking about this."

DO DO-GOODER LAWS DO GOOD?

The feel-goodism of the ADA does not come free, or even cheap. All indications are that the ADA simply cannot be obeyed in its entirety, which means every business, every public building, every government in the country is living under the shadow of a potentially exhausting and financially devastating lawsuit.

And for what? Like research into ADA's macro costs, research into its benefits has been thin. But the data that exist are not encouraging.

The National Organization on Disabilities conducted a survey on the status of the disabled in America in 1986 and again last year. The big numbers are numbing: 49 million disabled, more than one of six people of working age (defined as between fifteen and sixty-four). Fifteen percent, this survey says, have back problems as their only disability.

The specific figures are more striking. When Congress was considering the ADA, its advocates emphasized the benefits of making the disabled taxpayers, instead of tax consumers, by giving them freer access to jobs. But the ADA has had no appreciable effect on getting the disabled into the workforoo.

In fact, the percentage of working-age disabled actually working went down from the 1986 survey—31 percent were working in 1994, compared with 33 percent in 1986. A similar study done by Vocational Econometrics Inc. found that the percentage of disabled males working or actively looking for work dropped to 30 percent in 1993 from 33 percent in 1992.

Nor has the ADA shown any signs of stanching the flow of federal disability relief money. Total benefit payments from the Social Security's disability insurance trust fund were $40.4 billion for fiscal 1995, up substantially from the $30.4 billion in 1992, when the ADA went into effect.

The data don't prove the ADA has not had benefits in bringing the disabled into the workplace—perhaps without the ADA their employment rate would have been even lower. But there is certainly no evidence, despite all the costs, that the ADA has helped. . . .

The principled argument against the ADA is that it violates free association. And unlike more-traditional civil rights law, it sometimes forces people to bear huge costs while doing so.

The point of race- and sex-based civil rights law was to treat everybody the same; the ADA demands treating everybody differently. The disabled are not, in civil rights terms, analogous to blacks or women. It's one thing to say you must let into your restaurant, or hire, someone who in all practical aspects is just like any other customer or employee. It's another matter entirely to force you to build a ramp (instead of just giving someone a physical boost) at great expense to allow them easy access. And it is even more extreme to require that businesses allow employees to keep working if their emotional disturbances make them an unproductive nuisance. . . .

The standards for making new buildings handicapped accessible are reasonably clear (if overly detailed and sometimes silly), but there is essentially no way for someone operating a business in an old building to know if he is obeying the law. And while the employment part of the ADA applies only to businesses with fifteen or more employees, the access sections cover every public accommodation—and the meaning of public accommodation has been stretched to include nonphysical ''accommodations'' such as health care plans.

Clear and precise definitions of ''reasonable accommodation'' and ''undue burden''—such as dollar caps—are a necessary first step in ADA reform. The law ought to recognize that sometimes it makes more sense to help a person in a wheelchair up a step or two than to spend thousands of dollars on ramps. It ought to realize that if someone in a wheelchair can sit and eat in a restaurant, it's not necessary to force the owner to go to heroic measures to make sure that person can sit everywhere in the restaurant. . . .

ADA reform any time soon is a slim possibility. Lori Eisner of Representative DeLay's staff says, ''If one freshman got fired up they could very well get enough support to make something move.'' But even post-Contract, no such firebrand has arisen.

Now that Congress itself is officially bound to abide by the ADA, legislative change could be an ill-considered lawsuit away. But it's doubtful that disabled activists would be foolhardy enough to risk showing Congress directly how unreasonable and expensive full compliance can be.

The courts may, however, provide some redress. Currently, as New Haven ADA lawyer Patrick Shea puts it, ''The regulations don't say anything about cost-benefit analyses. You might have to spend $100,000 to accommodate someone on a job that is only worth $25,000 to you. Tough. You've been conscripted to provide opportunities.''

A decision by Seventh Circuit Appeals Judge Richard Posner, in *Lori L. Vande Zande v. State of Wisconsin Department of Administration*, may be the key to ending that conscription. Posner concluded that ''even if an employer is so large or wealthy . . . that it would not be able to plead 'undue hardship,' it would not be required to expend enormous sums in order to bring about a trivial improvement. . . . If the nation's employers have potentially unlimited financial obligations to [all] disabled persons, the ADA will have imposed an indirect tax potentially greater than the national debt.''

Instead of requiring an open-ended obligation, wrote Posner, ''The employee must show that the accommodation is reasonable in the sense both of efficacious and of proportional to costs. Even if the prima facie showing is made, the employer has an opportunity to prove that . . . the costs are excessive in relation either to the benefits of the accommodation or to the employer's financial survival or health.''

That precedent could go a long way toward clearing up the issues in Frank Cronin's cases of depressed secretaries, and providing a clearer understanding of what the employment aspect of the law requires. . . .

Sitting in the handicapped-accessible restaurant that cost him more months and more thousands of dollars and more grief than he could have imagined, Blair Taylor says, ''I want to be helpful because I'm a nice person. I don't want to be forced to do something to help you to the detriment of my own well-being.''

CHAPTER 6

Opening Up the Fed: Democratization of National Economic Policy—Economic Élites versus the Public Right to Know

The Federal Reserve Board has tremendous power in our economic system. The board helps set monetary policy and its decisions affect the money supply, interest rates, employment, and inflation rates of our nation's economy. The chairman directs policy by attempting to set the agenda and the priorities of the board.

Critics, such as Ralph Nader, state that Chairman Alan Greenspan has not made necessary reforms. In the following reading, Nader describes an agency that is inefficient, nonresponsive, and overly secretive. The independent nature of the Fed, instead of being protected, should give way to changes that would make it more accountable for its actions.

Why are economic élites hesitant to allow Congress to exercise more power over monetary policy? In what ways does the Federal Reserve Board impair democracy?

STATEMENT OF RALPH NADER ON THE NOMINATION OF ALAN GREENSPAN AS CHAIRMAN OF THE FEDERAL RESERVE BOARD

Mr. Chairman, thank you for this opportunity to comment on the renomination of Alan Greenspan as Chairman of the Federal Reserve Board and the present state of the Federal Reserve System under his tenure.

There is a need for change at the Federal Reserve. There is an overriding need to make the agency less wasteful, more open, more responsive to a broader segment of the American population.

The nomination of Alan Greenspan for a third term as chairman of the Federal Reserve Board comes against a backdrop of growing unease about job insecurity and corporate downsizing in a slow-growth economy characterized by wage stagnation and decline and growing disparities of wealth.

Pollsters, the media, and political candidates are becoming increasingly aware of the anger and disappointment of both blue-collar and white-collar workers who have lost jobs or been forced to uproot their families in search of new jobs with less pay and less satisfaction. In recent weeks, *The New York Times* used hundreds of column inches to chronicle the new era of economic insecurity in an unprecedented seven-part series.

The president—and I assume shortly the Senate—appear willing to answer these concerns with a "business as usual" message—or, more to the point, a "Federal Reserve as usual" response.

The reappointment of Alan Greenspan—who has controlled a major share of the government's economic policy-making machinery since 1987—can be interpreted only as a desire to maintain the status quo.

With two vacancies on the board and with the chairmanship open, the president had a golden opportunity to reshape the Federal Reserve and, at minimum, open a debate within the board about monetary policy options. It was also an opportunity to let sunlight in and turn the agency away from its obsession with

Committee on Banking, Housing and Urban Affairs
United States Senate
March 26, 1996
Reprinted with permission.
Ralph Nader is a consumer advocate and founder of Public Citizen and other citizen groups.

secrecy and its apparent unease with the right of the people to know what their government is doing.

But the president's decision to keep the monetary policy reins in the hands of Alan Greenspan effectively closes the door on the possibility for change at the Federal Reserve. And if the published predictions are correct, the Republican majority in the Senate will be happy to accept the president's decision that all is well at the Federal Reserve.

While disagreeing strongly, I have no illusions about the ultimate outcome of this nomination process. For eight long years, the Congress has seemed willing to accept most, if not all, of Alan Greenspan's bland assurances when he visits Capitol Hill twice each year to report on monetary policy.

These reports are invariably self-congratulatory messages from the Federal Reserve—reports from the battlefront against real or imagined inflation. If Congress sees problems in the economy, the Federal Reserve is quick to assign blame elsewhere.

In his testimony last month, Alan Greenspan was forced to concede that there was, indeed, growing anxiety about job security among the nation's middle class. The blame, he contended, was essentially "technological change"—an analysis that he hoped would send a message that neither the Fed nor the banks nor any large companies are part of the problem.

While accepting no responsibility, he did nonetheless dust off the subject with a note of what he must have regarded as compassion for the workers caught in corporate downsizing in a slow-growth economy.

"The phenomenon of [corporate] restructuring," he told the Congress, "can be *especially unfortunate* for those workers directly caught up in the process." A message to be read aloud when the corporate personnel office announces a new layoff.

Some of these workers may feel it was "especially unfortunate" that Alan Greenspan's Federal Reserve decided to increase interest rates sharply in rapid-fire actions between mid-1994 and early 1995.

As John Berry, *The Washington Post*'s reporter on the Federal Reserve beat, noted, many economists believe this interest rate shock accounts for the exceedingly slow economic growth last year. The inflation-adjusted gross domestic product rose just 1.4 percent from the end of 1994 to the end of last year—compared with 3.5 percent in 1994. The economy is continuing to experience slow growth, not to mention how the fruits of this growth are distributed.

Asked about the reasons for the big interest rate increase in the 1994–1995 period, Greenspan resorted to the Federal Reserve's age-old excuse—"inflationary expectations."

In an attempt to refute charges that the Fed's vision of inflation had been illusory, Greenspan, using the analogy of a river, told the House Banking Committee in February that he had seen a "flood crest" of inflation coming down the river and, as a result, felt the need to pile up interest rate sandbags.

The analogy was less than convincing to Representative Maurice Hinchey of

New York who replied that "many of us looked at the same river and saw a trickle of a stream, not threatening anyone at all, and the placing of sandbags up around such a benign trickle of a stream seemed in itself extreme. . . ."

But the Federal Reserve's repeated visions of inflation are nothing new. It is boiler plate to excuse monetary policy mistakes. The Federal Reserve's preoccupation with fighting "inflation ghosts" ignores the broader and specific mandate added to Federal Reserve Act on November 16, 1977, to "maintain the long run growth of monetary and credit aggregates commensurate with the economy's long run potential to increase production, so as to promote effectively the goals of maximum employment, stable prices and moderate long-term interest rates."

The ability of Alan Greenspan and his predecessors to ignore the Federal Reserve's broader responsibilities can be credited to the mystique that surrounds the agency and the general failure of the media and the Congress to explain the role of the Federal Reserve in anything but the most complex and confusing terms.

Few Americans are focused on the renomination of Alan Greenspan and even fewer understand the large power that the Federal Reserve exercises over their lives. The Fed makes sure that such a condition remains undisturbed by any of its actions.

Whether workers have jobs or families can afford shelter or young people can go to college depends, in a substantial way, on the decisions that are made on interest rates and monetary policy behind the closed doors of the Federal Reserve Board. The Federal Reserve, if it so chooses, can use monetary policy to literally negate—veto—fiscal policies that may be undertaken by the Congress.

This is also a board that makes key regulatory decisions affecting the safety and soundness of taxpayer-backed deposit insurance funds, and a board which has a critical say about what safeguards are enforced for consumers in the financial marketplace. For low- and moderate-income and minority citizens, the Federal Reserve's approach to the Community Reinvestment Act (CRA) and the Equal Credit Opportunity Act can be the difference between opportunity and despair.

The chairmanship of the Federal Reserve has always defined Federal Reserve policy, overshadowing the role of the other six members of the board and the twelve Federal Reserve Bank presidents. And the boards under most Federal Reserve chairmen have been relatively low-key with few public dissents.

This has been especially true under Chairman Greenspan. More and more, the votes of the board and the Federal Open Market Committee (FOMC) have taken on a monolithic appearance. On the public record, at least, it is lockstep with the chairman in a manner that would have made the old Soviet Politburo proud. Many believe that there are differences among the members, but that these are papered over and kept secret while only the unanimous agreement appears in the votes released to the media and Congress.

CLAIMS OF INDEPENDENCE

The Federal Reserve's statutory powers are magnified by the lack of effective ongoing congressional oversight, a heavy curtain of secrecy that builds the agency's mystique and hides its mistakes, and the lack of accountability that other agencies face in the budget and appropriation process.

But the biggest piece of armor in the possession of the Federal Reserve is its claim of absolute "independence." Challenged in any forum—congressional, presidential, or media—the Federal Reserve will invariably retreat behind its self-constructed wall of "independence."

The word "independent" does not appear in the Federal Reserve Act. But the Federal Reserve has assumed it and has given the word a new and powerful definition.

Proposals to change the Federal Reserve Act, board operating procedures, and other policies are always greeted with sounds of alarm from the Federal Reserve and its apologists proclaiming a threat to the "independence" of the agency. Any call for accountability and openness is interpreted as a threat to its "independence" and as an attempt to exert "political influence" over its decisions.

Never is the Federal Reserve's version of "independence" defined. Is it independence from the government, the executive branch and the legislative branch—and the American people? Tracking the expanding claims of "independence" leads one to wonder if the Federal Reserve regards itself as almost a "separate government"—autonomously setting its own rules without regard to the checks and balances that control our democratic system.

While the Federal Reserve may regard itself as "independent" from the rest of the government, it seems much less "independent" from the banking industry and big business. It appears quite solicitous of these areas of the economy. The majority of the members of the boards of directors of the twelve Federal Reserve Banks and their twenty-five branches are drawn from banking and business.

It was instructive to observe the reactions of Wall Street and the banking industry when rumors rose earlier this year to suggest that President Clinton might choose his own Federal Reserve chairman. The word immediately circulated that Wall Street would throw a full-scale tantrum unless Greenspan was reappointed. Never mind that the president and the American people might want someone else—Wall Street and the banks would riot. Clearly, the banks and Wall Street provide a ready and powerful lobbying arm for the Federal Reserve and its chairman—and this might just suggest that "independence" has a limit.

As this committee is aware, five members of the Federal Open Market Committee—the center of monetary policy making—are presidents of Federal Reserve Banks elected (with approval of the Fed Board) by boards of directors drawn in large part from banking and business corporations. (The president of the New York Federal Reserve Bank is a permanent member of the FOMC, and four other presidents serve as voting members of FOMC on a rotating basis.)

Such links certainly do not suggest "independence" from the banking and business corporations that hold seats on the district banks' boards of directors.

Let me note here, Mr. Chairman, that Senator Paul Sarbanes, the ranking Democrat on this committee, has introduced legislation that would remove this conflict of interest and limit the Open Market Committee solely to the seven members of the Federal Reserve Board who are appointed by the president of the United States.

In the final analysis, the Federal Reserve's "independence" is a shield against accountability. Challenged on any front, the Federal Reserve retreats behind this shield. Bad policy, outrageous mistakes, mismanagement can and are rendered immune from exposure by the Federal Reserve's invocation of "independence"—a device that exceeds even the most outlandish uses of "executive privilege" by presidents down through history.

SECRECY

Going hand in glove with "independence" as a source of Federal Reserve power is the agency's ability to maintain a CIA-like secrecy over virtually all of its operations.

The meetings of the Federal Open Market Committee—the body that establishes monetary policy—are shrouded in secrecy despite the fact that its decisions are critical to the well-being of all Americans.

The General Accounting Office—Congress's watchdog over federal agencies—is barred from examining anything at the Federal Reserve that remotely involves monetary policy. And as one would expect, the Federal Reserve stretches the definition of "monetary policy" as far as possible to keep the GAO locked out and the Federal Reserve's secrets safe from public scrutiny.

The real meat of monetary policy decisions—the debates of the Federal Open Market Committee (FOMC)—are withheld for five years. And even then the transcripts, in the words of the Federal Reserve, are "lightly edited." The full unedited transcripts are locked away for thirty years.

What this means is that the thinking behind some of the key decisions during Alan Greenspan's chairmanship will not be available to this committee when it considers the new nomination. And these decisions include the controversial move to ratchet interest rates up in 1994 and early 1995 at a time when inflation was relatively low.

I do not believe that this committee would accept this same secrecy from other agencies and departments under its jurisdiction. Would this committee tolerate "hidden agendas" and only vague sketches of policy decisions from the Department of Housing and Urban Development or the Securities and Exchange Commission? I doubt it seriously, and it should not do so with the Federal Reserve.

With most of the "final votes" behind the closed doors of the FOMC recorded as unanimous, it is critically important that the background, the debate, and the rationale contained in the FOMC transcripts be made available immediately after the meetings. Whatever happened to the concept that people in a democracy should know how and why their government is making decisions?

Representative Henry B. Gonzalez, both as chairman and ranking Democratic member of the House Banking committee, has made a valiant effort to break the Federal Reserve's secrecy. It was his efforts that uncovered the fact that full verbatim transcripts did exist.

Representative Gonzalez's investigations uncovered that the Fed has long operated a taping system at the secret FOMC meetings—apparently without the knowledge of some of the participants. Even with tapings admitted, the Federal Reserve contended that many of the tapes had been taped over and that there were no complete transcripts in existence. Ultimately, the hide-and-seek game ended with a concession by Chairman Greenspan to Representative Gonzalez that indeed the tapes existed and that seventeen years of full transcripts were at the Federal Reserve.

But they still remain a secret from the public for at least five years after the meetings of the Open Market Committee.

This is an absurdity which serves only to protect the Federal Reserve. There can be no public purpose in hiding the facts from the public for five long years.

Why does the Federal Reserve maintain such tight secrecy even years after the fact? And even after many of the participants have left the agency?

A quote in the January/February 1995 issue of the *Columbia Journalism Review* from Ted Balbach, a former research director for the St. Louis Federal Reserve Bank, may provide the real answer:

"Remember, secrecy is power."

WHERE'S THE PRESS? WHERE ARE THE WILLIAM GRIEDERS?

The head of most federal agencies that engaged in such an all encompassing game of governmental secrecy would be virtually hounded out of office by the Washington press corps.

But not Alan Greenspan. He lives in a charmed world where reporters don't demand press conferences and rarely complain about vague and confusing statements about policy issues. The very aura around the Federal Reserve is, itself, a controlling process.

As James Risen, a reporter for the *Los Angeles Times*, noted, "Greenspan takes great pride in his ability to reveal as little as possible."

This practice often delivers to the American public conflicting, if not totally inaccurate, information about what a major governmental agency is doing.

The latest example of this was last June when the confusing double-talk of Chairman Greenspan in a speech in New York City resulted in directly opposite stories in two of the major U.S. daily newspapers—*The Washington Post* and *The New York Times*.

The *Post* headline read: "Greenspan Hints Fed May Cut Rates."

The *New York Times* headline: "Doubts Voiced by Greenspan on a Rate Cut."

To cover his tracks with the press, Greenspan often calls in selected reporters for secret off-the-record sessions to give the Federal Reserve's special slant on the world and to answer critics of the agency.

Paul Starobin, a reporter for the *National Journal* writing for the *Columbia Journalism Review* last year, described the Greenspan media strategy as "soft spin, no fingerprints."

In an article entitled "The Lure of FEDTHINK," Starobin wrote: "Under the hush-hush ground rules set by the Fed chairman, the journalists are not even allowed to report that they have had a talk with a senior Fed official. It's as if the whole thing never happened."

Mr. Chairman, in passing on this nomination, I hope the committee will consider carefully where all of this massive game of secrecy, double-talk, and efforts to obscure what a government agency does fits in a democratic society. Again, I do not think the members of this committee, Republicans or Democrats, would accept such extreme secrecy and such tactics of obfuscation from any other agency that appears before this committee.

NO MONEY WORRIES AT THE FED

All of the claims of "independence" and all the convoluted tactics to ensure secrecy would mean less if the Federal Reserve did not have its own pot of money which allows it to bypass formal budget and appropriations processes.

Virtually all of the Federal Reserve's income comes directly from the U.S. Treasury in the form of interest payments on government securities it buys and sells in carrying out monetary policy through the Federal Open Market Committee.

That portfolio of government securities now totals nearly $400 billion annually—and the figure is rising year to year. There are no limits on what the agency can spend out of the Treasury's $20 billion in interest payments and the various fees collected for services. No formal budget is submitted and there are no tough questions to answer for appropriations committees on Capitol Hill. But every dime the Federal Reserve spends is money that doesn't go back to the Treasury.

Under the secrecy strictures and the lack of full congressional oversight, it is difficult to know how much unchecked waste there may be in the System.

The Federal Reserve System employs 25,000 people nationwide. This includes 730 economists on the permanent payroll. Every month the System expends on average an additional $100,000 on contracts for outside economists and related researchers.

When the Federal Reserve System was established in 1913, the twelve Federal Reserve Banks were scattered across the nation, many as political plums. Before the age of jet airplanes and the advent of instant communications and computer networks, the scattered district banks and branches had a modicum of rationale.

Today, the bank buildings in many cities stand on expensive mid-city property, maintain large staffs, and perform fewer and fewer essential functions. Former House Banking Chairman Henry Ruess proposed doing away with many of the banks and branches and selling the property.

While some functions may be eliminated in an information age, the Federal Reserve's publications empire goes on unabated. Earlier this year, the *Kansas City Business Journal* conducted a survey of Federal Reserve publications and described the system as a "virtual publishing machine." The Kansas City Federal Reserve Bank, alone, spent $295,000 on publications, the *Journal* said.

The *Journal* quoted Don Schilling, an associate professor of economics at the University of Missouri, as saying that the "Federal Reserve in essence talks to itself through its publications. I think there's an element of waste."

In dealing with complaints about waste and abuse in the System, Chairman Greenspan has apparently resorted to the simple tactic of "stonewalling" in some cases.

On January 8, 1996, Representative Henry Gonzalez, the ranking Democrat on the House Banking Committee, submitted a forty-one-page report to the Federal Reserve citing "waste and abuse" in operation of the agency's system for clearing and collecting checks.

The study, conducted by Dr. Robert Auerbach, the Democratic staff economist, detailed improper contracting practices, gifts to nonperforming contractors, overcharges to the U.S. Treasury, violations of the Monetary Control Act of 1980, and lack of controls over contracts for transporting checks across the nation in fleets of planes nightly. Backing up the allegations of waste and questionable practices were signed statements from employees in the Interdistrict Transportation System operated in the Federal Reserve Bank of Boston, Representative Gonzalez told Chairman Greenspan.

Was Mr. Greenspan concerned? Apparently not since Representative Gonzalez has yet to receive a reply—even an acknowledgment—to the report.

Mr. Chairman, I would like to submit a copy of the Gonzalez report for the record so that this committee will have an idea of how much concern the Federal Reserve places on waste and abuse in the system. Before this committee votes on the Greenspan nomination, it should have an answer on this issue. A charge of waste of public monies by a ranking member of the House Banking Committee should at least have an answer, if not a remedy.

CONSUMER ISSUES

Under Alan Greenspan, the Federal Reserve Board is essentially passive on consumer issues. If Congress gives the agency a consumer law to enforce, it will go through the motions. But rarely does the Fed knock on the doors of the legislative branch for solutions to consumer problems or put up battles to keep the banking industry from weakening existing protections. And even rarer are initiatives in utilizing existing powers to give consumers a fair break in the marketplace.

A prime example was in the news last week when the Federal Trade Commission announced it was launching a major effort to fight scam artists who are using "demand drafts" to rob consumers' bank accounts of tens of millions of dollars annually. The victims were consumers who had given out their bank account numbers and permission to use demand drafts for magazine subscriptions, various membership fees and similar outlays.

To make the scams work obviously required wide utilization of the banking system—right where the Federal Reserve's authority lies. But it was left to the Federal Trade Commission, not the well-staffed and well-financed Federal Reserve System, to take aggressive action to protect the consumer—even though the Federal Reserve shared identical enforcement power with the FTC under Section 18(f) of the FTC Act.

When the contest over consumer regulations is between consumers and the banking industry, the Federal Reserve can find some creative ways to support the industry.

The Congress, for example, recently asked the Federal Reserve to give it a report on regulations to limit the time that banks may hold checks before crediting the consumers' account.

In answer to the congressional request, the Federal Reserve decided to survey the banks and prepared a one-sided questionnaire that assures the results would be weighted to the banks' desire to lengthen the time they could hold checks.

The survey allows the banks to "estimate" their check losses instead of providing hard data—an open invitation for banks to exaggerate losses. And participation, the Federal Reserve decided, would be "voluntary." This means that the returns are likely to be heavier from those institutions most actively seeking changes in the checkhold law, rather than providing representative data for a cross section of banks.

The message for consumers from the Greenspan Federal Reserve: Don't expect proactive steps for consumers by the Federal Reserve and don't expect to win a battle with the industry over regulations when the Federal Reserve is the referee.

The Fed's implementation of the Equal Credit Opportunity Act (ECOA) provides a good example of the Fed's regulatory inertia when it comes to consumer, community, and civil rights interests. Although ECOA prohibits credit discrimination against small businesses as well as consumers, the Federal Reserve has never established any disclosure requirements that would permit monitoring of discrimination against small businesses. Indeed, the Fed's Regulation B, which implements ECOA, perversely prohibits lenders from collecting data on the distribution of their small business loans by race category.

Civil rights organizations, community groups, and even the Clinton administration have asked the Federal Reserve to revise Regulation B to require lenders to collect and make public race data on their small-business lending patterns. Under strong pressure from the Clinton administration, the Fed in April 1995 proposed to modify Regulation B to permit voluntary collection of race data on small-business loans and other types of credit. Yet one year later, the board has failed to act on even this extremely modest proposal.

Similarly, the Federal Reserve is looking the other way on the convenience and needs of communities as mergers sweep across the nation. Neighborhoods and communities are facing the loss of banking facilities, while borrowers in low- and moderate-income and minority neighborhoods, already starved for credit, are seeing lending decisions moved through distant lines of management in these new merged giants.

Eight hundred community organizations turned out on the West Coast to oppose the Wells Fargo-First Interstate merger on the grounds that the closure of 345 branches would severely wound local communities. The Federal Reserve heard the arguments and received the documentation, but in the end the wishes of Wells Fargo were granted—and 345 branches will be closed.

Interstate branching and the vast increase in mergers is cresting a new generation of problems for communities—but the Federal Reserve is not meeting its responsibility to examine fully the convenience and needs of communities as required by the Bank Holding Company Act.

DISSENT—IS IT ALLOWED ON THE GREENSPAN BOARD?

Are strong independent voices excluded from Greenspan's Federal Reserve Board?

Alan Blinder, the vice chairman appointed by President Clinton, unexpectedly resigned and returned to his job at Princeton, removing a voice from the Board for more openness and more concern about employment and consumer issues than may have been compatible with the Greenspan party line. And there were published reports (including one in the *Columbia Journalism Review*) that Greenspan's staff had leaked unflattering comments to the media that led to stories that Blinder was ''soft on inflation''—an episode that undoubtedly increased Blinder's frustration and desire to leave the Greenspan Board.

President Clinton's choice for Blinder's replacement was Felix Rohatyn, a New York investment banker with a reputation for strong stands on economic issues and a belief in progrowth monetary policy. After the opposition rose, including some from members of this committee, Rohatyn's name was dropped and the possibility of a counterweight to Greenspan's conservative views was removed.

Two years ago, Dr. Alicia Munnell was slated for a spot on the Federal Reserve Board. But as an employee of the Federal Reserve Bank of Boston, she had conducted a significant study on discriminatory lending patterns by commercial banks—and this gained her the lasting enmity of the banking industry, a fact that probably reduced her chances for a spot on the board.

CONCLUSION

The public interest would best be served by a change in the chairmanship of the Federal Reserve Board.

Alan Greenspan has served two full terms, stretching back to President Ronald Reagan's administration and including a reappointment by President George Bush. No other head of a major federal agency today has served longer than Alan Greenspan. As an agency cloaked in secrecy, term limits make particular sense.

Many of the problems I have cited were not invented by Alan Greenspan. But he has done little to correct shortcomings and institute change that would open up the Federal Reserve and make it a more responsive agency subject to the checks and balances of a democratic system.

While the consensus is for approval of the president's choice, I urge this committee to defer action until it has an opportunity to fully explore Alan Greenspan's administration of the Federal Reserve Board. The confirmation process gives the Senate this opportunity and it should not be bypassed for the Federal Reserve.

In addition to his monetary policy duties, Alan Greenspan is also charged with major responsibilities in the area of bank supervision. His earlier confirmation hearings have failed to explain fully his role as a consultant to a number of savings and loan associations, including the ill-fated Lincoln Savings during the 1980s and his battle against Federal Home Loan Bank Board Chairman Ed Gray's efforts to curb the investment powers of Lincoln Savings and other savings and loans.

The exhibits of the Special Counsel to the Senate Ethics Committee in the investigation of the five senators involved with Lincoln Savings contain a number of letters, billings, agendas, and other items related to Alan Greenspan's activity during this period. Among these is an endorsement by Mr. Greenspan of Lincoln Savings as a "financially strong institution that presents no foreseeable risk to the Federal Savings and Loan Insurance Corporation" contained in a letter of February 13, 1985, to Thomas J. Sharkey, principal supervisory agent of the Federal Home Loan Bank of San Francisco.

These materials do not reflect the mind of a financial industry leader who weighs heavily the integrity of a financial institution, effective government regulation, and protection of taxpayer interests.

In light of the large regulatory role of the Federal Reserve, it is pertinent for the committee to examine this area and determine whether Alan Greenspan's approaches to the savings and loan problems in the 1980s reflect an insensitivity to the overriding need to protect the deposit insurance funds and the taxpayers who have paid for several hundreds of billions of dollars of losses, including at least $2 billion in the failure of Lincoln.

(And on the question of deposit insurance currently, it would be interesting to know where the Federal Reserve chairman stands on the decision of the

Federal Deposit Insurance Corporation [FDIC] to cap the reserves of the Bank Insurance Fund [BIF] and allow the majority of banks to pay no premiums for government insurance.)

Beyond these issues, it is important for this committee to insist on changes at the Federal Reserve as a condition for confirmation—particularly changes that would remove some of the thick walls of secrecy that separate the agency from the people and the Congress.

If Alan Greenspan is confirmed, he will control the Federal Reserve into the year 2000. It is unlikely that there will be change in the agency unless the committee insists on it now.

Thank you.

CHAPTER 7

Corporate Welfare

Corporate welfare is a relatively new concept in American politics. Usually, welfare is thought of as strictly government aid to poor individuals. However, when mounting deficits forced budget decisions to become more difficult in the 1980s, observers began to closely examine the relationship between businesses and government.

Defined as government action, which can take the form of tax breaks, specific exemptions from regulations or subsidies, corporate welfare is increasingly being critically analyzed.

The reading describes recent attempts by Congress and the Clinton administration to reduce corporate welfare.

Would you consider businesses that receive special legislation welfare recipients? Why is it politically so difficult to take on corporate welfare?

BUSINESS' CLOUT KEEPS THE GOVERNMENT BREAKS COMING

AARON ZITNER AND CHARLES M. SENNOTT

Two weeks after his party was swamped in the mid-term elections of 1994, Robert B. Reich issued a simple dare. You Republicans won control of Congress by attacking welfare, the U.S. labor secretary asserted. Why not cut "corporate welfare" and move business off the dole as well?

But Reich's own colleagues were uneasy with the challenge. Treasury Secretary Lloyd M. Bentsen and Commerce Secretary Ronald H. Brown quickly distanced themselves. And President Clinton, while calling it an "attractive idea," made it clear he had not endorsed cutbacks in benefits to business.

While Democratic party leaders cringed at Reich's gambit and most Republicans dismissed it as liberal rhetoric, Reich got a warm phone call from a key congressman: John R. Kasich of Ohio, chairman of the House Budget Committee. The two men could not be more different—Reich, a classic liberal from Harvard University, and Kasich, the son of a mailman and a leading light in Speaker Newt Gingrich's "Republican revolution."

"You're on to something," Kasich said, urging Reich to keep pushing the idea and promising to do his best to put corporate welfare on the Republican agenda as well.

It was a unique meeting of minds at opposite ends of the political spectrum to take on the labyrinth of subsidies and tax breaks for businesses that cost the government about $150 billion a year. More lawmakers, buttressed by key Washington think tanks that provide the ideological underpinning for political action, later lined up against this underwriting of corporations.

But over the course of a year, the resolve to root out corporate welfare would dissipate. First, it would falter, and then it would sink amid parochial politics, big-money lobbying and a campaign finance system that together conspire to keep corporate welfare as constant as the tide.

By March of this year, after most of his subsidy cutbacks had been rejected in a brutal two-month budget negotiation, an exasperated Kasich said at a hearing: "I think it is an absolute outrage that some of this crap is still in this budget, and it just infuriates me every day when I think about it."

By May, the Cato Institute, a libertarian think tank which rode the crest of bipartisan wave last year by challenging Congress to cut $85 billion in corporate

Reprinted courtesy of *The Boston Globe*, July 9, 1996.

welfare programs—declared the battle all but over in a report titled "How Corporate Welfare Won."

The story of how Reich, Kasich and their allies lost the battle begins after the 1994 elections with both parties claiming they wanted to balance the federal budget. It lingers into last winter, when snow blanketed Washington through December and January, and the government shut down twice over how to cut costs. Within both parties, key figures like Reich, Kasich, Republican Sen. John McCain of Arizona, Democrat Edward M. Kennedy of Massachusetts—even centrist Colin Powell—pointed again and again to corporate welfare.

They attacked the sugar and peanut price-support programs that raise food prices for consumers. They attacked the Export Enhancement Program, which gives $800 million a year to giant agriculture firms to sell wheat and grains at a discount overseas. While no two lists of targets were identical, nearly all cited the Market Promotion Program, which gives $100 million annually to Gallo, McDonald's, Ocean Spray and other food companies for international advertising.

Moreover, the Republican plan for reining in Medicare and welfare gave lawmakers of both parties ammunition to argue that cutting corporate subsidies was only fair and moral. For awhile, it seemed like deep cuts were inevitable. But corporate welfare, it became clear, is not a partisan issue. Rather, Republican is set against Republican, Democrat against Democrat when programs in a politician's home state are threatened.

Not enough lawmakers were willing to vote against home-state businesses and jobs. "One person's pork is another person's prize," said Sen. Fred Thompson, a Republican from Tennessee. "No one wants to give up their prize if there isn't shared sacrifice."

AN ADMINISTRATION DIVIDED

For Reich, the 50-year-old longtime friend and economic adviser to Clinton, the corporate welfare fight began long before he joined the Cabinet. As a lecturer at Harvard, he chastised policy makers for confusing aid to American workers with aid to American companies. U.S. firms were sending more jobs overseas, while foreign companies were creating jobs here. "Our primary concern should be the training and development of the American workforce, not the protection of the American-owned corporation," he wrote in 1990. Four years later, Reich replayed that theme with a twist. Voters rebuked Clinton and the Democrats, he told an influential Democratic group just after the 1994 elections, because many Americans feared their paychecks were shrinking.

"The middle class has become an anxious class," he said. The solution: invest in jobs and training. Give people the skills to move from welfare to work, as Republican rhetoric argues. Help them move from low-paying jobs to more lucrative ones. How to pay for it? Cut corporate welfare. Ask business, not just welfare recipients, to become more self sufficient.

Reich's theme struck a chord across the ideological spectrum. Answering his challenge, the Cato Institute issued its report on the 125 corporate welfare subsidy programs worth $85 billion. The Progressive Policy Institute, allied with the centrist Democratic Leadership Council, found $265 billion in savings over five years. To the right, the Heritage Foundation came up with its own plan to eliminate, not just shave, unnecessary spending. And to the left, the Ralph Nader group, Essential Information, identified 153 sources of subsidies as well as tax breaks costing $167 billion a year.

Vice President Al Gore weighed in with approval for Reich's ideas. But Treasury Secretary Bentsen, a Texan whose home-state oil and energy industries take millions of dollars each year in tax breaks, opposed cutbacks on business assistance. And Robert E. Rubin, who replaced Bentsen in January 1995, also was reluctant. After fighting to shed the Democrats' anti-business image, many in the party worried Reich would undo their work.

The gulf was between classic liberals and the more centrist, pro-business "New Democrats." Clinton initially wanted to make a strong statement on corporate welfare but backed away, an administration source said. He eschewed the words "corporate welfare" in public, the source said, adding "He uses the phrase in private and Cabinet meetings, but the phrase is too combative for him."

Kasich, still boyish-looking at age 43, was one of the populist upstarts who helped make Gingrich speaker of the House. Now, with the Republican takeover of Congress, the six-term representative had been named chairman of the important Budget Committee. It was no small task.

Kasich had to find $200 billion to pay for tax cuts in the "Contract With America." On top of that, he had to design a federal budget to eliminate the deficit by 2002. Corporate welfare seemed one place to start looking for money.

But there was little question Kasich was bound to clash with Ways and Means chairman Bill Archer. As representative of a wealthy Texas district, Archer long had argued that tax breaks helped keep the nation and economy strong. No tax break, he says, meets the definition of pork. "Corporate welfare" was not in Archer's lexicon.

Kasich believed business subsidies and tax breaks were more than a source of savings. If Republicans truly wanted to balance the budget, he argued, they had to do more than tap Medicaid, welfare and other social programs. While some Democrats feared that attacking corporate welfare would hurt them politically, there were Republicans who worried that if business did not share the pain of budget cuts, voters would accuse them of unfairness.

Archer, on the other hand, argued that eliminating tax breaks amounted to a tax increase. Supporting him were many Republicans who have backed big business, a longtime GOP constituency.

REPUBLICAN SHUTDOWN

The shutdown came at a GOP retreat in May 1995 in Leesburg, Va. It was the first time House Republicans saw Kasich's plan to balance the budget. Proposing ways to save money, Kasich said tax breaks for business ought to be cut or modified by $25 billion over seven years. Kasich cited tax concessions to energy, timber and other interests that he said did not benefit the public. Some were the very tax breaks Archer had championed. Archer spoke against Kasich's plan, and his argument that repealing such inducements would be, in effect, a tax increase for businesses was persuasive. Two weeks later, when Kasich's budget hit the House floor, corporate welfare savings were all but gone.

But that was not the end of the issue. As Republicans moved further into details of how to balance the budget, it became harder to ignore the money that could be recouped from corporate tax breaks and subsidies. Equally important was the GOP's image. Polls showed the public hated corporate welfare, said Frank Luntz, a Republican pollster. They may even hate it more than social welfare, he said, adding: "Republicans don't want to appear to be in bed with big business."

In November, two Republicans brought the issue to the Senate. McCain and Thompson proposed a "dirty dozen" list of programs to be eliminated. From agriculture, they selected the Market Promotion Program. From the defense budget, the B-2 bomber and military export subsidies. From transportation, they chose highway demonstration projects.

McCain and Thompson won support from conservative Republican Phil Gramm from Texas, along with Democrats Kennedy and John F. Kerry of Massachusetts, and Bill Bradley of New Jersey.

But they lost, 74–25. Voting to uphold the subsidies were such progressives as Barbara Boxer and Dianne Feinstein, the California Democrats, whose state benefits from millions of dollars in subsidies to the Gallo and Wente Brothers wineries, Sunkist orange cooperative, almond growers and others.

As Republicans pushed for a balanced budget and limits on social service programs, the annual budget process continued long past its deadline. By fall, the authority for most government agencies to spend money expired. In November and December, the GOP and Clinton administration chose to let most of the government shut down because they could not agree on a budget. Within the Democratic Party, meanwhile, debate continued over how much corporate welfare should be redirected to social programs and how much to deficit-cutting.

At times, Clinton professed great interest in corporate welfare. On Dec. 16, the first day of what would be a three-week government shutdown, he met with top advisors and Democratic congressional leaders at Blair House, the historic guest house steps from the White House. Dressed in sweaters and clutching cups of hot coffee, they tried to develop a strategy to balance the budget.

Liberal standard-bearers, like Sen. Kennedy, believed corporate welfare was the place to start. He argued for a plan to save $50 billion to $60 billion by eliminating many tax breaks. He gave them names like the "runaway plant loophole," which he said encourages companies to send U.S. jobs overseas, and the "billionaires' loophole," which allows people to renounce U.S. citizenship as a tax ploy.

Clinton was interested. At the end of the session, he buttonholed Kennedy and asked him to send details to the White House, a source at the meeting said. But the next afternoon, as administration and congressional leaders met at the Capitol without the president, it was clear the White House had backtracked.

When Kennedy again argued to close tax breaks, aides to Secretary Rubin and Laura Tyson, the president's chief economic advisor, were working the room, talking privately with lawmakers. They were arguing, "Don't touch corporate welfare," recalled one person who was there.

At one point Lawrence Summers, Rubin's deputy secretary for tax policy, leaned over the table and argued against Kennedy's plan to cut the "runaway plant loophole," the "title passage loophole" that allows companies to shift profits overseas and a third tax break for exports. Summers said those provisions helped the leading employers in their states.

According to several people at the meeting, Sen. Boxer responded: "We've got to raise revenue and this is the way to do it. If we can't abolish them, then we should at least change them or alter them." Summers answered: "Barbara, do you have any idea how Silicon Valley will react to this?"

In an interview, Kennedy accused Rubin and Tyson of intentionally obscuring the corporate welfare debate to make sure nothing gets done. "They don't want to do it because they basically are a spokesman for many of these industries," he said. "I would like Bob Rubin to tell me the best ones to cut. I would like him to tell me, and tell the president, how to do it. But he is representing a different kind of constituency. He knows it. I know it. The president sort of knows it. So that makes it a political issue."

In time, the Democrats did nudge Clinton. After starting with a proposal last December to end $28 billion worth of tax breaks for businesses, the president later increased the number to $62 billion for the 1997 budget, which begins in October. But the budget was equally noteworthy for what it allowed to survive including: sugar and peanut subsidies, tax breaks for the ethanol industry and the Advanced Technology program, which grants money to companies for research and development.

"If the Congress' performance was a disappointment, the Clinton administration's was dismal," Stephen Moore and Dean Stansel of the Cato Institute wrote in May. "With few exceptions, the administration has shown itself hostile to even the modest corporate welfare cutbacks proposed by Congress."

The sugar industry, which gave $5.5 million to federal campaigns in the last seven years, managed to kill a bipartisan attack on price supports mounted by Reps. Charles Schumer, a New York Democrat, and Dan Miller, a Republican from Florida. And Congress, bowing to the wine industry, actually increased funding for the Market Promotion Program, which supports overseas advertising.

Archer Daniels Midland Co. of Illinois beat back an attempt to kill a tax break for ethanol, an alcohol-based fuel. ADM controls about 80 percent of the ethanol market. Killing the subsidy would save $3.6 billion over five years. According to Common Cause, the government watchdog group, ADM gave more than $480,000 to the Democratic Party and more than $345,000 to the Republican Party in the 1994 elections, on top of donations to individual candidates. The company and the family of its chairman have given more than $250,000 to former Sen. Bob Dole's campaign committees over the years. ADM chairman Dwayne O. Andreas has raised money for Clinton as well.

Even Kennedy, who criticizes the subsidies to sugar and peanut farmers or federal support of giant power companies in the Southwest, speaks quite differently when it comes to programs that help high-tech companies in Massachusetts. Virtually all of these so-called "high-tech handout" programs—the Advanced Technology Program, the Technology Reinvestment Project and the Small Business Innovative Research program—have been in the cross hairs of conservatives, especially Kasich and the Cato Institute. "These programs are modest in size in comparison to the others," Kennedy said.

THE CAMPAIGN CONNECTION

Overall, Robert J. Shapiro of the Progressive Policy Institute calculates Congress was ready to cut $300 billion from social programs like Head Start and welfare, but only $30 billion in corporate welfare. Those cuts would have become law had Clinton not vetoed the Republicans' budget for 1996 and general spending plans through 2002. Instead, the president and Republican leaders fought for so many months over the budget that corporate welfare cuts and other long-term spending decisions were put off until later this year. "Each of these cuts is a knockdown, drag-out fight," Reich said in a recent interview. "Why? Because the issue of corporate welfare is intimately tied to campaign finance. Why do we have so many targeted subsidies and tax breaks with no public justification or the thinnest justification? It's because companies and industries have managed to effectively lobby for their little piece of public largesse. Why have they been so effective? Because they support campaigns."

In short, many argue, Congress cannot cut subsidies and raise campaign funds at the same time. And changes to the campaign finance system do not appear to be coming soon. The Senate killed a campaign spending reform plan pushed, among others, by senators McCain and Thompson, who also targeted the "dirty dozen" corporate subsidies.

Recently McCain, Thompson, Kerry, Bradley, Kennedy and others have been pushing a new approach on corporate welfare: a bipartisan commission that would draw up a list of subsidy programs to cut. After approval by the president, Congress would vote on the list—all or nothing. The idea is patterned after the commission that chose what military bases to close, another politically sensitive problem that called for shared sacrifice.

"I don't know any other way that we can attack this issue," McCain said this year at a hearing on the proposal. An independent commission "would depoliticize the process, guarantee that the pain is shared, and might be the only realistic means of achieving a meaningful reform, which the public and our dire fiscal circumstances demand."

CHAPTER 8

Health Care

"It was the best of times and the worst of times." The state of the American health care system can be compared to these opening lines of Charles Dickens' novel *A Tale of Two Cities*.

Our health care system has some of the best technology, hospitals, and doctors in the world. However, it leaves many citizens uninsured and underinsured. Moreover, skyrocketing health care costs have put tremendous pressure on the medical community to reduce expenses, sometimes at the loss of quality. Publicly funded drug and alcohol rehabilitation centers are constantly short of funds as the demand for them increases. President Clinton's plan for national health insurance for all Americans was successfully aborted in 1994 through a combination of poor legislative strategy and intense interest group opposition.

For lower prices than traditional fee-for-service practices, many businesses and individuals have turned to health maintenance organizations (HMOs) for medical care. The first reading describes the potential negative consequences for increasing amounts of individuals relying on HMOs.

The second and third readings describe positive actions taken to meet different needs. The second reading describes aspects of the 1996 Kassebaum-Kennedy law, which ensures transportable health insurance, limits rejections for preexisting conditions, and helps individuals and small-business employers afford health insurance.

The third reading presents the health care work of the Salvation Army. A genuine community designed to treat people with "tough love," they are a nonbureaucratic open door for drug addicts and alcoholics to receive help.

Should the profit motive operate in the same way in medicine as it does in other parts of the economy? Should basic health insurance be a right for all Americans? What responsibility to society do individuals have in maintaining their health? Is the Salvation Army a good model for community health care?

WALL STREET IN HOSPITAL SCRUBS

JULIA RAISKIN

MANAGED CARE AND AMERICAN HEALTH

Three years ago, Christine deMeuers was diagnosed with metastatic breast cancer. Her only hope was a new type of therapy, the harvest and retransplantation of her own bone marrow. After receiving her diagnosis, Christine and her husband, Alan, sat down to read the ominously thick contract they had signed when they enrolled in Health Net, a California-based health maintenance organization (HMO). Like most members, they had never opened the book; now they were poring over its pages. And although their despair was briefly interrupted by Alan's exclamation, ''It's covered!,'' the fight for treatment was to continue for the next two years. Christine had to travel from clinic to clinic, plead with HMO officials, implore her doctors for a right to treatment and, astonishingly, question the veracity of their opinions and prescriptions. She died on March 10, 1995.

The growing frequency of experiences like deMeuers's—the failure of the HMO, the uncertainty surrounding the doctor-patient relationship, the anxiety about coverage—raises the obvious question: ''What's happening to America's health care?'' You don't have to be Oliver Stone to spot a story behind this story. The truth of the matter is that our medicine is less and less about trust and care, or even doctors and patients; the dictates of profit maximization are our medicine's new guiding principles. ''It's a paradigm shift,'' states . . . William Popik, chief medical officer of a large HMO, ''What's shifting is patients can't drive it anymore; patients can't decide, 'My ear hurts, so I'm going to go to the doctor today.' '' While this executive may be justified in trivializing earaches, his attitude borders on monstrous when one considers that life-threatening conditions are often discovered through the examination of minor complaints.

Of course, ruthless moneymaking is the stuff of which our American dream is made. Open a business and amass millions; you are well on your way to fulfilling the dream. In a society where people hold Michael Milken and Bill Gates as cultural icons, and commodification is regarded as a form of creativity, allegiance to profit appears morally commendable. However, when the commodities are Life and Death, our laissez-faire attitudes run up against some ethical dilemmas.

Until a few decades ago, America had been a fee-for-service type of land, where medical care consisted of transactions between khaki-clad doctors and

From *Perspectives*, June 1996. Reprinted with permission.

trusting patients; these could cost anywhere from $50 for a routine visit to hundreds of thousands of dollars for complex procedures such as transplants. For the insured, much, or at least a part, of this tab was picked up by the traditional insurance companies; the uninsured often had to rely on charity care.

That was then. Now, "managed health care" plans have been widely introduced to counteract the escalating costs of medical procedures and to allow coverage for patients unable to afford traditional insurance plans. For the privately insured, this managed care comes largely in the form of health maintenance organizations. The idea is very attractive: for a reasonable fee ($5–10 for a routine doctor visit) patients are able to obtain care from a designated circle of physicians. Behind the veil of affordability, however, hides the boardroom decision making of big business. In order to "manage" this health care, doctors have been turned into marionettes by behind-the-scenes entrepreneurs whose tight fists often prohibit costly treatments, regardless of patient need. In the jargon of market-driven medicine, patients are "covered lives," and physicians are "gatekeepers." The rise of market forces, with their exclusive focus on profit, threatens to transform the language of medicine into Wall Street newspeak.

HMO care is radically different from fee-for-service care because it merges two traditionally separate sectors—health care providers and insurers—into one. Patient premiums and payments to doctors are now controlled by the same set of executives. Conventional insurance companies operate through perpetual rounds of Russian roulette: they collect premiums calculated according to life models, smoking patterns, and general health risks in the population, and then hope the money they receive exceeds the funds they are forced to hand over to doctors. Since HMOs collect the premiums and employ the doctors, the risks that they assume are internally controlled by their managers.

HMO executives frequently use questionable methods to further their corporate goals. Most HMOs cut premiums to attract more patients, which, of course, requires internal costs to be reduced in order to maintain profits. So HMOs frequently resort to a cost-cutting measure dubbed "capitation." Capitation is, crudely put, much like giving a child with a sweet tooth a bag of candy, instructing her to give out as much as she wants and to keep the rest. Primary doctors are budgeted a fixed amount of money, a flat fee to treat each patient. And, since they are the "gatekeepers" to further care, they must share this sum with specialists. As a result, every time a doctor refers a patient to a specialist or performs a costly procedure, her take-home pay is docked. If the doctor spends less than the capitated rate, she keeps the difference. Those thrifty doctors who help to restrain health spending often receive bonuses or other financial rewards from the grateful HMO.

This practice pits patients and doctors against each other and, needless to say, breeds problems bigger than big business. "Understand, every time a patient comes into the doctor's office it's a liability, not an asset, because [the doctor] is on a fixed income," says David Robinson, a doctor hired by a California

HMO. Dr. Herbert Lang, an internist who was formerly employed by the Share Health Plan of Illinois, claims that he had to quit because "when I did not order some expensive test like CAT scan, I was forever asking myself if I did that because it was not medically indicated or because I wanted to save money. In the end, I would over-order tests, and I didn't make as much as some of the other doctors."

Unstated limitations on medical services offered to patients are a logical consequence of the capitation "fat trimming" method. General practitioners control patient access to further medical care, including treatment by specialists. A further problem, however, is that the gatekeepers themselves are limited in their options because they, too, must consult a "higher authority"—HMO managers—for permission to administer and refer. One physician recalls "requesting a CAT scan for a boy who had experienced seizures and occasional losses of consciousness, possible warnings of a brain tumor, only to have his request denied."

Patients are also restricted in their options by the limited coverage of "experimental procedures," as defined by their HMOs; this was Christine deMeuers's predicament. The managed care system abhors complexity and innovation. Breakthroughs tend to be expensive, and so there is virtually no talk of funding research. Health Net recently rejected a proposal to support a study on ovarian cancer claiming: "If we put money into ovarian cancer research and the word gets out, then it isn't going to be long before AIDS groups or prostate-cancer groups start having a field day." The reluctance to invest in new treatments is peculiarly selective, and always dictated by cost concerns. While adamantly refusing to support expensive systematic clinical research or to cover transplants and innovative pharmacotherapies, some health care providers experiment with cheaper "miracle cures" by paying for visits to faith healers and acupuncturists.

As a result, HMOs have a perverse incentive to cheer for negative trial outcomes. In response to a trial showing transplants were an effective treatment for breast cancer–treatment that would become standard in the near future–a chief health official of an HMO reacted with despair. He was "very disappointed" to discover that the treatment was "not experimental." He even "raised a little hell" about the results.

We are caught in a situation in which the HMO benefits from patient ignorance. "You put yourself in a position where you don't discuss it, or else discuss it and, worse yet, indicate that all the data is negative or that there is not a significant amount of data about this," says Dr. Jones, a Colorado physician, "I think you are irreparably damaging the very thing that makes you as a physician so valuable to patients." The more the patient is kept in the dark about her treatment options, the more the doctor and the HMO stand to benefit.

All of this would be less disturbing if patients had the right to know about the devil's kitchen behind the polished HMO facade. But patients often do not even have the option of knowing about the "standard practices" of managed care providers. By law, HMOs are permitted to limit the information which doctors may disclose to their patients. The use of "gag clauses" in contracts with doctors is an increasingly common practice. These clauses—which doctors often must sign as part of their contracts—give HMOs the right to regulate the level of disclosure. HMOs claim that this practice is intended to protect proprietary and trade secrets, as well as to divert doctors' venting of their frustrations from patients to management.

The practical consequence is that many doctors who want to advocate on behalf of their patients are muzzled. A standard "gag clause" found in a contract of Choice Care in Cincinnati reads: "Physicians shall take no action nor make any communication which undermines or could undermine the confidence of enrollees, potential enrollees, their employers, plan sponsors or the public in Choice Care, or in the quality of care which Choice Care enrollees receive." Some contracts, such as those offered to physicians by Kaiser Permanente of Ohio, do not even permit doctors to discuss any proposed treatments with patients before receiving authorization, while others bar doctors from making "disparaging" or "derogatory remarks" about the HMO.

Though many doctors are forced to accept the terms of the HMOs' contract for financial reasons, resistance has been significant. Doctors in New York recently filed a law suit claiming that confidentiality clauses destroy "the physician's liberty to convey needed information to patients concerning HMO operations." The deputy director of Medical Society of New Jersey, Neil Weisfield, added that "these gag clauses intimidate physicians and discourage them from talking openly to patients about the need for specialty care and the role of managed care companies in limiting tests and treatments. It's more like managed silence than managed care."

Even as care is severely restricted, corporate profits are soaring, and executives are receiving hefty pay raises. Last year Health Net's director earned a base salary of $815,000, an additional bonus of nearly $300,000, and other incentive-plan rewards that brought his yearly total to nearly $1.9 million. Massive mergers are continually boosting these corporate salaries by turning large HMOs into sprawling monopolies, as smaller insurers are pushed to the limits of fiscal viability.

How many more Christine deMeuerses will it take for us to realize that health care should not be tied to the fluctuations of the market? Since we cannot radically alter our entrepreneurial mentality, the government should become more proactive in ensuring that medicine does not become a "growing economic field." Tough regulation is imperative. Legislation limiting HMOs' control over patient-doctor communication and enforcing coverage for particular procedures and support for research is long overdue. If this appears to be disadvantageous for big business, it is because, clearly, medicine must not be solely about big business. As Christine deMeuers's experience shows, the consequences of corporate strategizing in medicine may be lethal.

HEALTH INSURANCE REFORM ACT

SENATOR JOE BIDEN (D-DEL.), SENATOR JOHN KERRY (D-MASS.), AND SENATOR HOWELL HEFLIN (D-ALA.).

MR. BIDEN. Mr. President, when comprehensive health care reform went down to defeat in 1994, many of us in the Senate were frustrated because we had let yet another opportunity for reforming the health care system slip away.

At that time, there was wide agreement on some elements of health care reform. I, for one, wanted to go forward with those items—even if they fell short of addressing all of the problems in the health care system. Unfortunately, political considerations on both sides of the aisle and at both ends of Pennsylvania Avenue prevented us from passing even those things we all agreed on.

Who would have believed less than two years ago that we would be on the verge of passing a bipartisan health care bill. And, who would have believed that the bill would provide real reform by addressing the most pressing problem faced by middle-class Americans—the possibility that they will lose their health insurance just because they change jobs or get sick.

Four years ago, a national survey showed that nearly one-third of all Americans had at some time in their lives been the victim of "job lock." Fearing the loss of health insurance, they stayed in a job they did not want and did not like. Two years ago, I asked Delawareans that same question—and in responding to my questionnaire, 21 percent of Delawareans said they had experienced job lock. Addressing this problem is long overdue. But it may finally happen.

With the bipartisan Kassebaum-Kennedy bill, no longer will insurance companies be able to deny coverage for most pre-existing conditions. No longer will Americans be locked in jobs they do not want because changing jobs means losing health insurance. And no longer will insurance companies be able to cancel a person's policy just because they get sick. . . .

Mr. President, the Kassebaum-Kennedy bill also provides some important help to small businesses—those who have been most devastated by the rapidly rising costs of health care. First, the bill would increase the self-employed health insurance tax deduction to 80 percent. I am a cosponsor of legislation to increase the deduction to a full 100 percent. This bill falls short of that goal, but it continues to move us in the right direction.

Second, the bill would make it easier for small businesses to join together to purchase health insurance. By pooling their employees, small businesses can

From the *Congressional Record*: April 23, 1996 (Senate).

spread the health risks among a large number of people and get cheaper insurance rates as a result.

And, third, the bill guarantees that all small businesses will have health insurance available to them. It prohibits insurance companies from cherry picking the businesses with the healthiest employees and refusing to sell to all other businesses. This sounds simple—even unnecessary. But, in the real world, it is crucial. When just one employee in a small business has a problem pregnancy, or has a disabled child, or suffers from some other medical condition, it often means that no one that works in that small business can get health insurance. . . .

MR. KERRY. Mr. President, I want to thank Senators Kassebaum and Kennedy for their leadership in putting together this bill which the General Accounting Office (GAO) estimates will help over 21 million people.

I also want to talk today about a woman from Florence, Massachusetts, who wrote me about her daughter. She supports this bill, she said, because her daughter has diabetes and the family had a terrible time finding health insurance that would cover her. In her letter she told me, "I think it's immoral for health insurance companies to cut off coverage even while the people they cover are paying their premiums. No health insurance company should have the power to do this to their clients."

Millions of Americans have medical histories or preexisting conditions that make it difficult to get comprehensive insurance coverage. As many as 81 million Americans have preexisting medical conditions that could affect their insurability. Many people are locked in their jobs because they fear they will be unable to obtain comprehensive insurance in new jobs. And many people who work in small businesses often have trouble getting insurance especially if one employee has medical problems. . . .

This bill takes very important steps forward. But we must do more, so that ultimately we have coverage for all Americans. Currently, 40 million Americans live without health insurance, and 23 million of the 40 million are workers, according to a study by the Tulane University School of Public Health. Furthermore, an average of more than 1 million children a year have been losing private health insurance since 1987. In Massachusetts alone, there are more than 130,000 children—one-tenth of all the children in my state—who are without any health insurance, private or public, for the entire year. And many more children lack health insurance for part of the year. A recent study in the *Journal of the American Medical Association* reported that almost one-quarter of U.S. three-year-olds in 1991 lacked health insurance for at least a month during their first three years, and almost 60 percent of those lacked insurance for six or more months. . . .

MR. HEFLIN. . . . In light of all the money spent on the provision of health care in the nation, it is surprising that we have not already found a way to deliver a sufficient level of care to the millions of citizens who do not have health insurance. The Department of Health and Human Services estimates that between 32 and 37 million Americans have no health insurance, and an additional 50 to 60 million are underinsured. As translated by the Office of Management and Budget, a total of 13 percent of all Americans are completely uninsured, with as many as 28 percent without insurance for one month or more. The Labor Department reports that each year, one million people lose their health insurance.

As currently structured, the private health insurance market provides an insufficient level of coverage for individuals and families with major health problems and makes it difficult for employers to obtain adequate coverage for their employees. This is especially true of small businesses.

The bill before us—S.1028, The Health Insurance Reform Act—will reduce many of the existing barriers to obtaining insurance coverage by making it easier for people who change jobs or lose their jobs to maintain adequate coverage. It will also provide increased purchasing power to small businesses and individuals. I am proud to support this legislation, which is aimed at covering millions of those who do not have insurance or who have an inadequate level by addressing the issues of portability and preexisting conditions.

S.1028 builds upon innovative and successful state reforms and enhances the private market by requiring health plans to compete based on quality, price, and service instead of refusing to offer coverage to those who are in poor health and need it the most. Passage of this measure is being called a relatively modest first step toward the kind of comprehensive reform legislation we tried to pass in 1994. I agree that it is only a first step, but feel instead that it is a rather major first step in that it goes a long way toward reaching the goal of universal health care. . . .

Enactment of S.1028 . . . would also provide much-needed momentum for future reform efforts. Equally important, it would not increase federal spending, impose new or expensive requirements on individuals, employers, or states, or create new federal layers of bureaucracy. . . .

IN PRAISE OF UNLIKELY CAPITALISTS

JOAN RETSINAS

Here is a health care riddle for the 90s: What 10,688-bed rehabilitation organization served 50,171 addicts last year, accepts no insurance payments, demands no government stipend—yet takes indigent applicants? Answer: The Salvation Army.

Unlike the Skid Row alcoholics of thirty years ago, who lost family and friends and jobs to a bottle, today's addicts are younger, less skilled, less literate, more troubled, and addicted not just to alcohol, but to a pharmacopoeia of drugs. They—men and women—come to the 146 Salvation Army Rehabilitation Centers to get clean. They want sobriety enough to embrace a regimen that most Americans would reject as anachronistic, totalitarian, and certainly not politically correct.

The Salvation Army operates outside the world of managed care and psychojargon. The men and women who enter the Salvation Army doors are not "patients," or "consumers," or "clients," but "beneficiaries"—beneficiaries of the benevolence of a corps of caring people, or benevolence of a loving God, depending upon perspective. In either case, the corps expects gratitude, as well as obedience to a list of mandatories: mandatory religious participation (morning prayer, midweek vespers, regular Bible study), mandatory support group meetings, mandatory work (called "work therapy"), mandatory cleanliness and orderliness, mandatory counseling, mandatory courtesy.

The behavioral canons hark back to nineteenth-century etiquette: beneficiaries shall dress and behave like "ladies and gentlemen." Beneficiaries cannot swear, copulate, or complain. Nor can they relapse. This treatment world is not a democratic one.

Yet so long as the person follows the straight and narrow path toward sobriety, the Corps supports him. New beneficiaries commit to ninety days, with many staying longer, working not just on shaking their monkeys, but on learning to read, mastering a skill, working with other people. When counselors fear a person is growing so comfortably acclimated to this community that s/he shrinks from leaving, counselors nudge him, or her, out—but help him find a home and job. Even employing him. No treatment timetables force people out at twenty-eight days. No insurers restrict treatment to once, or twice. An addict can stay, leave, relapse, return, stay, leave, relapse, return. . . . In the Army's lexicon, "hopeless" must not exist.

From *The Progressive Populist*, August 1996. Reprinted with permission.

The "community"—the most overused word of today—is genuine. Staff and beneficiaries work and eat and pray together. They celebrate birthdays and holidays. Walk into a thrift store cafeteria; and pick out the beneficiaries from the employees. You can't. Or go through the thrift store and differentiate beneficiary from employee. You can't. The contribution of one person is as important as the other; all sustain each other and the business.

The business that keeps the rehabilitation centers afloat is discards: old furniture, outgrown clothes, broken appliances, often junk. From the tons of donated stuff, the Salvation Army sells some, recycles some, and dumps the rest (what some donors should have done from the start, thereby sparing the Army hefty dumping fees). The profits support room and board and counseling for the beneficiaries, as well as salaries for staff. The Providence, Rhode Island, Pitman Street operation is not atypical: With a $4.5 million budget, the thrift stores are a solvent business, employing 148 people, 103 of them recovering addicts.

No insurers underwrite the rehabilitation. Few of the addicts have insurance anyway. Nor do public moneys contribute. Although the Army might be able to negotiate welfare stipends for some residents (thereby getting them Medicaid, food stamps, and a monthly check, which could then reimburse the Army for room and board), the Salvation Army has spurned government entanglement. This is a textbook entrepreneurial marvel.

I don't know whether in the long run the rehabilitation works. In the short run the beneficiaries get to live and work among people who respect them and their labor.

Most importantly, though, nobody else is reaching out to help these addicts. The government is retrenching on the limited money it spends on rehabilitation, though it does feed and house these people, as inmates, under the corrections budget. The private rehabilitation sector treats paying "clients." Period. As for private charity—the stuff of Republican enthusiasm—young male addicts fall below endangered whales on the public Richter scale of concern. The addicts represent society's discards.

So it is fitting that the Salvation Army, which salvages millions of dollars from the detritus of our affluence, uses that money to salvage the lives of these people. And it is comforting to know that, when the Dow Jones slips and the megahealth conglomerates retreat from residential addiction treatment, the Salvation Army will simply expand.

CHAPTER 9

A Concluding Speech from a True Believer

It would be difficult to find a better representative of the original economic populism of the late nineteenth century than Byron Dorgan. Dorgan is a Democratic U.S. Senator from North Dakota, a state where prairie populism was particularly powerful. Dorgan talks about the legacy of populism and how some Republicans are trying to claim its heritage.

He also talks about contemporary populism's relationship to such issues as the standard of living, the trade deficit, tax laws, the importance of production in our economy, how value is created and rewarded, the policies of the Federal Reserve Board, and farm policy.

Populists distrust large organizations, whether they are public or private. Would it be possible for a politician with Dorgan's views to represent a larger state, with more people and industries than North Dakota? What interests would stand to lose the most if U.S. trade policy was reoriented towards "fair trade"? Is Dorgan's emphasis on production, rather than consumption, compatible with expanding international trade?

POPULISM

SENATOR BYRON DORGAN (D-N. DAKOTA).

Mr. DORGAN. There is an old axiom in politics, when your adversaries are having a healthy feud, never walk across the street and get involved in it. I will not do that this morning. I am tempted to. However, I wanted to discuss, at least a bit, the issue of populism. I will not discuss so much the details of the feud that is going on in the Republican party and in the primaries, but I do want to talk about the issue of populism.

What propelled me to do that today was *Time* magazine. There is a picture of Pat Buchanan in a hard hat and work shirt, and Lamar Alexander peeking over his shoulder in his plaid shirt, and then Bob Dole and Steve Forbes behind them.

It says, "Grand Old Populists." So I am presuming, I guess, that GOP means "Grand Old Populists." I wanted to talk a little about this issue of populism. It is a fascinating concept to see these, as one of my colleagues in the Senate calls them, Grey Poupon-eating, Jacuzzi, country-club folks, wearing hard hats and work shirts and calling themselves populists.

Let us put all this in perspective. About 80 or 90 million years ago, the brontosaurus and triceratops and tyrannosaurus rex were running across southwestern North Dakota. They are digging some of them up, by the way. Then we skipped and fast forwarded, and it was about 5,000 years ago that we discovered there were people around, and about 2,000 years ago Jesus was alive. About 500 years ago Columbus was relatively lost and stumbled onto the southern part of this continent, and despite the fact that the folks who were living here greeted his boat, he was credited with discovering something or another.

And 200 years ago our country was born. Then 100 years ago we created planes, trains, and automobiles, roughly speaking. And seventy-five and fifty years ago it was the radio, then television. And twenty-five years ago we put a man on the moon. Then ten years ago the computer became something that you could have in your home and then later carry on your lap as you traveled. And now in the Republican party "GOP" means "Grand Old Populists." And it is causing quite a stir, actually.

I noticed in this morning's paper one of the strategists, William Kristol, who speaks more often than most on politics from the conservative side, spoke of this issue.

He is speaking now about the turmoil that is going on in the Republican

From the *Congressional Record*, February 23, 1996 (Senate).

primaries. "William Kristol," according to the story this morning as a result of something he wrote recently—I guess this week—"sees no need for the Republican Establishment to succumb, in Pat Buchanan's phrase, to 'terminal panic.' A junior member of that Establishment, Kristol doesn't cower when the high-riding presidential contender thunders about the terrified knights and barons of the GOP," et cetera, et cetera.

"Someone needs to stand up and defend the Establishment," says Kristol, a sometime strategist, party ideologist and editor of the conservative *Weekly Standard* magazine. "In the last couple of weeks, there's been too much pseudo-populism, almost too much concern and attention for, quote, the people—that is, the people's will, their prejudices and their foolish opinions. And in a certain sense, we're all paying the price for that now.... After all, we conservatives are on the side of the lords and the barons." He says there is "almost too much concern and attention for the people . . . we are on the side of the lords and barons."

Well, what to make of this: The grand old populist with the hard hat and the honest conservative who says, "Wait a second, there's too much attention being paid to the people here, the people and their foolish opinions," Mr. Kristol says. "We are on the side of the lords and the barons."

God bless the lords and the barons. They are a good group of folks, but it is the people who run this country. It is the people for whom elections are held, because the Constitution gives the people in this country the right to grab the steering wheel and decide in Montana or North Dakota or Nevada or New York or Texas in which direction they want America to move. They nudge that steering wheel by collectively voting. It is the people, not the lords and barons, the people who grab the American steering wheel every even-numbered year. That is part of the miracle of the American Constitution. It is a miracle guaranteed every even-numbered year to the people in this country.

What of this issue of populism? It is interesting to me, coming from a state where populism had its roots. In North Dakota, in the early 1900s, nineteen-teens, there was a legislator named Treadwill Twitchell who stood up in the chamber of the state legislature and told the farmers to "go home and slop your hogs with great arrogance." He was someone who represented one of the big cities in our state. "Go home and slop your hogs," he said.

They went home all right, and two years later, they organized section line by section line all across North Dakota. They came back and took over in North Dakota in the nineteen-teens. They were populists. There is a book written about it called *Prairie Fire*, in which the people took hold and said, "This is our destiny."

They built themselves in North Dakota a bank saying, "We're tired of having public money put in private cronies' banks. We will have our own bank which belongs to people." My state is the only state in America that still has a Bank of North Dakota, and all public money goes into that bank is used for the public good. It is not a case in our State where some of the State's money goes into some crony's bank someplace. It goes into the bank the populists created in the nineteen-teens.

They built a mill and elevator because they were sick and tired of the big mills in the East taking advantage of our farmers. They said, "We are going to build a mill and elevator." They passed a farmers bill where they said, "We want farmers, not corporations; we want yard lights where families live on the farm."

The populist legacy in our state is a legacy about people having power. Part of what I find heartening these days is the discussion in the political system, especially in the Republican primaries, but also in our party, the Democratic party, a discussion about what kind of economic system does this country have. For whose benefit does it operate? Who reaps the rewards of this economic system?

There are some things I have heard and seen in recent weeks that trouble me greatly, and I am sure that is true of many in this chamber: Top advisers to campaigners out there who give speeches to white supremacist groups and use code words. Those kinds of things really bother me a lot, because there is a dark tinge to some of this discussion, and that ought to be rejected, and rejected quickly, by the American people.

But there is also, in my judgment, an arrow headed straight to the center of what ought to be the economic debate in this country, and the center of the economic debate is how are American families doing? Are they advancing? Is their standard of living improving? When they sit down for dinner with the family to talk about their circumstance, are they able to say, "Our jobs are secure; we have good jobs with good incomes; we have decent health care at affordable prices; we go to good schools"? Are they able to say that? Or do they say, "Too often these days, we're not so sure about our job security. We worked for the same company for twenty-two years, but the company just reported record profits, the CEO makes $4 million, just got a $2 million raise and laid off 8,000 people, because they call that progress."

So, too many families now sit down at dinner and understand the companies they have worked for twenty years see them like they see a wrench or a punch press: as a tool, perfectly expendable and completely expendable once the company has decided it is in their interest to decide to get rid of them now and hire another tool or another worker.

All too often in China, Malaysia, Indonesia, Bangladesh, Sri Lanka, somewhere where they can hire someone without the restrictions on age—you can hire a kid if you wish—without the nettlesome restrictions that you have to pay a living wage—you can pay fourteen cents an hour to someone who makes tennis shoes in Malaysia—without the restriction that you have to have a safe workplace, without the restriction that you cannot dump chemicals into the air or dump chemicals into the water.

So people now understand that they are expendable, and that is the sadness of the lack of security in the job place in America. Not only do they see they have less security, they also see that they make less money; they work harder, but they make less money. If one adjusts their wage for inflation and goes back twenty years and measures it, what has happened is they are working harder and twenty years later they are making less money and have less purchasing power than they had twenty years ago.

Is there any reason that the American people have some anxiety about that? We can talk forever that the GDP numbers are up, America is on the move, our economy is growing, and it does not matter if the standard of living for American families is not advancing.

I have spoken on the floor previously about this—I know it is repetitive— but it is important to say you do not and cannot measure America's economic health and its future promise by what it consumes. I am just flat sick and tired of hearing the news reports that the Commerce Department said this, the Federal Reserve Board this or that, car sales are up, home sales are up, shoes sales are up. At issue is not how much we bought, how much we consumed.

The issue is what did we produce in this country? It is production that gives you good jobs. Good jobs come from our productive sector and, as our manufacturing jobs are moving, we are losing manufacturing jobs. They are being moved by international economic enterprises who do not say the Pledge of Allegiance and they do not sing the national anthem. They are interested in international profits. They do not care whether they produce in Pittsburgh or Malaysia. They will produce where it is the most profitable to produce, and manufacturing jobs are leaving America in droves. Witness the trade deficit we have.

Last year, the trade deficit was larger than our budget deficit. There is nobody saying much about it, and it is almost a conspiracy of silence. The trade deficit means we buy from abroad more than we sell abroad. What that means is jobs that would have been here are instead somewhere else in another country.

Corporations that are producing are producing elsewhere, and the American people have some role in this as well. It is not unusual to find somebody wearing a Chinese shirt, slacks from Taiwan, shoes from Italy, shorts from Mexico, driving a Japanese car, and then saying, ''Where on earth have American jobs gone?'' You are wearing where it has gone. So there is enough responsibility to go around.

But the center of the economic debate in this country has to come to this issue about what is fair trade and how do we construct a circumstance in which we have a healthy, vibrant growing manufacturing base in our country.

To those out on the campaign trail these days wearing hard hats and preaching populism, I say to them, ''Come here and help us.''

I offered an amendment in the U.S. Senate, and it was as simple as could be. No one could misunderstand it and no one could even, in my judgment, mistakenly vote wrong on it. I lost on a partisan vote.

The amendment very simply was to say: Let us stop providing tax breaks so that companies can close their American plants and open up plants overseas. Let us stop providing tax breaks so that American corporations can move their jobs to foreign countries. Let us put an end to the insidious giveaway in our Tax Code that allows companies to do that: Fire American workers, hire foreign workers, become more profitable, and destroy job security in our country.

I could not even get that adopted in the Senate. Mr. President, to all of those who voted and voted wrong, they are going to get a chance six, eight, ten, twelve more times, if I have my way, this year to rectify that, because this country should not and cannot continue to have economic incentives in its tax laws to say "it is our aim to encourage you to move your jobs overseas."

It is my aim to encourage American companies to invest here, to produce here, and to hire here in this country.

There are twin responsibilities that we have. The American worker has a responsibility, but productivity is on the rise. Workers are working harder. Workers do have a responsibility to be motivated, educated, dedicated, and to be good workers. But companies then have the responsibility, as well, to care about the people who make up that company, to care about the people who make the products that the company sells with that company's name on it.

About a month or so ago, I read a piece in the *Minneapolis Tribune* as I was going through the airport. I came to the floor of the Senate and told, briefly, about what I had read because it was so foreign to everything that is going on in this country. It was about a fellow who had owned the company that make inline skates called Rollerblades. He and his wife had purchased this company and built it into something substantial, an enormously successful company, making inline skates. Rollerblades is the name of the company. And then this fellow, named Bob, sold the company some months ago. He had made a substantial amount of money because the company was enormously successful. Of course, all of us understand what has happened with inline skates. At Christmastime, some of the workers at this company began getting in the mail a letter from the fellow who had owned this company. They began to open their Christmas greeting from this fellow and his wife, and it turned out that he had sent them money. He no longer owned the company, but he sent all of the employees—I think something like 270 employees who worked for that company in the factory lines, custodial, the painters, and everything—if memory is correct, he sent them $160 for every month they worked for the company.

In some cases, those folks on the factory lines, who had been there all the time he had the company, got up to a $20,000 check from this fellow and his wife. Do you know what else he did? He prepaid the taxes on it. So he said to them, "This gift is for you. You owe no taxes on it. I have prepaid the taxes."

I called him and said, "This is remarkable, at a time when we hear about all of the selfishness and layoffs and moving jobs overseas. I want to tell you how remarkable it is to hear about what you did." What he said to me was perfectly understandable. He said, "I made money with that company because all of those folks helped make that company work. They worked on the factory lines. They are the ones who made the company; it was not just me, it was them as well, and I wanted to share something with them. I wanted to tell them that they contributed something significant in the success of that company.''

I thought, ''What a hero.'' He did not have to do that. We do not hear many stories like that—stories that are unselfish, where the CEO says, ''You people really make this company work. When we put our company name on the product, we are proud because you helped make the product.'' That is almost unheard of these days. Nowadays it is, ''Well, you worked for us, but tomorrow you are like a used wrench. You might be out of here with no security, no health care, and maybe no pension. We might be hiring your replacement 6,000 or 8,000 miles away.''

Well, would it not be nice to hear more people do what that man did, and recognize that part of this country's success is to have a vibrant, expanding, growing manufacturing base, and to recognize the workers out there on the line producing products, doing good work, working hard, and are also part of the success and part of the competitive team?

I just think that we have kind of gone in a different direction in this country, in which we have had economists, CEOs, and others develop an economic model that says that it is fine if we produce elsewhere and sell here as long as we are buying cheap. That is not fine. Major jobs are gone, and a major future is gone with it. That needs to be the center of the economic debate. How could we create conditions in which manufacturing in this country expands again, in which there is fair international competition, in which we reduce the trade deficit, bring jobs back to this country, and rev up the American economy to a reasonable economic growth.

On a related but slightly different issue, yesterday, the President reappointed Alan Greenspan to head the Federal Reserve Board for another term. He is going to submit his name to us. Certainly, the Congress will accept that. I am terribly disappointed by that. I have great respect for Mr. Greenspan, but I have profound disagreements with him, as well. I agree with Jack Kemp on the issue of economic growth. The Federal Reserve Board sees itself as a set of human brake pads. That is their mission in life. They say America cannot have an unemployment limit below 6 percent because it is inflationary, or economic growth above 2.5 or 3 percent because it is inflationary. But wages are going down, not up, so that is nonsense.

When you consign our economy to a meager growth rate of 2.5 percent, you consign an economy to an anemic future that is far less than what it should be for all Americans. It means fewer jobs and less opportunity. I am very disappointed the president has seen fit—not that Mr. Greenspan is a bad person, I have great respect for him. But I would have much preferred new leadership at the Fed—not leadership that says inflation is not important because, of course, it is. We have seen stable prices and a growing economy. Inflation has been going down—under 3 percent for four years in a row. Yet, the Fed has its foot on the brakes with higher interest rates than the producers in this country should be paying.

Mr. President, I notice my friend from Nevada on the floor. He has some things to say today. So let me finish with a couple of other brief comments. This issue of populism, or the power that people have in this country to affect their lives and to force this political system to debate what it ought to debate, is a very important concept. We just finished debating a farm bill in the U.S. Senate. A fellow named Robert Greene, an Associated Press writer—somebody who I think does an excellent job of synthesizing what we do with foreign policy in the Congress. He wrote a piece that is probably the best piece I know of describing what we did on the farm policy. We passed the so-called freedom-to-farm bill, which I fought against and voted against because I think it is a terrible piece of legislation. Here is what he said about it: "With a mix of luck, work and unusual organization, the lobby for the big grain companies, railroads, meat companies, millers and shippers scored a big win in the Senate-passed overhaul of farm programs."

The freedom-to-farm bill is a serious act of mislabeling. It is everything that big railroads wanted, that big grain trading farms wanted, that all the millers wanted, that all the food processors wanted. Guess what it means to the family with the yard light on at night trying to figure out how to operate the family farm? These large interests want lower grain prices. Talk about economic populism, about putting jam on the lower shelf so everybody can reach it. This sort of nonsense, the freedom-to-farm bill, which gives everything they want to the big grain trading firms, and shortchanges family farmers is the wrong way, not the right way, to address the issue of whether we should have family farmers in our future. If it becomes law, we will have large agrifactories from coast to coast, and you will see precious few yard lights on because family farmers will not be able to make a living.

I was going to talk about other economic issues that relate to the same thing—who gets, who gives, who has the power, and who does not. As Mr. Kristol says, "Who are the lords and barons, and what do they get?" I will end where I began with not so much surprise at the message, but at the candor in the article this morning where Mr. Kristol says, "Someone needs to stand up and defend the establishment. In the last couple of weeks there has been too much pseudo-populism, almost too much concern and attention for 'the people.' "

Mr. Kristol has not served in the House or the Senate, but the people control the House and the Senate. This is their Chamber; it is their body. They, by their election, determine who serves here. I guess maybe some people, who have not run for county sheriff or Congress, for that matter, probably sometimes dismiss the interests of the people.

There is a desk here that I was assigned to the first day I came to the Senate, and I have since been reassigned. It was temporary. I opened the drawer and, as is the custom, deep in the drawers, in the history of the Senate, everyone carves their names in the desk. That is not a practice we recommend to schoolchildren, but the history is that we do that. The desk that I was assigned to the first day I was here indicates that Harry Truman carved his name in the desk. A desk I was assigned to later says that Warren Harding sat in that desk. He later became President. Below his name is the name of one of the great populists in this country, Robert La Follette from Wisconsin. He understood about economic power. He understood about the people, and he would understand when I express enormous surprise that there is anyone who comments on, is interested in, or is involved in politics, who believes that there is too much concern and attention being paid to the people in our political campaigns.

Frankly, there is not enough concern and attention being paid to the center issues that affect people, who, every day, are trying to figure out how do we get a good education, how do we afford decent health care, how do we find a good job that pays well, how do we find a company to work for that will value and trust us and keep us and appreciate our work? Those are the center concerns of a lot of people in this country, who believe that over two centuries of growth, through innovation and through hard work, America has succeeded beyond the dreams of most when you look at two centuries; but who also believe that the best days in this country are still ahead of us, if its best days are consigned to the interests of the people in this country, who still have the opportunity to control its direction and still have the opportunity to tell us what they think is important and what they think will make America a better country in which to live. . . .

CHAPTER 10

Postscript

The appeal of economic populism, to a large extent, will depend on how well the American economy distributes benefits to its citizens. At this point, the discourse on free trade is largely symbolic: the effects of the World Trade Organization (WTO) on a majority of Americans is minimal. But that could change quickly if there is a dramatic change in the economy. For example, if there is weak growth or a recession, then there will be calls for governmental action. If the WTO is seen as impeding national or state action, then the issue of sovereignty might arise. However, if the trend towards expanding free trade coincides with economic prosperity, then questions of sovereignty will not be as pressing.

A possible dispute could develop between Massachusetts and the WTO. Massachusetts forbids any state procurement from companies doing business with Burma. Burma has been cited for its lack of democracy and human rights abuses. The European Union is threatening to use the WTO to punish Massachusetts, claiming that their law violates the principle of universal rules for commerce. See "Boston's Stand on Human Rights" by Fred Hiatt, *The Washington Post* (August 25, 1997).

Information on the World Trade Organization can be accessed electronically on the world wide web (http://www.wto.org). For critical views of the relationship between free trade and sovereignty, see Ian Robinson's "Globalization and Democracy," *Dissent* (Summer 1995); several articles in *The Nation*, July 15/22, 1996; and William Greider's *One World, Ready or Not* (Simon and Schuster, 1997). For a critical view of the relationship between the World Trade Organization and the free market, see *The WTO Reader* (The Ludwig von Mises Institute, Auburn, Alabama 36849–5301). Analyses of the overall impact of free trade, including positive steps that can reassert sovereignty, are available from Public Citizen/Global Trade Watch (http://www.essential.org/public__citizen/

pctrade/tradehome.html). An organization that promotes and supports American products is The Made in the USA Foundation (http://www.madeusa.org) A social history of modern American trade policy can be found in Susan Ariel Aaronson's *Trade and the American Dream* (University Press of Kentucky, 1996). Links to a wide range of information on state governments are available from Governing magazine (http://www.governing.com/state.htm).

Investigate for yourself how the Chicago Board of Trade operates by accessing their website (http://www.cbot.com/menu.htm).

The 1996 Farm bill is analyzed from a populist perspective in Larry Swartz and Katherine Ozer's "FAIR is Foul for Farmers and Consumers," *The Progressive Populist* (May 1996). Corporate concentration in agriculture is one of the concerns of the National Farmers Union (http://www.nfu.org).

If corporate domination of the mass media provides consumers with a wide variety of reasonably priced services, then concerns over diversity of information become insubstantial. However, it is not clear that this will necessarily happen. Judge for yourself at the Time-Warner electronic site (http://pathfinder.com). A detailed look at how parts of the 1996 Telecommunications Act came about is provided by Joshua Wolf Shenk in "The Robber Barons of the Information Highway," *The Washington Monthly* (June 1995). A one-year evaluation of the Telecommunications Act can be found in "A Year Later, Still Lots of Static" by Mike Mills and Paul Farhi, *The Washington Post National Weekly Edition* (January 27, 1997). James Boyle writes about the potential corporate domination of the Internet in "Is Congress Turning the Internet into an Information Toll Road?" *Insight* (January 15, 1996). Three groups that study the effect of media policy on consumers are the Center for Media Education (cme@access. digex.net), the Consumer Federation of America (1424 16th Street, NW, Suite 604, Washington, D.C. 20036) and the Consumer Project on Technology (http://www.cptech.org/cpt.html).

The Americans with Disabilities Act is one of those sacred cows in American politics. What politician wants to be seen as discriminating against the handicapped? Some of the law's problems are covered in Phillip K. Howard's *The Death of Common Sense* (Random House, 1994). A wide range of information on ADA accessibility compliance is provided by Access by Design (http://www.access-by-design.coml).

Alan Greenspan was confirmed as the head of the Federal Reserve Board in 1996. Some of his toughest critics on Capitol Hill continue to be Senators Byron Dorgan (D-N.D.), Tom Harkin (D-Iowa) and Rep. Henry Gonzalez (D-Tex.). The secrecy of the Federal Reserve is well documented in an investigation by Congress (U.S. House, 1994. *The Federal Reserve's 17-year Secret*. 103d Cong., 2d sess.). How the press interacts with the Federal Reserve is the subject of several articles in the *Columbia Journalism Review* (January/February 1995). An excellent book that describes the power that the Federal Reserve Board exercises is William Greider's *Secrets of the Temple* (Touchstone, 1987).

Economic populism's appeal is also dependent upon what government does.

If budget deficits force a reduction in entitlements, then corporate welfare programs might look unfair to a majority. TaxWatch (910 17th Street, NW, Suite 413, Washington, D.C. 20006), Taxpayers for Common Sense (http://www.taxpayer.net), and The Cato Institute (http://www.cato.org) are three organizations that monitor corporate welfare. Corporate welfare is a favorite topic for Former Texas Agriculture Commissioner Jim Hightower (http://www.essential.org/hightower/today.html). A. V. Krebs writes about Archer Daniels Midland (ADM), one of the biggest recipients of corporate welfare, and price-fixing in "Supermarket Sweeps: Unraveling the 'Best Documented Corporate Crime in American History,'" *The Progressive Populist* (April 1997, http://www.eden.com/~reporter). A good book that lists the specifics of corporate welfare is *Take the Rich off Welfare* by Mark Zepezauer and Arthur Naiman (Odonian Press, 1996).

There has been political action by the federal and numerous state governments that seek to address public concerns about HMOs. In early 1997, President Clinton issued an order which prohibits "gag clauses" by HMOs which treat Medicaid patients. A 1996 California referendum which would have restrained HMOs from dissuading doctors from providing treatment was defeated at the polls. However, New York and New Jersey recently adopted new consumer protection regulations on HMOs. The relationship between HMOs and Medicare is explored in Joan Retsinas's "Jane Austen Congress Needs You!" *The Progressive Populist* (September 1996). The pressures that HMOs bring to doctors are explored in Nat Hentoff's "The Shackling of Managed Doctors," *The Village Voice* (June 18, 1996). One person's struggle with an HMO is described in "How I Fought My HMO and Won—Without a Lawyer" (http://members.aol.com/jasonwolff/hmo.main.htm). Regina Herzlinger writes about the winners and losers of modern American health care in *Market Driven Health Care* (AddisonWesley, 1997). A group which tracks these movements and seeks to promote "the ability of the patient and the physician to do all that is medically necessary without interference" is Clinical Freedom (http: clinical freedom.org/INDEX.HTM). More information on the Salvation Army can be accessed on the world wide web (http://www.salvationarmy.org/).

In 1997, the federal government enacted a new health care reform measure. Low-income children received $24 billion in expanded health care programs.

One of the most important groups which wants to reclaim the historical legacy of the Populist movement is The Alliance (http://www.igc.apc.org.). It seeks to challenge corporate power through building a grassroots network of supporters nationwide. There are many groups that are studying corporate responsibility including the Institute for Local Self-Reliance (http://www.ilsr.orgSustainableMN: http://www.me3.org), the Program on Corporations, Law & Democracy (P.O. Box 806, Cambridge, Massachusetts 02140) and Democracy Unlimited of Wisconsin Cooperative (888–299–9119). The power of corporations is one of the subjects of *When Corporations Rule the World* by David Korten (Berrett-Koehler, 1995). An independent and critical analysis of business and society is the Left

Business Observer (http://www.Panix.com/~dhenwood/LBO_home.html). For a view that suggests that the media do not focus enough on job creation, see Peter Lynch's "The Upsizing of America," *The Wall Street Journal* (September 20, 1996). For a humorous perspective, see Michael Moore's motion picture, *Roger and Me* or his television program, *TV Nation*, or read his book *Downsize This!* (Crown, 1996).

The key to economic populism's power is found in one vital relationship: how the majority views the relationship between their general economic condition and how big business and government interact with each other. If the majority view government as being captured by big business, then the responsibility for their economic condition can be shifted to an outside, illegitimate force. This force can be described as an elite constellation of government and business interests, which challenges majority rule.

CHAPTER 11

Contemporary Cultural Populism

A public philosophy for the twenty-first century will have to give more weight to the community than to the right of private decision. It will have to emphasize responsibilities rather than rights.

—Historian Christopher Lasch

Is this type of philosophy more conservative or liberal? Some fear that it would weaken our respect for diversity. Those fears usually come from liberals. Others fear that this type of philosophy would dilute our commitment to the market. Those fears usually come from conservatives.

In reality, cultural populism recognizes the interconnectiveness of concepts that most view as opposites: private decisions play a key role in the make-up of a community and rights are dependent upon people taking responsibility for the consequences of exercising them. But in politics, one has to stand for a particular vision of change: from which perspective should reform be pushed? Cultural populists emphasize strengthening community and responsibility as the primary means to improve American society.

Populists are disturbed how economic markets encourage individuals and companies. Triggered by competition, the need to differentiate too often gives way to the impulse to shock, providing a powerful incentive for the mass media to crudely appeal to sex and violence. Chapter 12 calls for the entertainment industry to take more responsibility for how its products might be negatively effecting our culture.

There is a "fine line" between protecting the feelings of individuals and paternalistically censoring the free flow of information and ideas. Chapter 13 describes a proposed speech code at a major American university, and the potential effect it would have on free speech.

The destructive potential of unfettered capitalism is increasingly being realized by communities across the United States. The pressures of competition are forcing governments and businesses to consider revenue-raising schemes that may infringe upon deeply held values of their communities. Some of these proposals include expanding legalized gambling, moving pro-sports teams, and opening up communities to potentially job-destroying megastores. Chapters 14, 15, and 16 describe these developments and how some forces are trying to fight them.

The concept of work brings out strong feelings in many citizens. Many feel guilty if they are not working full time because they cannot afford to adequately support themselves or their families otherwise. Others, who are employed full time, have a nagging suspicion that they should be spending more time with their families or communities. Additionally, there are people who resent having to work full time at a job which they get little satisfaction from. Chapter 17 argues that societal structures and incentives concerning work should be changed, in order to make them fit more closely the needs of the majority of the people.

Identifying the establishment is a primary goal of cultural populists. However, attacking how the establishment illegitimately shapes key societal ideas or institutions is their key objective. In Chapter 18, Pat Buchanan argues that the American dream has been hijacked by both economic and cultural élitists. He believes these élitists have denigrated morality and personal responsibility in the pursuit of individual gain.

CHAPTER 12

The Mass Media, Sex, and Violence

The growth, and progressively dominating nature, of the mass media is one of the most significant social developments that has affected American society in the last fifteen years. Whether through music lyrics, television programs, motion pictures, or computer images, many U.S. citizens are concerned over the increasingly violent and sexual content contained in them. Parents, in particular, are worried over the potential affect that the language and pictures have on their children's development. Politicians have responded by expressing their concern and directing their anger towards the creators of these images.

In the first two readings, former Kansas U.S. Senator and 1996 Republican presidential nominee Bob Dole speaks out on Hollywood's responsibility to American society. In the third reading, a newspaper columnist accuses some TV talk shows of emotionally exploiting children in order to gain viewers.

Gangsta rapper Willie D is profiled in the fourth reading. While his music is known for its celebration of violence and sex, he has recently transformed himself into a radio personality who preaches individual responsibility.

What happens when community values conflict with freedom of expression? Should artists take into account how their creative expression might harm someone? Does the free market in entertainment contribute to the breakdown of the traditional family?

REMARKS BY SENATOR BOB DOLE ON HOLLYWOOD AND AMERICAN VALUES

Thank you very much. John, I appreciate that kind introduction. I appreciate all the work that Lod Cook and others have done tonight—Jim Montgomery and many of my friends who are here.

I want to talk about a specific matter tonight. I may not win an Oscar, but I'll talk about it anyway. I want to talk to you tonight about the future of America—about the issues of moral importance, matters of social consequence.

Last month, during my announcement tour, I gave voice to concerns held across this country about what is happening to our popular culture. I made what I thought was an obvious point, a point that worries countless American parents: that one of the greatest threats to American family values is the way our popular culture ridicules them. Our music, movies, television and advertising regularly push the limits of decency, bombarding our children with destructive messages of casual violence and even more casual sex. And I concluded that we must hold Hollywood and the entire industry accountable for putting profit ahead of common decency.

So here I am in California—the home of the entertainment industry and to many of the people who shape our popular culture. And I'm asking for their help. I believe our country is crying out for leaders who will call us as a people to our better nature, not to profit from our weaknesses; who will bring back our confidence in the good, not play on our fears of life's dark corners. This is true for those of us who seek public office. And it is true for those who are blessed with the talent to lead America's vaunted entertainment industry.

Actors and producers, writers and directors, people of talent around the world dream of coming to Hollywood. Because if you are the best, this is where you are. Americans were pioneers of film, and dominate world-wide competition today. The American entertainment industry is at the cutting edge of creative excellence, but also too often the leading edge of a culture becoming dangerously coarse.

I have two goals tonight. One is to make crystal clear to you the effect this industry has on America's children, in the hope that it will rise to their defense. And the other is to speak more broadly to America about the corporate execu-

Los Angeles, California, May 31, 1995.
Reprinted with permission.

tives who hide behind the lofty language of free speech in order to profit from the debasing of America.

There is often heard in Hollywood a kind of "aw shucks" response to attempts to link societal effects with causes in the culture. It's the "we just make movies people want" response. I'll take that up in a minute. But when they go to work tomorrow, when they sift through competing proposals for their time and their money, when they consider how badly they need the next job, I want the leaders of the entertainment industry to think about the influence they have on America's children.

Let there be no mistake: televisions and movie screens, boomboxes and headsets are windows on the world for our children. If you are too old, or too sophisticated, or too close to the problem, just ask a parent. What to some is art, to our children is a nightly news report of the world outside their limited experience. What to some is make believe, to them is the "real skinny" on the adult world they are so eager to experience. Kids know firsthand what they see in their families, their schools, their immediate communities. But our popular culture shapes their view of the "real world." Our children believe those paintings in celluloid are reflections of reality. But I don't recognize America in much of what I see.

My voice and the rising voices of millions of other Americans who share this view represent more than the codgy old attempt of one generation to steal the fun of another. A line has been crossed—not just of taste, but of human dignity and decency. It is crossed every time sexual violence is given a catchy tune. When teen suicide is set to an appealing beat. When Hollywood's dream factories turn out nightmares of depravity.

You know what I mean. I mean *Natural Born Killers. True Romance*. Films that revel in mindless violence and loveless sex. I'm talking about groups like Cannibal Corpse, Geto Boys and 2 Live Crew. About a culture business that makes money from "music" extolling the pleasures of raping, torturing and mutilating women; from "songs" about killing policemen and rejecting law. The mainstreaming of deviancy must come to an end, but it will only stop when the leaders of the entertainment industry recognize and shoulder their responsibility.

But let me be very clear; I am not saying that our growing social problems are entirely Hollywood's fault. They are not. People are responsible for their actions. Movies and music do not make children into murderers. But a numbing exposure to graphic violence and immorality does steal away innocence, smothering our instinct for outrage. And I think we have reached the point where our popular culture threatens to undermine our character as a nation.

Which brings me to my second point tonight. Our freedom is precious. I have risked my life to defend it, and would do so again. We must always be proud that in America we have the freedom to speak without Big Brother's permission. Our freedom to reap the rewards of our capitalist system has raised the standard of living around the world. The profit motive is the engine of that system, and is honorable. But those who cultivate moral confusion for profit should understand this: we will name their names and shame them as they deserve to be shamed. We will contest them for the heart and soul of every child, in every neighborhood. For we who are outraged also have the freedom to speak. If we refuse to condemn evil, it is not tolerance but surrender. And we will never surrender.

Let me be specific. One of the companies on the leading edge of coarseness and violence is Time Warner. It is a symbol of how much we have lost. In the 1930s its corporate predecessor, Warner Brothers, made a series of movies, including *G-Men*, for the purpose of restoring "dignity and public confidence in the police." It made movies to help the war effort in the early 1940s. Its company slogan, put on a billboard across from the studio, was "Combining Good Citizenship with Good Picture Making."

Today Time Warner owns a company called Interscope Records which columnist John Leo called the "cultural equivalent of owning half the world's mustard gas factories." Ice-T of "Cop Killer" fame is one of Time Warner's "stars." I cannot bring myself to repeat the lyrics of some of the "music" Time Warner promotes. But our children do. There is a difference between the description of evil through art, and the marketing of evil through commerce. I would like to ask the executives of Time Warner a question: Is this what you intended to accomplish with your careers? Must you debase our nation and threaten our children for the sake of corporate profits?

And please don't answer that you are simply responding to the market. Because that is not true. In the movie business, as Michael Medved points out, the most profitable films are the ones most friendly to the family. Last year, the top five grossing films were the blockbusters *The Lion King, Forrest Gump, True Lies, The Santa Clause* and *The Flintstones*. To put it in perspective, it has been reported that *The Lion King* made six times as much money as *Natural Born Killers*.

The corporate executives who dismiss my criticism should not misunderstand. Mine is not the objection of some tiny group of zealots or an ideological fringe. From inner city mothers to suburban mothers to families in rural America—parents are afraid, and growing angry. There once was a time when parents felt the community of adults was on their side. Now they feel surrounded by forces assaulting their children and their code of values.

This is not a partisan matter. I am a conservative Republican, but I am joined in this fight by moderates, independents and liberal Democrats. Senator Bill Bradley has spoken eloquently on this subject, as has Senator Paul Simon, who talks of our nation's "crisis of glamorized violence." And leaders of the entertainment industry are beginning to speak up, as well.

Mark Canton, the president of Universal Pictures, said, "Any smart business person can see what we must do—make more 'PG'-rated films." He said, "Together . . . we can make the needed changes. If we don't, this decade will be noted in the history books as the embarrassing legacy of what began as a great art form. We will be labeled, 'the decline of an empire.' "

Change is possible—in Hollywood, and across the entertainment industry. There are few national priorities more urgent. I know that good and caring people work in this industry. If they are deaf to the concerns I have raised tonight, it must be because they do not fully understand what is at stake. But we must make them understand. We must make it clear that tolerance does not mean neutrality between love and cruelty, between peace and violence, between right and wrong. Ours is not a crusade for censorship, it's a call for good citizenship.

When I announced I was running for President, I said that my mission is to rein in our government, to reconnect the powerful with the values which have made America strong and to reassert America's place as a great nation in the world. Tonight I am speaking beyond this room to some of the most powerful arbiters of our values. Tonight my challenge to the entertainment industry is to accept a calling above and beyond the bottom line—to fulfill a duty to the society which provides its profits. Help our nation maintain the innocence of its children. Prove to us that courage and conscience are alive and well in Hollywood.

Thank you for listening to me tonight. I am grateful for the support you have shown by being here, and feel a great sense of hope and confidence that together we will succeed—not only in this Presidential race, but in our larger mission to reaffirm the goodness and greatness of the United States of America.

Thank you very much.

REMARKS BY BOB DOLE, REPUBLICAN CANDIDATE FOR PRESIDENT OF THE UNITED STATES, ON HOLLYWOOD AND AMERICAN VALUES

Thank you very much. I'm proud to be here today with all of you. Bill, I appreciate those kind words. Bill Bennett has had an impact on our country, not just as Secretary of Education under President Reagan, but as Drug Czar under President Bush, and, more recently, as the man who gave us the *Book of Virtues*.

And please say hello to the next First Lady of the United States, Elizabeth Dole. Yesterday was her birthday. She reached voting age just in time for the election.

This is a town of sequels, and I'm here today with one of my own. A little over a year ago, I came here with a message from the great and not-so-silent majority of the American people. Hollywood, after all, is in the business of sending out messages to the people in the form of art and entertainment. But it runs both ways, and sometimes a message comes back from the people.

In my remarks last year, I pointed to those in Hollywood who don't seem to care about the social consequences of what they do. I spoke of movies, music, art, and advertisements that push the limits of decency. I challenged the view that art occurs in a void; that those who revel in violence and depravity on the screen or in song bear no responsibility when that spirit spreads out into our culture—as it clearly does.

And I asked those in Hollywood who make their living that way, heart to heart, if that is really what they want to do with their lives—if that is really how they want to make their money.

That speech began a national debate. From some quarters the criticism came quick and harsh. But elsewhere it clearly struck a chord. It raised questions a lot of people here and around America had been asking themselves. Far from raising any thought of "censorship," it invited thoughtful people to consider how we might defend both artistic freedom *and* the larger culture. It was a

Los Angeles, California, Tuesday, July 30, 1996.
Reprinted with permission.

message not of restricting freedom, but extending freedom and accepting its responsibilities.

I've been gratified that a number of influential Americans at different points of the ideological spectrum have helped lead that debate. I came here today with a few more thoughts to add to the dialogue.

Let me begin by explaining just why I think these questions are so important. The people in this town have such power over our culture, such enormous influence over what people see and think and feel. Yes, you are entertainment and business people—but let's not be too modest here: Often you are much more than that. You have the power to alter moral sensibilities, to shape attitudes, outlooks, and habits of mind and heart.

The kind of power you have today is at times greater than laws and governments. Indeed that influence reaches straight into the homes and hearts of people across the world.

No, that doesn't mean that Hollywood alone is responsible when things go wrong in our culture. A violence-filled movie does not by itself cause a viewer to kill. Life and causation are not so simple. But neither should we deny the obvious: Hollywood is the site in our culture where our most powerful forces of imagination come together—for good or ill. All the gifts, the opportunities, and the freedom you enjoy—they don't come free. Something is expected of you in return.

Your freedom is yours to use as you wish. So let's dispense with a familiar myth. It's the usual response offered in defense of gratuitous violence, casual sex, and generally cheap behavior in some movies. I'm referring to that familiar line, "We're only giving the public what it wants." We've all heard that line.

There are other lines I find much more convincing—the lines outside America's theaters. It's clear that by far most of the public wants something better. And we know that Hollywood is capable of producing better. Now, some in the industry may wish to produce movies that are degrading, debasing, tawdry, second-rate, anti-heroic. But I would ask them to spare us the "market made me do it" excuse. This is a free country. No one is forcing you to do anything.

Besides, in Hollywood today, the big story is that respectability is good business. You can watch your ratings rise and your box-office receipts go up, and still look yourself in the mirror. You can put your money at risk, while still keeping your artistic integrity. If our ticket windows are a kind of cultural ballot box, then the results are in and we can call a winner. By a landslide, Americans are choosing the good over the grotesque. Excellence over exploitation. Quiet virtue over gratuitous violence, and character over pointless cruelty.

Sure, there are fears about our culture and those who influence it. There is an uneasy feeling shared by millions—people of all parties, races, and creeds— that too many lines have been crossed, too many restraints abandoned in our popular culture. But there is something even bigger running through American culture today. You can feel it: there is a yearning for better things. There is a call—a demand as strong as any in our free market—for things that affirm our

lives instead of cheapening life. Things that lift up our country instead of dragging it down. Things that appeal to the best in the human heart, and not to the
worst.

Just look at the box-office receipts. What do they tell us? Americans hailed
the adventure and courage of *Apollo 13*. We loved the faithfulness and humility
of *Forrest Gump*. And the most popular "Babe" in Hollywood is a pig that
goes by that name. We were touched by the story of tolerance and human
kindness. We were inspired in *Braveheart*, a story of love, honor—and yes,
violent battle. But it was violence true to the story, a story of men fighting for
freedom, not just brutality thrown in there for the shock and thrill of it. And
like me just yesterday, Americans by the millions are turning out to see *Independence Day*—a high-tech thriller about patriotism and humankind at its best.

Meanwhile, something called *Striptease* is playing to empty theaters everywhere. That movie was billed as a story of empowerment and freedom for
women. But what a sad waste of talent and human energy! Is *that* what women
have been fighting so hard for all these years—the right to be degraded and
exploited for profit? I don't think so—and apparently neither do the women of
America.

After all, a lot of Americans when they go to movies like to bring the kids
along, without feeling embarrassed or nervous about those powerful images up
there on the screen. Some social critics tell parents not to worry, not to be too
protective of what their kids might see and hear. They say "this is life in the
real world. Kids need to see it."

But if it's all the same to these social critics, the parents of America will
decide for themselves what's best for their children. And childhood innocence
is worth protecting. Parenthood these days is hard enough without our kids being
exposed to a constant stream of foul language offered as "reality"; rudeness
palmed off as self-expression; license hailed as liberation; and brutality disguised
as strength.

Now, I'm a realist. I know that where the standard of taste and decency is
concerned, there are still some in this industry who seem to operate by the
reverse of the famous line in *Field of Dreams*, believing that "If your tear it
down, they will come." I suppose that works sometimes. But more often than
not—far more often than not—it doesn't.

And it doesn't take a marketing genius to see why. Around this country today
are hard-working mothers and fathers whose choices seem to be narrowing with
every year. Many are working in two jobs—not always by choice. They pay a
third or more of their income in taxes, leaving less money for leisure and less
time for their families.

Meanwhile, they look to the public schools and see their authority disregarded
and their values dismissed. They see government programs destroying families
instead of helping them. They see violence and crime going unpunished. Even
more troubling, they see the violent ones getting younger every year.

But art and entertainment is one area where parents still *do* have the power of choice. And it's clear what they're saying: Give us films and music and television that *help* us raise our families instead of hurting us. Give us art worthy of our lives; worthy of your own talents; and worthy of a country to which we all owe so much.

More with every year, that "R" on some movies should stand for "Reject." Increasingly, the people of America are *rejecting* entertainment that insults our intelligence and offends our sense of decency. We are *rejecting* films that deride our country and our values. As consumers with choices and as people with standards, the great majority of us are *rejecting* the very idea that art must offend and degrade, instead of uplift and inspire.

There are many people in this town who have been producing art that Americans can watch or hear without wincing, or casting a worried glance at their kids. And if I may speak for families across this country, I would encourage those artists and producers to keep up the good work. There is after all, a time to criticize. And there is also a time to praise. And that's my main purpose in coming here today—to praise what is best in your industry. I do so in the hope that others will follow your example. For remembering the good things about this country and what it stands for—we applaud you. For making movies that raise our vision of life instead of dragging us down—we thank you.

I want to be as clear as possible about what I am *not* saying. I am not saying that all the films you produce should be what they call "feel-good" movies. Nor should we make the mistake of assuming that "feel-good" always means "excellence."

None of us wants to live in a Muzak culture without variety, tension, or depth. Obviously, like other great works of art, many great movies have explored the dark side of human nature. I am thinking here of movies like *Schindler's List*. What is distinctive about these works of art is that there is a depth to them. They enlarge our understanding of humanity, of goodness and evil, of suffering and courage. Unlike so much else that is passed off as "reality," they are not gratuitous, cheap, debasing, or mindless.

In the real world, most people have learned that character is what usually makes the difference between rising and falling. And when someone falls, there is not "fade out" and roll of the credits. In our streets and homes, some of the qualities glorified on screen don't work out so well.

You can see it in the violence of teenagers emulating Hollywood's violent "heroes." But those kids don't get an Oscar or big paycheck for their performance. Often they get a prison sentence. Or a spot in the cemetery. You can see it in the lives of kids who picked up from the television or the CD player the idea that life is all about "making your own rules." That attitude doesn't land them on talk shows, magazine covers, or invitation lists to state dinners. Usually, it lands them in a lot of trouble.

The values I have spoken about in this campaign—and which I will continue to speak about, in confident and unapologetic ways—are not intolerant values: They're what make us kind and civil toward one another. They're what make tolerance possible in a country of many faiths, and unity possible in a country with one future. Far from being divisive, those principles are what keep this country together.

So I would just leave you with a reminder that cynicism is contagious—but so too is decency. Anyone with influence over our culture has to choose one or the other. And maybe no one expressed that choice better than Clark Gable's character, Rhett Butler, in *Gone With the Wind*. He says: "What most people don't seem to realize is that there is just as much money to be made out of the wreckage of a civilization as from the upbuilding of one. I'm making my fortune out of the wreckage."

I believe that applies to all of us who would lead this country, whether it's in art, politics, or anything else. Every last one of us who lays claim to the public trust has to face the same questions: Does our fortune come from the wreckage of our culture, or from its defense? Are we just looking out for number one—or are we looking out for America too? Enjoying the best a free society can offer, living in the greatest country on the face of the Earth—what are we giving back?

To those of you who have cast your lot with the upbuilding of civilization—to things that are honorable, worthy of praise, and worthy of America—I salute you.

Thank you very much, and God bless America.

WHEN TV TALK SHOWS WERE MERELY TASTELESS

SUZANNE FIELDS

I've changed my treadmill schedule from the evening, when I watched "The News Hour with Jim Lehrer," to the morning so I can get a sampling of the talkshow fare and stay in touch with "real people" outside Washington. No offense to Jim Lehrer, but I can watch him at night without the help of endorphins.

But if my morning energy level has gone up, my tolerance for talk television has sharply declined. In the weeks since I began surfing for the morning shows the absolute worst, yet quite typical, was about identical ten-year-old twins. Two girls and two boys were videotaped by their parents showing how nasty they could be to each other, kicking and biting and pulling each other's hair. Then we meet the twins live, in the television studio to hear and see them tell the audience why they hate one another. Each boy and girl wish they weren't stuck with a horrible double.

To give this junk morally redeeming value, we're told that after the commercial break these twins are going to want to shape up and learn the meaning of brotherly (or sisterly) love. When we return we're introduced to the tutors for the twins.

One is a tragic mother who ran over her son, a twin, when he was four years old. She didn't see him as she backed the van out of the driveway. She felt a bump and wondered if she had hit the dog. She thought both boys were asleep upstairs in their room. Her son, sitting by her side, describes almost inaudibly how lonely he is and wishes he could bring his brother back. By now everybody is crying, the twins, their mothers, and the audience. I confess, me too.

I've written about child abuse on television before and this time I'm not even going to castigate the hosts of such shows. They only offer what the guests and the public of the idiot culture will bear. But what can we say about the exploitative parents of these children? Do they have no responsibility?

Maybe less should be written about the effects of television sex and violence on children and more about the ill effects of putting children on display before the cameras. This is a long way from *Sesame Street* or silly home videos.

We eagerly write child labor laws. We lock up pornographic photographers of children. Isn't it obscene to portray children violently taunting each other in

From *The Washington Times National Weekly Edition*, June 2, 1996.
Reprinted with permission.

scenes of sibling rivalry and then on cue parade their feelings before their friends and millions of others?

The last time I complained about child abuse on television, it occurred on a show where children, ages six and nine, were trotted out to explain how and why they wanted to kill their mothers. Greek tragedy this was not.

The hosts usually make a pretense of offering such families "a therapeutic environment," with bright lights and microphones, lots of supportive gasps, sympathetic applause, and of course ample commercial breaks. Frequently a resident expert is recruited to say that killing mothers is bad for their health, or that beating up a sibling is not nice, either.

These shows are sometimes defended as "the democratization of culture," a harmless low-brow pleasure—like watching Christians being fed to lions? Or defended as giving those who don't have much to feel good about an opportunity to feel superior to someone else: At least my kids don't want to kill me or each other! They've even been called popular theater with an Aristotelian catharsis: There, but for the grace of God and television producers, go I.

But no matter how you look at it from an audience's point of view, the children placed in front of that camera are abused children. We should worry about the psychological impact on their lives.

Now that we've bid our farewell to Phil Donahue, who started this abuse, we can wax nostalgic about a more innocent time when the host merely wore a skirt and brought male strippers into our homes. Tastelessness beats beating up kids.

WILLIE D: A GANGSTA RAPPER GOES STRAIGHT UP ON THE RADIO

CYNTHIA THOMAS

HOUSTON—In many ways, it sounded like just another radio call-in show. Host, guest, and callers railed against abuse of the welfare system—particularly women who have baby after baby and rob taxpayers of hard-earned money.

What made some listeners do a double-take was the host. He wasn't Rush Limbaugh or one of his colleagues, but "gangsta" rapper Willie D, one of the Geto Boys, a nationally known rap group.

"Tonight I'm going to offend a lot of people by the comments I'm going to make. But guess what? I don't give a damn. It's going down tonight," he warned. "I'm tired of footing the bill for these fools that don't want to work, you know what I'm saying?"

His "Reality Check" show has dealt with such topics as the death of Tupac Shakur and getting out the vote.

Some of the shows have unleashed an emotional response, such as when callers raged against comments made by two guests—"professional" carjackers called Red Boy and K—Dog.

When Willie asked K—Dog what went through his mind before he took a car, he said: "Nothing really goes through my mind. It's something that I really like and I want and I don't have. He got it, why can't I have it, know what I'm saying?"

With topics like this, the discourse is not the detached dialogue of most current-affairs shows.

"I want to hear what people on the streets are saying. The ones that don't really get a chance to voice their opinions are the ones that don't think that their opinions count," he says. "That's why I think rap music is so important, because before rap music came along, there was no way to really hear the pain from the inner city."

A rap fan used to seeing Willie D on his album covers might not recognize him behind the mike at the radio station. The gangsta look is gone. With a closely trimmed beard, wire-rim glasses, and short-sleeve cotton shirt, he looks more like a literature professor ready to deconstruct the work of James Baldwin than the author of "[Expletive] Rodney King."

From *The Houston Chronicle*, December 2, 1996.

The Geto Boys became nationally famous in 1992 with their hit song "Mind Playing Tricks on Me" and quickly became a symbol of the most violent of gangsta rappers. They were singled out in Bob Dole's attack on the movie and music industries as one of the groups that "revel in mindless violence and loveless sex."

The Geto Boys' and Willie D's songs have raged against women and white people and have poked fun at black leaders.

On "Reality Check," Willie D is refashioning himself as a calm talk-show host. But sometimes the anger of his music still comes through, as it did in his most controversial show to date, the one about welfare mothers.

"These people that's just laying up on their [expletive]s, ain't never worked a day in their life, dropping out of school and sitting back popping out babies that's killing our babies," Willie D said. "Hey, I ain't with that at all."

Outraged listeners called the station for an hour after the show ended.

The following week, Willie D apologized for the way he had expressed himself. He said he became emotional because he had watched welfare "destroy two or three generations of my family." A few of his aunts and uncles, he said, had been mostly content to live on welfare.

Community activist Ada Edwards, who appeared on one of his shows, said, "I'm sure a lot of people don't like the way Willie D puts things, because he says exactly what he feels, and people aren't used to that. I don't agree with everything he says, but he is one person in this town who can get younger people to think about things they wouldn't ordinarily think about."

Willie D hasn't given up the gangsta persona entirely. His latest album with the Geto Boys, *The Resurrection*, came out in the spring. It was a reunion album for the group, whose members had gone their separate ways. The language is angry and raw.

But in real life, he's a husband and the father of a two-year-old, with a nice house in the Houston area. His wife, who has a job at an airline, is pursuing a degree in engineering at Prairie View A&M University.

When he was asked about the welfare show and his views on how much responsibility men have for children they have fathered, he said, "If more men took care of their kids and was part of their kids' life, we wouldn't have as much crime as we have, the AIDS epidemic, so many kids using drugs."

He said the point he was trying to make is that women have to take care of themselves and not depend on men, "because it's a proven fact that men are dogs."

Later he called from his car phone to clarify his statement.

"OK, I've been thinking about this. This is the quote: 'I think men who neglect their fatherhood responsibilities should be taken out into a field and shot like a dog.' "

CHAPTER 13

The University Élite and Political Correctness: The Proposed University of Massachusetts Speech Code

One of the strongest appeals that colleges and universities have is their image as islands of pure idealism—a place where thoughts and ideas are given the highest institutional priority. Academic freedom means allowing students to develop their minds to the fullest extent, unencumbered by fear that their expression would be punished if it wasn't rationally thought out or popular.

In recent years, there have been calls to protect certain groups from hateful or at least hurtful speech. The culmination of these efforts has sometimes led to "speech codes" being set up on campuses. The intent has been to create an academic environment where learning could take place free from any form of discrimination.

In 1995, the University of Massachusetts at Amherst announced a speech code. In the reading, UMass economics professor Robert Costrell describes his reaction to the proposal and the potential it could have on curbing free speech and learning on the campus.

Are there certain subjects that you feel never get brought up in classes because they are too controversial? What alternative methods, besides speech codes, can colleges use to help create an atmosphere of tolerance and respect?

A NEW SPEECH CODE PROPOSED AT THE UNIVERSITY OF MASSACHUSETTS

ROBERT M. COSTRELL, PROFESSOR OF ECONOMICS, UNIVERSITY OF MASSACHUSETTS AT AMHERST, NOVEMBER 6, 1995

[The UMass administration newspaper, *The Campus Chronicle*, published a shorter version of this article on November 10, 1995.]

When we arrived at our offices on October 18–19, the UMass faculty found that an attempted coup d'état, to curtail campus civil liberties, is apparently now underway. Our mailboxes held a document, dated a month earlier, proposing to circumscribe the freedom of speech on campus. Incredibly, the proposal represents the fruits of one and one-half years of negotiations between the administration and the Graduate Employee Organization (GEO), a union of teaching assistants organized in 1991 by the United Auto Workers. Almost as an afterthought, the faculty and the rest of the University community were given three weeks to react to a document which has already obtained unanimous consent from a group of administrators, including two deans. Facing a virtual fait accompli, the faculty is informed by the administration that this document will serve as the basis for a revised policy to be implemented by the spring.

While I have seen many strange things at UMass in my eighteen years here, one never ceases to be amazed at the misuse or outright abdication of authority among those charged with running the campus. In the present instance, Orwell's *Animal Farm* clearly comes to mind. Why on earth would the administration negotiate a speech code with a group of graduate student activists, bringing the faculty in only as a postscript? Surely the protection of academic freedom, to which the document gives truly Orwellian lip service, is first and foremost the responsibility of the faculty. A responsible administration, with the students' true interests at heart, would have gently, but firmly persuaded these n-th year grad students to write their dissertations instead of speech codes. Instead, the administration sat down with them to regulate the rest of us.

It should be no surprise that such a fundamentally flawed process would produce a document which is so entirely unacceptable. As Professor Herbert Gintis and Professor Daphne Patai have argued elsewhere, the proposed policy attempts to regulate that which cannot be regulated in the area of such verbal conduct as "negative stereotypes," and regulates that which is already regulated in the area of threats, assaults, and intimidation. The policy elevates group status to equal or greater importance than individual status, completely contrary to the principles of American Constitutional government, and thereby exacerbates the very stereotyping the document intends to combat.

Contrary to the administration's presumption, this palpably unconstitutional document cannot be revised, and it should be discarded forthwith. Indeed, we have been given no explanation whatsoever regarding any putative rationale for such a document, other than pressure from the graduate student union. The basis for discarding this document is fundamental, and does not rest on one passage or another. However, to illustrate its illiberal cast, I will examine some excerpts from this fourteen-page document, which reads like an amateur version of the Federal Register (though with approximately the same verve).

For starters, the document is embarrassingly flawed by such elementary errors as circular definitions ("harassment is defined as verbal or physical conduct . . . that serves to harass") and inconsistent stipulations (classroom conduct is actionable in one passage and protected in another).

The proposed code defines offenses in the vaguest, most open-ended fashion, including, but "not limited to" epithets, "negative stereotyping," and unspecified "ritual and unspoken behaviors." The operative passage, hopelessly amorphous, proscribes verbal conduct which might be judged by a member of one group or another to "discriminatorily alter the condition" of participation in the University. While it remains unclear whether white males have standing to grieve against negative stereotyping under this document [see Note], it is quite clear that virtually everyone else does, given the incredibly expansive, self-parodying list of protected categories. The list not only includes the usual categories, but also "citizenship, culture, HIV status, language, parental status . . . and pregnancy status." GEO wants these added, while the administration believes they are already covered.

To take but one example, consider "parental status" and "pregnancy status." Heaven only knows what the code-writers had in mind here, but that's exactly the point: who knows what is proscribed? A reasonably intelligent reading of these protections might well infer that, taken together with "marital status," they provide the basis for grievance against negative stereotyping of unwed mothers, absent fathers, or perhaps their children.

Suppose an unwed mother overcomes the odds against her and manages to arrive on the UMass campus. Now suppose she is present at a classroom or lunchroom discussion of family breakdown. She may well hear a statement like the following:

there is one unmistakable lesson in American history; a community that allows a large number of young men to grow up in broken families, dominated by women, never acquiring any stable relationship to male authority, never acquiring any set of rational expectations about the future—that community asks for and gets chaos. Crime, violence, unrest, disorder . . . that is not only to be expected; it is very near to inevitable. And it is richly deserved.

Quite likely, and quite understandably, she will find this an upsetting experience. She might well find the speech so stigmatizing that it bothers her the rest of the day, or longer, and disturbs her concentration in doing her course work. Referring to the proposed code, a "reasonable person" might well conclude that such a speech had indeed "altered the conditions" of her participation at the University. Is this "discriminatory," and therefore actionable? In short, could Daniel Patrick Moynihan (author of the above 1965 statement) teach at UMass? Could he visit here and eat lunch with students? Could his host be punished? Could he offer such views as a student here? Who knows?

Unfortunately, this example is all too realistic: in 1991, the economics profession received "guidelines" from a similarly illiberal (though unofficial) committee of "bias" arbiters. Among other things, the committee explicitly warned us against introducing Moynihan-type analyses of female-headed households into our teaching and research.

To be sure, one passage of the UMass code protects classroom speech "which the instructor deems relevant." But outside the classroom, all bets are off. More importantly, student speech inside the classroom is not protected if the student's judgment differs from the instructor regarding relevance. Suppose the instructor attributes high crime rates to economic deprivation, but a student argues that high rates of illegitimacy are more important. A dogmatic instructor (unfortunately, there are a few around) may well judge the student's argument irrelevant, or worse ("blaming the victim"). The student may not only be at risk of actionably offending on the basis of parental and marital status, but of also stereotyping a different "culture," which is yet another protected category.

Given the uncertainty, the prudent choice might be to steer clear of the topics of family breakdown. Thus, with a stroke of the pen, this document could chill or still discussion of one of our era's most pressing social problems. The codemakers' intent here is unknown, but ultimately irrelevant. The basic problem is the unavoidable uncertainty created by any such speech code, which can stifle legitimate discourse whether or not it is, in any meaningful sense, "harassing."

As another indication of the brave new jurisprudence which the administration would impose on this campus, consider this curiosum from the "scope" of who is covered by the code: on the one hand, individuals whose *visitors* run afoul of the code will themselves be held culpable (guilt by association?); by contrast, if the visiting bigot is invited to address a public forum on campus, then anything goes. The administration's message is clear: if you're going to bring a bigot to campus, you had better do it big-time.

Now consider the elaborate bureaucratic machinery established by this code to process charges. The procedure seems designed to maximize the probability of conviction, with little regard to due process. Charges can be filed as long as twelve months after the alleged event, long after witnesses may have graduated and disappeared. The standard of proof is "preponderance of evidence," which simply means "more likely than not," rather than the much stricter "beyond a reasonable doubt."

Moreover, charges under even this weak standard of proof are to be adjudicated by a simple majority of a three- or five-member Hearing Panel, under the aegis of the Affirmative Action Office. Defendants are specifically NOT to be judged by juries of their peers. For example, a custodian could readily be hauled before a panel with a majority of students. So could a faculty member, in flat violation of the American Association of University Professors (AAUP) guidelines.

Lest any defendants consider challenging the proceedings, one finds they may have only "supervised access" to the tapes of the hearings—they are not to be given copies. Nor does the policy stipulate that any other records of the proceedings be made available to the defendant—only to various administrators. UMass thus proposes to advance from Orwell to Kafka.

Once convicted, the proposed code threatens an open-ended host of sanctions including, but "not limited to," suspension without pay or even *dismissal*. The administration asks us to trust them to implement such sanctions in accord with "the severity of the violation," which, of course, is left totally unspecified.

Once could easily continue dissecting this document, but the whole exercise strikes one as somewhat disconnected from the world-at-large. Is no one in the UMass administration aware of the enormous difficulties similar codes have caused at major universities across the country? At the University of Pennsylvania, charges were brought against a student for calling other students "water buffaloes," when their loud socializing disrupted the midnight study efforts of dorm residents. Penn pressed this case for months, putting the student's future at risk, until eventually the case was dropped due to public ridicule. Penn subsequently scrapped their speech code. The courts have struck down similar codes at Stanford and the Universities of Michigan and Wisconsin.

No such speech code is compatible with free speech and academic freedom. This proposed code will not stand, nor should it. The only question is how it will fall. One might yet hope that the administration will quickly withdraw the proposal as it sees the light of day. But the latest pronouncement from Chancellor Scott offers little hope in this direction. Indeed, he informs us that this policy is just the first of a whole set of such policies that will shortly be presented for our perusal, including "guidelines for gender-neutral language in publications, and a Statement on Religious Displays and Religious Holidays." We are asked to consider these documents' "relationship to one another and the totality of the statement that they make about the kind of institution we want UMass Amherst to be."

Fortunately, the "kind of institution" UMass Amherst will be is still constrained, for the better, by the more freedom-loving institutions of American society. Prior to the court roll-back of campus speech codes, some American universities were described as "islands of repression in a sea of liberty." It is sad to say, at this late date, that the liberation of UMass from the attempted coup that is underway will probably have to come from beyond the confines of our own little utopia gone awry Until then, the casualties on campus may well include free speech and academic freedom.

NOTE [September 1996]: As it turned out, the administration quite candidly declared its intention to apply the code with a double standard, depending on the group membership of those at the receiving end of objectionable speech. In a Boston radio interview, the associate chancellor who had negotiated the proposed speech code with the graduate student union explicitly stated that it would be applied on behalf of those belonging to groups characterized by their "powerlessness" and "vulnerability" in society, but not to those from any other groups. Thus, First Amendment rights were to be protected for some, but not others, as pointed out by the constitutional scholar who appeared on the show to debate the associate chancellor.

CHAPTER 14

The Growth of Legalized Gambling: Unkept Promises at What Cost?

In recent years, many states and cities have turned to legalized gambling as a method to stimulate economic growth and create employment. Critics claim that the social effects of making gambling more accessible are often overlooked when the issue is debated. This reading describes the price that individuals and communities often pay for the growth of legalized gambling—addiction, debt, and family breakdown.

One of gambling's appeals is that it encourages people to think that they can get ahead by luck. Is this a message that government should promote? What is the relationship between gambling and morality? Some feel that gambling taxes are preferable to other types of taxes, like income or property, because there is a choice of whether to pay it. In what ways does society pay for the repercussions associated with "problem gamblers"?

THE DICEMAN COMETH: WILL GAMBLING BE A BAD BET FOR YOUR TOWN?

RONALD A. RENO

FROM CASH COW TO TROJAN HORSE: GAMBLING COULD RIVAL DRUGS AS THE ADDICTION OF CHOICE AMONG TEENS

Flush with a handful of money he had just won at a bowling tournament, Joe Koslowski invited some friends to celebrate with him at the nearby Atlantic City casinos. Joe, then sixteen, and all his buddies were allowed in despite the age limit of twenty-one. Once inside, Joe's good fortune continued; he parlayed his bowling winnings into a couple of thousand dollars.

After his initial success, Joe returned to the casinos frequently. His winning streak eventually ended, but his taste for the thrill of gambling did not. Once out of cash, he opened credit accounts under family members' names, using cash advances from the credit cards to gamble.

The whole scheme finally came crashing in on Joe last year, after he had amassed $20,000 in debt. Now at age twenty, Joe, who had no prior criminal record, is serving time in a Pennsylvania federal prison for credit-card fraud.

Joe is one of tens of thousands of young people who fall victim to America's gambling obsession every year. At least three-quarters of the nation's teens engage in some form of gambling. Much of it, of course, is fairly innocuous and occurs among peers: weekend poker games, betting on football, the annual NCAA basketball tournament pool. Adolescents have become increasingly adept, however, at gaining access to state-sanctioned gambling—lotteries, casinos, electronic poker—which often becomes a bridge to compulsive or addictive behavior. In 1995, University of Minnesota researchers reported that more than half of underage Minnesota teens surveyed had participated in some form of legalized gambling. An earlier survey of Atlantic City high-school students revealed that nearly two-thirds had gambled at the city's casinos.

It is becoming painfully apparent that the only jackpot awaiting many of these young people is a life out of control: More than a million adolescents are already addicted to gambling, according to Durand Jacobs, a professor of clinical psychiatry at Loma Linda University Medical School and an expert on youth gambling. Further, Jacobs says, the gambling addiction rate among teens is three

Policy Review, March/April 1996.
Reprinted with permission.

times that among adults. In a recent review of major youth-gambling studies in North America, Howard Shaffer, director of the Center for Addiction Studies at Harvard Medical School, concluded that roughly one in six teens experiences gambling-related problems, while about 6 percent are actually addicted, or pathological, gamblers.

The New Jersey Council on Compulsive Gambling, which operates a national toll-free hotline (1–800–GAMBLER), reports that callers under twenty-one phoned the hotline 4,300 times in 1994, accounting for 11 percent of total calls. Ed Looney, the council's executive director, says many of these young people find themselves in desperate straits. He tells of a call regarding a sixteen-year-old who had slit his wrists after losing $6,000—four years of newspaper delivery earnings—on the lottery in a single day. He tells of the college student from the Midwest who dropped out of school because he lost his tuition money gambling; of the nineteen-year-old New Jersey youth who sold his car for a fraction of its value so he could get back into the casinos; of the numerous calls from kids too scared to go back to school because they can't pay back their bookies.

The phenomenon of youth gambling is not entirely new, but its rapid growth and startling magnitude is alarming. Says Valerie Lorenz, head of Baltimore's Center for Compulsive Gambling, ''We never saw a teenage gambler ten years ago. Now we see them regularly.'' Moreover, the most addictive forms of gambling—eagerly promoted by more and more state governments in search of tax revenue—can produce ripple effects in young lives that undermine families, communities, and civic order. As we move into the next century, Shaffer says, ''We're going to have major issues with youth gambling that will equal or eclipse the problems that we have with substance abuse.''

A SLIPPERY SLOPE?

Experts draw a distinction between the ''problem'' gambler and the ''pathological'' gambler. According to Shaffer, pathological gamblers exhibit three basic characteristics: an inability to stop gambling despite massive losses, a sense of lost control, and a compulsion or craving to gamble. Problem gamblers can be affected in less severe ways, including difficulty concentrating, failure to fulfill family, school, or work obligations, general irritability, and sleeplessness. The two, however, are closely connected. Shaffer refers to problem gamblers as being ''in transition,'' either moving toward or away from pathological gambling behaviors. Individuals may frequently move in and out of these designations. It is estimated that 1 to 3 percent of the adult population are pathological gamblers, but nearly twice that number are problem gamblers.

Probably 90 percent of the population can gamble ''recreationally,'' but a significant minority cannot. Moreover, all forms of gambling can be addictive for teens, as well as adults, though they vary in their potency. The most addictive, such as electronic poker, contain the element of rapid ''action'' and occur in relative isolation, Shaffer says. Video gambling and slot machines are inherently more dangerous than bingo or the lottery. But the lottery frequently serves as a gateway to other gambling activities for teens. Once exposed to even a relatively benign form of gambling such as the lottery, many find themselves craving greater excitement. Studies bear this out: participation in other forms of gambling is higher in those states that have lotteries.

Many problem and pathological gamblers—adolescents or adults—become debtors. Once they get in over their heads, teen gamblers follow the cue of their elders: they turn to crime. Jacobs contends that at least one in ten juveniles has used illegal means such as stealing, shoplifting, selling drugs, or prostitution to obtain money to pay off gambling-related debts. A 1994 study of Massachusetts youth found that 5 percent had been arrested for gambling-related problems.

Despite the extent and impact of youth gambling, Jacobs says, the level of public awareness is "absolutely abysmal." A few recent high-profile press reports, along with a meeting last spring of the North American Think Tank on Youth Gambling Issues at Harvard, have begun to bring the issue to the public's attention. Teens themselves remain largely unaware of the dangers associated with gambling. Shaffer found that only one-quarter of Massachusetts youth surveyed rated gambling as potentially dangerous, compared with 60 percent or more who perceived the dangers in alcohol, tobacco, and drugs.

Gambling in all its forms is proving to be nearly irresistible to a rising generation that frequently tells pollsters of its apprehensions about a bleak economic outlook. Traditional forms of gambling such as church bingo have generally been able to restrain compulsive betting. Government promotion of gambling, including the $350 million states spend advertising the lottery, has been more pernicious. It communicates to young people the subtly destructive notion that the work ethic is passé, that all they need is "a dollar and a dream," as one lottery advertisement puts it. Perhaps that's why an average of 200,000 minors have been turned away from Atlantic City casinos every year for the past decade, according to figures from the New Jersey Casino Control Commission. Another 24,000 underage gamblers are escorted from the casino floor annually. Many more gamble in the casinos undetected. Ironically, many state lotteries are pitched to the electorate as a honey pot for public education.

"By sending young people the message that they need to gamble to get ahead," Shaffer says, "we're telling them not to study calculus, not to study science, and we shouldn't be surprised that America is now falling behind other cultures in terms of intellectual pursuits."

A NATIONAL COMPULSION

If young people follow the lead of the adult gambling culture around them, they'll squander much more than their intellectual energy. Americans will legally wager more money this year than they will spend on groceries—some $500 billion. That number represents a 3,000 percent increase since 1976. Utah and Hawaii are the only states that prohibit all forms of gambling, though Hawaii is considering casinos. Casinos are now legal in about half the states and constitute nearly half of total gambling revenues, which are growing at the rate of 15 percent annually.

"America is on a gambling binge," says Congressman Frank Wolf, who is pushing legislation to establish a national commission to study the effects of legalized gambling. The growth will undoubtedly continue, at least in the short run, as state and local governments scramble for an even bigger slice of the gambling revenue pie. In 1994, governments received $1.4 billion from casinos alone. Lotteries contributed another $10 billion to state coffers. That same year, revenue-hungry state legislatures considered more than 1,600 gambling-related bills.

Unfortunately, government's addiction to gambling has been transmitted to the public. Nationwide, it is estimated that about 10 million Americans have a gambling habit that is out of control. A recent surge in the number of problem and pathological gamblers is strongly correlated with the explosion of legalized gambling opportunities. An unlikely source for a case study is Iowa. A 1989 survey indicated that 1.7 percent of Iowa residents were problem or pathological gamblers. Shortly thereafter the state added riverboat casinos and casinos on Indian lands and also expanded parimutuel wagering. A subsequent survey last year showed the percentage of Iowans with a serious gambling problem had ballooned to 5.4 percent. An additional 78,000 Iowa adults had become hooked on gambling in that six-year period.

The Iowa study is consistent with other findings. John Kindt, a professor of commerce and legal policy at the University of Illinois, says that when gambling activities are legalized and made accessible to new jurisdictions, increases in the numbers of addicted gamblers range between 100 and 550 percent. These newly created addicts are turning in overwhelming numbers for help—help that the mental health community is ill equipped to supply. According to the National Council on Problem Gambling, there are fewer than a hundred treatment programs nationwide for pathological gamblers, as compared with some 13,000 such programs for alcoholism and other substance-abuse problems. Tens of thousands are seeking help through local Gamblers Anonymous (GA) groups; GA has added four hundred new chapters in the United States in the last five years.

Testifying before the House Judiciary Committee last September, American Gaming Association (AGA) president Frank Fahrenkopf Jr. claimed that the gambling industry is making substantial efforts to address the problem. So far, however, little has been done. "The casino industry is heavily dependent on the revenues of psychologically sick people," says Earl Grinols, an economist at the University of Illinois, who calculates that more than half of a casino's take comes from problem and pathological gamblers. University of Minnesota researchers found that a mere 2 percent of gamblers in that state accounted for nearly two-thirds of all money spent on the state's casinos, charitable pulltab games, lottery, and the like.

Experts warn that the number of gambling addicts has yet to crest. In fact, Jacobs predicts that it will be the nation's fastest growing addictive behavior. In addition to greater availability of traditional gambling venues, the emergence of high-tech video gambling machines, gambling on the Internet, and interactive telephone and television gambling will undoubtedly contribute to the problem. These addictions will come with enormous social and economic price tags, as social scientists and researchers—and millions of families—have already discovered.

GAMBLING WITH THE FAMILY

In August 1993, Mike and Sharon James (not their real names) and their two preschool children left a successful business in East Liverpool, Ohio, for promising job prospects in Charleston, South Carolina. The couple had been in Charleston one month when Sharon received an overdrawn notice from the bank. Puzzled, she contacted the bank to clear up the "error"; the couple had several thousand dollars in their checking account set aside for a down payment on a house.

Sharon discovered that her husband of ten years had made several withdrawals in recent weeks, many in the neighborhood of $1,000. When she questioned Mike, she learned that he had spent the money on South Carolina's ubiquitous video poker machines. Despite Sharon's pleas and attempts at treatment, Mike couldn't kick the habit. He squandered the family's remaining savings, hocked many of their possessions, even cashed in the children's savings bonds, and left the family $20,000 in debt. Finally, Sharon filed for divorce. Mike wound up in the county jail for delinquency in child-support payments and for writing bad checks.

"This man was a wonderful person, a very caring father," says Sharon. "I really believe he didn't realize what he was doing, because he was never like that before. This addiction just grabs you and twists you. It destroyed him and us."

Similar stories abound in gambling communities across the nation. Yet the scope of the problem is tragically underestimated, largely because so little research has been undertaken regarding gambling's impact on the family. The meager available data comes primarily from surveys of small groups of compulsive gamblers seeking treatment.

Last year the Illinois Council on Compulsive Gambling surveyed nearly 200 Gamblers Anonymous members and found that 16 percent were divorced due to their gambling addictions; another 10 percent had separated as a result. In an earlier study of spouses of compulsive gamblers, Valerie Lorenz discovered that 78 percent had threatened separation or divorce, and half had carried through on their threats. Jacobs surveyed 850 high-school students in Southern California and found that children of compulsive gamblers were almost twice as likely to experience the trauma of a broken home.

In Harrison County, Mississippi, the hub of the state's casino industry, the number of divorces rose from 440 in 1992 to nearly 1,100 in 1993, the first full year after casinos. Judge William L. Stewart, who has served on chancery court along Mississippi's Gulf Coast for seventeen years, says he knows gambling to be a factor in about a third of the divorce cases he now oversees. "Other than the general decline of morality in society, I don't believe there has been a single factor [affecting divorce rates] like this. It's just not a normal thing. This thing is huge. It has a tremendous effect on a community."

Spousal and child abuse and neglect are other problems attendant to gambling addiction, as reports from social-service agencies in gambling communities consistently attest. The Gulf Coast Women's Center in Biloxi, Mississippi, has averaged 400 additional crisis calls per month since the advent of casinos there. Central City, Colorado, reported a six-fold rise in child protection cases in the year after casinos arrived. Jeffrey Bloomberg, former state's attorney for the Deadwood, South Dakota, area, cited a similar increase in his September 1994 congressional testimony, and described how children were being left in cars all night while their parents gambled. Earl Grinols points out that Nevada led the nation in deaths of children attributable to abuse from 1979 to 1988, a period when casino gambling was illegal everywhere else except in Atlantic City.

Children of compulsive gamblers also suffer in other ways. Jacobs found that such youth have a greater propensity for substance abuse, lower academic achievement, juvenile delinquency, and poorer mental health. They are also far more likely to develop gambling addictions themselves.

Compulsive gamblers are at much greater risk for other harmful behaviors. According to Henry Lesieur, about half of compulsive gamblers experience problems with alcohol and substance abuse. Lesieur also notes that compulsive gamblers are five to ten times more likely to attempt suicide than is the general population. The National Council on Problem Gambling states that 20 percent of compulsive gamblers attempt suicide. Many succeed. A nineteen-year-old Iowa college student, a St. Louis-area housewife and church volunteer, and an Illinois businessman are a few of the recent self-inflicted casualties that have received press attention, but hundreds of others go relatively unnoticed year after year. Nevada has the highest suicide rate in the nation. In Gulfport, Mississippi, attempted suicides rose more than 200 percent in the first two years of casinos, while suicide attempts soared from six to sixty-six in nearby Biloxi in the first year alone. Family members of compulsive gamblers are also at greatly increased risk for suicide, according to Lesieur.

SHOWDOWN IN RIVER CITY

Over the last decade the gambling industry has done a phenomenal job of selling itself as an economic elixir to communities strapped for revenue. Inflated promises of jobs, tourism, and additional tax monies have seduced politicians and citizens in dozens of states and communities. The numbers, however, are beginning to catch up with the gambling forces. As Americans become more aware of the societal devastation wrought by legalized gambling, the industry is finding it increasingly difficult, and ever more expensive, to peddle its wares. In recent elections, gambling interests have outspent opponents by margins of ten, twenty, even fifty to one, and are still losing far more often than not.

Jefferson City, Missouri, which voted for casino riverboats in 1992, voted them out last November. Fledgling efforts are underway in Louisiana, Wisconsin, and elsewhere to repeal legalized gambling. Even the industry's own polls show that gambling's acceptance appears to be waning.

The issue, however, is far from decided. Gambling interests have targeted several key states again this year—California, Florida, Illinois, Maryland, New York, Ohio, Pennsylvania, and Texas, among others—for expansion. In New York, the gambling lobby last year helped introduce a form of keno called "Quick Draw." It puts casino-style gambling right in front of teens, appearing in bowling alleys, supermarkets, and even candy shops to lure kids into shooting high-tech craps. If these and other efforts are successful, it will be a sure bet that millions more Americans—many of them children—will slip into addiction, and the destitution and darkness that go with it.

CHAPTER 15

Professional Football, Loyalty, and the Power of the Average Fan: The Betrayal of Cleveland— The "Browns" Move to Baltimore

In November 1995, sports fans were shocked to find out that the Cleveland Browns were moving to Baltimore. The Browns were one of the National Football League's oldest and well-supported franchises. Losing money and frustrated with the lack of a new stadium in Cleveland, owner Art Modell secretly negotiated with Maryland officials throughout 1995. Baltimore, hungry for professional football ever since the Colts left for Indianapolis in 1984, promised Modell a new stadium and favorable tax breaks if he would move his team.

The readings describe congressional reaction to the Browns' move in particular, and the overall environment of professional sports franchise instability in general. U.S. Senator Mike DeWine and former U.S. Representative Martin Hoke, both Republicans from Ohio, introduce legislation that would strengthen the power of communities and fans to keep franchises when their owners threaten to move them out of town. Their proposed bills directly address how Congress has helped the National Football League (NFL) prosper through the use of tax laws and antitrust exemptions and the responsibility that pro sports franchises owe their community.

The NFL's Green Bay Packers are a nonprofit, community organization owned by their fans. Would more community-owned teams enhance franchise stability in professional sports? Does money have too much influence in how pro sports operate? What power do fans have?

FANS RIGHTS ACT OF 1995

SENATOR MIKE DEWINE

S. 1439. A BILL TO REQUIRE THE CONSIDERATION OF CERTAIN CRITERIA IN DECISIONS TO RELOCATE PROFESSIONAL SPORTS TEAMS, AND FOR OTHER PURPOSES; TO THE COMMITTEE ON COMMERCE, SCIENCE, AND TRANSPORTATION

Mr. DeWINE. Mr. President, I am very proud to join my colleague from Ohio today in cosponsoring this piece of legislation. . . . Let me . . . talk about a few items that I feel are important, because this legislation is not just about the Cleveland Browns. Really, this legislation is about how tax dollars are spent. This legislation is about equity. It is about fairness. It is a bill that would ultimately help protect professional football fans everywhere. The question is asked many times . . . why should Congress even think about becoming involved in professional sports? I think the answer is threefold.

First, in 1966, the NFL-AFL wanted to merge, and they came to this Congress to ask for specific exemption of the antitrust law, and that was granted. Later on, when they wanted to pool their resources, pool the TV money, again the NFL came to this Congress, to the House and the Senate, to the American people, and said we want special legislation. That legislation was passed and signed into law, and they operate under that law today. In virtually every move that is contemplated today in professional sports, certainly in regard to the purported move by the Browns from Cleveland to Baltimore, tax dollars are involved, federal tax dollars indirectly, local tax dollars both indirectly and directly. No move takes place today without subsidization by the taxpayers. In the case of the Baltimore-Cleveland situation, you have the Cleveland community that has not only supported the Browns with its individual money by the people who go to the game, not only watch the game on TV, not only the great loyalty of almost fifty years of the Cleveland Browns fans, but the community through tax dollars has put tax dollars back into Municipal Stadium over the years, and there has been a contribution. And so we see that case now in Baltimore with additional tax dollars. Yes, I know they are called lottery dollars. They are. But again they are public funds that were used to lure Cleveland over to Baltimore. So public dollars are involved and involved in virtually every single move. And so these are three good reasons I believe why Congress is

From the *Congressional Record*: November 30, 1995 (Senate).

already involved in the NFL, already involved in professional football. The only question before us is to what extent we want to be involved. . . . The one provision which will give a limited antitrust exemption to the NFL owners if they turn down a move is . . . very limited, and it does have the effect, in my opinion, of facilitating the NFL in doing what they ought to do anyway, and that is, frankly, follow their own nine-point criteria. That is all anyone can expect them to do. When anyone looks at the nine-point criteria that the NFL drew up to guide them, that they did in lieu of the Al Davis case and they drew up nine points, very objective criteria it is abundantly clear that if you objectively apply the criteria, the Cleveland Browns would simply never be allowed to move. It is not even a close call. Here we have a community that has put an average of 70,000 people in the stands Sunday after Sunday after Sunday in good years and some years that maybe were not football in Cleveland. The day after it was announced that the Browns wanted to move to Baltimore, a day after the infamous press conference in Baltimore was held, less than twenty-four hours later, the voters of Cleveland, in Cuyahoga County, voted by a 72 percent margin to tax themselves to keep the Browns in Cleveland—72 percent in 1995, with the antitax climate that we have today. Here is a team that is rated number 1 in the NFL in TV penetration of their market. They get a bigger share of the TV market in the Cleveland area, throughout the Cleveland market, northeast Ohio, central Ohio, than any other team in the NFL. So if you look at the criteria that is applied, objective criteria, how well has the community supported the team, how willing is the community willing to try to negotiate and to provide the things that are needed for the team to solve any problems the team might have, when you look at all the criteria, it is abundantly clear, on an objective basis, the Browns did not qualify. It is not even close. Baltimore should get a team, but it should not be the Cleveland Browns.

Let me turn, Mr. President, to another provision in this bill, and it has to do with something that I discussed yesterday with Commissioner Tagliabue when he testified in front of our Judiciary Committee, and that is this thing that is called the franchise relocation fee. This is, in essence, to boil it down, money that is given by the team that is moving to all the other NFL owners. The last time this was done, the amount was, if you count the direct money and the indirect money, $46 million. The last time there was a move in the NFL, $46 million, they spread it among the other NFL teams. These are the same owners, same teams that have to judge whether or not it is in the best interest of football and for a team to be able to move. What this bill does is say you cannot have this franchise relocation fee. It is not right. It is not fair. It does not accomplish anything for the fans, for professional football, and certainly it does not make the decision-making process any more objective as carried on by the owners. The deal between the Cleveland Browns and Baltimore in Maryland provides a specific provision. In that contract it provides that up to $75 million can be used for a franchise relocation fee, up to $75 million. I would submit, Mr. President, that it is not too far a stretch of the imagination to argue that the lottery funds, other public money, from Baltimore, from Maryland, will then go to the Browns, the Browns would then turn around and distribute this, on this relocation fee, to the other owners. I think it is abundantly clear what the problem is with this franchise relocation fee.

Mr. President, we are not in any way with this bill arguing or saying that teams should not be able to move. Teams should be able to move. They should be able to move if the market is not good, if there are problems locally that cannot be resolved. What we are simply saying, though, is that the movement should be based on merit, and there should be some logic behind that. In yesterday's hearing, Mr. President, I talked with some of the witnesses, particularly witness Tagliabue, the commissioner of the NFL, about a couple changes I thought the NFL could make without any intervention by Congress. The franchise relocation fee is one. The NFL does not have to wait for legislation. They could do that tomorrow. They could change the rules and do away with that. And I think they should. Another thing that the NFL could do would be to change their very, very strange I do not know, Mr. President, a better word to describe it but the very, very strange structure by which they share revenues in regard to people who go into those coliseums and ballparks every weekend.

Mr. President, if you or I buy a ticket, go in to see an NFL football game this coming Sunday, if we just buy a regular ticket, part of the money from that ticket will go to the visiting team, part will go to the home team. It is the way most professional sports divide the money up. The home team does get more, but there is a certain percentage. It works no matter where you buy the ticket. There is one exception to that. This has to do with the luxury boxes. If you are lucky enough to be seated up in a luxury box, in comfort, looking down, the money you have paid or the money someone else has paid for that luxury box, for that seat, whatever you want to call it, that all goes to the home team. Well, this was a decision made apparently a few years ago by the NFL.

It did not take the owners and teams very long to figure this out. And so if you got extra money, if you got all the money from the luxury boxes, it put a premium on building more luxury boxes, in fact, put a lot of pressure on the teams to build these luxury boxes, because not only, Mr. President, do the teams get all of the money instead of just part of the money— . . .

Not only does all this money for the luxury boxes then go to the individual owner of the home team, but it also has the effect, I will not take the time on the floor of the Senate today to explain all the math of this, but it has the effect of driving up these salary caps because that salary cap is based on total gross revenue and based on formulas. Basically, it is 62 percent times the designated amount of revenue. And so if one team, let us say team A, has no luxury boxes, but team B builds luxury boxes, not only does team B get all the money for the luxury boxes, not split at all with team A, who they might be playing that weekend, but team B, by getting that luxury box money, drives up the salary cap, not just for them but for everybody. So team A has their costs go up. So it is almost like being on a treadmill. The NFL has created a system by which everybody has a real incentive to go out and build luxury boxes. What that means is they are either going to build them in the home coliseum or the home park, or they are going to make the incentive to move somewhere else.

So the NFL has created a situation with this structure that really puts a premium on movement, and I do not think it is in the best interest of football. Again, it is something that the NFL should change and can change themselves, and I think it is a fair representation of Commissioner Tagliabue's testimony yesterday that he simply did not disagree with this at all.

Mr. President, let me conclude by stating that the thing that I have found most interesting in the last several weeks in regard to the controversy surrounding the Cleveland Browns' reported move to Baltimore has not been the reaction of fans in Ohio and that has been absolutely unbelievable. People are up in arms. But we sort of expected that. What I think is interesting is that people across this country, who are sports fans, and who are not Browns, have looked at this and said this is not right, something is wrong, there is a problem. Maybe this move or attempt to move by the Browns to Baltimore is sort of, or should be, a wake-up signal to the NFL that something is absolutely wrong. . . .

THE FAN FREEDOM AND COMMUNITY PROTECTION ACT OF 1995

TESTIMONY BY REPRESENTATIVE MARTIN R. HOKE ON H.R. 2740

I ask unanimous consent to place my prepared statement in the record. Rather than read it, I intend to use my five minutes to set the record straight and rebut the misinformation and disinformation campaign that has been mounted against the Fan Freedom and Community Protection Act by the NFL and its surrogates.

CLAIM #1. This is private enterprise and Congress has no business in it.

If that were true it would be a mighty compelling argument, but the fact is that the pro sports leagues are about as far from free enterprise as you can get in America. In 1961 and 1966, the leagues came to Congress and asked for what amounted to a private bill. They wanted special legislation just for them to shield and exempt them from federal antitrust laws. They said the exemptions would give them financial stability and thereby allow them to protect fans and communities—which they passionately promised to do.

In fact, Pete Rozelle testified before Congress in 1966 that preserving existing franchises was of considerable public interest to local economies, stadium authorities, consumers. Without the plan, franchise moves and/or franchise failures will occur as a matter of course within the next few years.

Congress took them at their word and gave about 100 very wealthy individuals one of the most spectacular pieces of corporate welfare ever enacted, The Sports Broadcasting Act of 1961 and The Football Merger Act of 1966.

They certainly achieved financial stability, which is not really all that hard when the federal government hands you an unregulated monopoly.

The NFL's TV contract made possible by the Sports Broadcasting Act was worth $1.1 billion in 1995. Now that's corporate welfare. In other words, Congress is already up to its neck in federal legislation with regard to professional sports.

So they got their financial stability, but what about their end of the bargain—protecting fans and communities? Not hardly! What we have gotten is what you ultimately get from all monopolies: ever escalating and more outrageous demands; arrogant behavior; monopoly pricing; lousy service; and a poor quality product. . . . If $350 million, including the debt service, goes to a new stadium,

From the House Commerce Subcommittee on Commerce, Trade and Hazardous Materials, May 16, 1996.

that's $350 million that's not going into schools, or streets and sidewalks, or public safety, or social safety nets, or other meritorious projects.

In Cincinnati it meant immediate cuts—real cuts, not Washington cuts—for the Cincinnati Zoo, the Riverfront Music Center, and the Cincinnati Museum of Art.

In Cleveland, school officials just laid off 451 teachers, 10 percent of the faculty, because of the dire financial straits the school system is in.

And who wins: superrich owners who can pay very rich players to be watched by well-off spectators in magnificent play palaces paid for with the taxes of working men and women who can't afford to buy tickets to the game—all because Congress gave the leagues a private bill exempting them from antitrust laws and neglected to place any conditions in the bill that would make the leagues' promise of community protection enforceable.

Well, that's what my bill does; it re-levels the playing field ever so slightly by giving communities a modicum of negotiating leverage, the opportunity—under very tough conditions—to get a replacement team.

It's simple; it's fair; it's effective.

CLAIM #2. The Leagues will put an end to franchise free agency immediately if Congress gives them an additional antitrust exemption.

I won't go into a long discussion about where the case law is today on this issue of franchise movement restriction. The 9th Circuit Federal Court of Appeals has made it clear that leagues can restrict team movements today. That is made clear by reading Raiders I & II and Clippers—and so does the NFL's own actions preventing Georgia Fontiere from moving the L.A. Rams to St. Louis until the pot for the owners was sweetened by $24 million and the NFL's recent decision to prevent Seattle from moving to Los Angeles. And my bill does codify the case law and make the leagues' ability to do this crystal clear. But that's not the problem! The problem is that franchise free agency makes the owners lots and lots of money.

When Art Modell moved his team to Baltimore its value increased by $40 million. Ditto the Rams move to St. Louis. So the promise made in the sixties of maintaining existing franchises was in direct opposition to the economic interests of team owners.

Owners know this. They also know that this time it is Art Modell and (Oilers' owner) Bud Adams. Next time it could be their turn. This owner's form of free agency is making rich those who take advantage of it. It simply goes against human nature to expect team owners to suddenly begin to act irrationally and oppose team moves. An individual owner is not going to oppose any move by another owner because he may need that owner's vote himself someday.

In short, maybe we can change the antitrust laws, but we can't change the laws of economics and we certainly can't change human nature.

CLAIM #3. The bill mandates forced expansion.

This is the NFL's mantra and it is completely untrue.

H.R. 2740 gives cities an opportunity for an expansion team provided that a tough but fundamental market test is met—a new investor willing to risk big bucks, $200–$300 million in the case of the NFL, comes forward. It's that simple. No government regulators, no bureaucracy, no new federal employees. Just a simple market test that makes sure that the old owner is leaving because the city won't support his team or that particular sport. And while this mechanism absolutely does not mandate forced expansion, it will help stabilize the leagues by reducing team movement as promised thirty-five years ago by Pete Rozelle. Why? Because the other team owners will be motivated by a competing self-interest—the interest of not seeing their share of league revenues diluted as a result of increasing the number of teams.

The league will be motivated to step in and help mediate a solution when a franchise first encounters problems—not after a crisis has developed, with the owner threatening to leave and the league faced with the potential of having to fill a void in the abandoned city.

CLAIM #4. The bill is an unfunded mandate.

Of all the misinterpretations, this is the most outrageous.

Those who say that have the right description, but they apply it to the wrong bill. The federal anti-trust exemptions granted to the leagues have become an unfunded mandate on host cities that cost billions and billions of dollars.

Of the 113 professional sports franchises, thirty-nine are demanding new stadiums and arenas—this is on top of the thirty-one built since 1989. And as long as team owners can negotiate from a—take it or leave it, build a new stadium or I'm out of here—position, the price of this unfunded mandate will continue to skyrocket.

Let's be clear what we're talking about here. This unfunded mandate involves the taking of scarce tax dollars from hard-working families to further enrich very wealthy team owners. H.R. 2740 ends that madness, ends unfunded mandates, and stops the extortions of cities and taxpayers.

Perhaps that's why the NFL is so opposed.

In closing, some people may wonder why I'm still involved in this. After all, Cleveland will have its team by 1999. So why do I care?

Because pro sports is becoming one more thing that is wrong with America. Powerful special interests obtain special legislation for special benefits from Congress on the promise that they will use the legislation to protect communities, consumers, citizens, taxpayers. But just the opposite happens. It is used to exploit cities and taxpayers into bidding wars against each other in a massive and subtle wealth transfer scheme that transfers tax dollars from millions of hard-working families to a handful of very wealthy team owners and in the bargain disrupts and distorts a community's priorities by placing it in an untenable no-win situation.

The fact is that Congress created this mess. Congress is responsible for the impossible bargaining position cities find themselves in. And Congress is obligated to fix that. So let's do what we can to make professional sports once again something that's right about America.

CHAPTER 16

Protecting Community from the Power of Unrestrained Economic Freedom

One of the oldest political beliefs is that unrestrained power, if left unchecked, will eventually lead to despotism. Our founding fathers realized this and created a public system of separated power and checks and balances.

However, there are many who believe that private economic power, if unchallenged, can lead to the same result. The first reading criticizes the totalitarian nature of contemporary capitalism, with its single-minded emphasis on short-term considerations and greed. It explores how the Republican party may represent this development by furthering its goals at the expense of sustaining community and encouraging cooperation.

The second reading describes the actions taken by a group of citizens who tried to stop Wal-Mart from opening a store in their town. The citizen effort was successful as the community effectively exercised its right to control its development.

Cynics are fond of saying, "Everything has its price." Is that true? Does American society recognize the value of activities that are not related to economics? Does the Republican party have room for people who are skeptical of business? In what way do megastores weaken small communities?

AMERICAN CAPITALISM IS DANGEROUS

MICHAEL GRAY

It's ironic that while the former Soviet Union tries to change from communist dictatorship to something resembling democracy, America, long considered a democratic society, is becoming a capitalist dictatorship fueled by ruinous economic "principles" and Republicanism.

Essayist/poet and Kentucky farmer Wendell Berry recognized this change in America in 1989. American economic principles, he wrote, have become "elevated to the position of ultimate justifier and explainer of all the affairs of our daily life, and competition enshrined as the supreme principle and ideal of economics."

Berry reveals the fatal error of capitalism: unrestrained competition that ultimately subjugates people and dehumanizes them in the same way that people became merely anonymous, joyless cogs in the machinery of the former Soviet Union.

"It seems that we have been reduced almost to a state of absolute economics," says Berry, "in which people and all other creatures and things may be considered purely as economic units, or integers of productivity in which a human being may be dealt with, as John Ruskin put it, 'merely as a covetous machine.' "

Berry is correct: capitalism gone mad is ruining America. But don't think this is just the view of philosophers. Ordinary people are waking up to the dangers of unrestrained capitalism. Mal Evans of Madison Heights felt strongly enough about America's wrong turn that he recently sent a letter to the editor to the *Detroit Free Press*.

Evans recalled: "when there were fewer controls over corporate America, we suffered from the worst depression the country has ever seen . . . unless something is done to curb the greed of the movers and shakers, we may be headed toward a repeat. Does every generation have to learn the bitter lesson that uncontrolled free enterprise brings nothing but misery and grief?"

Greed. It's the core of Republicanism. Greed is what makes capitalism, in its current primitive American form, only marginally better than Soviet communism, a system Winston Churchill so aptly called "foul baboonery."

Greed, whether in American capitalism or Soviet communism, forces a society

From *The Herald* (Western Michigan University), October 23, 1995.
Reprinted with permission.

to degenerate into economic tribal warfare—winners and losers, according to Berry.

"Economic anarchy," Berry says, like any other free-for-all, tends inevitably toward dominance by the strongest. If it is normal for economic activity to divide the community into a class of winners and a class of losers, then the inescapable implication is that the class of winners will become ever smaller, the class of losers ever larger."

House Speaker Newt Gingrich, (R-Ga.), and his Republican henchmen and henchwomen in Congress are doing their best to enrich the class of winners at the expense of the class of losers, which, generally, includes the elderly, students, women, and minorities.

Nations that once admired America have begun to realize that American capitalism is dangerously flawed, as political observer William Pfaff pointed out recently in *The Chicago Tribune*.

"This American ethic of the primacy of self-interest is spread abroad . . . by the worldwide doctrine that societies everywhere must subordinate themselves to market forces," Pfaff says. "There is a significant turning away from the United States by its allies, which rests on a conviction that the United States has put itself on a dangerous and destructive course." America's insistence on spreading capitalism around the world is not much different than the former Soviet Union's efforts to export communism. Both systems seek to install governing forces that benefit a privileged few at the expense and labor of a disadvantaged majority.

Unfortunately, the prospects for America returning to democracy are poor as long as Republicanism flourishes, and so Americans must stand up to the tyrannical minority of big business and its Republican servants and send the message that capitalism's unlimited competition principle is destroying American families and communities. Unrestricted capitalism is producing an economic battlefield that may yet resemble the Civil War.

Berry succinctly characterizes capitalism as a war that "pits neighbor against neighbor as readily as it pits buyer against seller. If one person is willing to take another's property and to accept another's ruin as a normal result of economic enterprise, then he is willing to destroy that other person's life as it is and as it desires to be."

Now that Republicans appear to control America (as lackeys for the insidious, intolerant Religious Right, the National Rifle Association and the rich), the throttle of the capitalism machine has been flung wide open. Republicans will stop at nothing in their quest to change laws—or get rid of them—that protect average citizens in order to replace them with laws that enrich the ability of Big Business to make even greater short-term profits.

Republicans, no doubt, will whine that people who criticize capitalism must be communists. That would simply be a lie, but then Republicans are fond of lies. Remember, these are the same people who piously claim that nothing is more precious than their children, and yet these same people routinely refuse to pass state budgets that adequately fund education, thus denying children safe schools and productive learning environments. Or maybe it's just that they can afford to send their children to private schools.

After all, Republicans seem to think that there's no profit to be mined from education, so they neglect it and concentrate on helping big business get bigger.

Because Republicans are interested only in the taking of short-term profit, they fail to understand that education is the key to maintaining societal health in the long run. Or maybe they realize that as more people are educated the chances increase that people will reject unhealthy, unrestricted competition in favor of cooperation. That would be a revolution against the Republican revolution of greed, and it would modify capitalism into something better—responsible capitalism, perhaps?

But don't bet on the Republicans letting it happen.

BUCKING THE ESTABLISHMENT: GREENFIELD, MASSACHUSETTS

CONSTANCE E. BEAUMONT

What do you do when your local newspaper won't cover your side of the story? When your town council glosses over the downside of a proposed development? When downtown businesses likely to be hurt by superstore sprawl are afraid to speak out for fear of offending customers? All of these problems and more beset citizens in Greenfield, a working-class town of 19,000 in northwestern Massachusetts, in late 1992 and 1993.

Sometime during the summer of 1992, Andree Clearwater learned of Wal-Mart's plans to build a 116,097-square-foot store (slated to expand later to 134,272 feet) and up to two more buildings on the edge of Greenfield. With its 1,372-car parking lot, the total project would equal 264,272 square feet and spread over 63 acres.

Clearwater had managed a shopping mall about ten years earlier and seen firsthand the damage that outlying commercial centers do to downtowns. "I had already seen the waste that this type of development causes," said Clearwater. "This new project would create major traffic problems. It would hurt the downtown. It would decimate the natural landscape. Their original plan was to remove the top twenty-eight feet of a ridge overlooking the Connecticut River (which they quickly backed down from after public outcry), opting to 'tuck it into the hillside' where it would be less visible. It was badly designed."

Clearwater began circulating a petition against the project in October 1992. After gathering what she considered a respectable number of signatures, she sent the petition with a letter to the editor of *The Recorder*. The paper printed her letter. Soon thereafter, Clearwater organized a meeting for Greenfield residents who shared her concerns. Fifty people showed up and formed a group called Citizens for Responsible Development (CRD). Phase One of Greenfield's battle against superstore sprawl had gotten under way.

Since the town had previously zoned the proposed development site for industrial purposes and had limited the size of buildings, Wal-Mart and its partner-developer needed to get the land rezoned commercially before building. That was controversial, so the twenty-seven-member town council decided to consult the electorate first through a nonbuilding referendum scheduled for April 6, 1993. Wal-Mart, meanwhile, had been inviting opinion leaders in town to small group meetings in the office of its local attorney.

Between November 1992 and April 1993, CRD concentrated on winning the referendum. It circulated petitions, distributed "Wal-Mart Goodbye" bumper stickers, and spoke out at public hearings. It produced a TV documentary featuring a panel discussion on the proposed development. It increased public awareness. But all the while, CRD members felt frustrated by the reluctance of local business people to speak out. They also felt hobbled by the general perception that the development would go forward no matter what. "The main thing we had to counteract was the feeling of inevitability," says Clearwater.

Meanwhile, several local residents persuaded the town to conduct an independent analysis of the store's fiscal and economic impacts before approving the rezoning. Wal-Mart agreed to pay for the $36,900 study, and the town hired RKG Associates, Inc., a Durham, New Hampshire, firm, to do the research.

The study was supposed to be completed in time to educate the citizenry before the referendum, but it was not actually released until April 2, just four days before the vote—too late for people to read and digest a dry, dense, technical report. The local paper ran an editorial favoring the rezoning and carried a special eight-page supplement on the issue. Conspicuously absent from the supplement, however, was the newly released economic and fiscal impact data. According to the April 6, 1993, *Recorder*, a Wal-Mart-funded group distributed a flier asserting that a "yes" vote would mean the creation of stringent development controls to protect environmental and aesthetic concerns. Without the benefit of the study findings, the voters approved the rezoning by a two-to-one margin.

The referendum itself did not mention Wal-Mart; it simply asked voters:

Shall the zoning bylaws be amended or changed to allow commercial development along the French King Highway?

Although CRD supporters felt many voters probably did not fully understand all the issues involved, they clearly had lost Round One in the battle against sprawl. As of April, most of Greenfield's citizens appeared to want the new superstore . . . or they were unconcerned about the effects of outlying development.

Soon after the vote, RKG's economic data began to circulate. The report said Wal-Mart would mean a net gain in Greenfield's commercial tax base of $6.9 million and a net increase of 177 jobs over ten years.[1] But it also included some troubling predictions. For example, under a "low-impact" scenario, 91,900 square feet of Greenfield's existing retail space would become vacant as Wal-Mart captured sales from existing merchants. After analyzing and discussing RKG's findings with other economists and retail experts, local business leaders concluded that the new superstore would cause several negative consequences:

- A capture by Wal-Mart of between $15 million and $24 million in existing retail sales, with 65 percent of these sales taken from Greenfield's stores (versus stores elsewhere in Franklin County)

- An increase of up to 16,000 car trips per day

- A 33 percent reduction in Greenfield's commercial property values due to increased store vacancies

- An increase of only eight new (lower paying) jobs after jobs lost through the displacement of existing businesses were taken into account

- The displacement of up to 239,000 square feet^2 of existing retail space in Franklin County (This would result in the vacancy of 65 percent of all retail space devoted to selling department store type merchandise.)

- A net gain of as little as $33,800 in tax revenue (a 1/10 of one percent increase on the annual $24 million town budget)

- A drop in residential property values[3]

Many Greenfield residents became concerned that the proposed rezoning would leave them with too little space for local industry to grow. They also thought Greenfield didn't need a fourth commercial center, since it already had a struggling downtown, one "dead mall" on the northern end of town, and commercial sprawl on the western edge. Why create yet a fourth retail hub, especially one that would further weaken existing centers?

As the minuses for local commerce and sense of community became apparent, so did the need for business leaders to become involved in the debate. Together with other concerned citizens, they formed what would become CRD's successor as the leading superstore opponent: the Greenfield Community Preservation Coalition. Its mission was to sway the town council, which would ultimately have to approve the required rezoning by a two-thirds majority.

Among the coalition's most prominent players were David L. Bete Sr. and Kevin O'Neil. Bete is president of Bete Fog Nozzle, which produces industrial spray nozzles and employs 140 people. Bete had voted for the rezoning in April because he thought the downtown didn't offer much and that no one was doing anything to improve it. The new economic data troubled him, however. "We really didn't have enough time in April to digest the RKG report," he said. "What I didn't realize then was that jobs would simply be shifted from one side of town to the Wal-Mart area. The negative impacts suggested by the report were not readily obvious. You had to think about how the proposed development would affect the town, its traffic patterns, etc." Bete also observed that while the report had assumed only one Wal-Mart store in the Greenfield area, it later became apparent there would be one every twenty miles or so, including at least one other store in Franklin County. Thus Greenfield could not expect to capture sales from the larger region, as the report had suggested.

O'Neil is president of Wilson's Department Store, a downtown retailer. O'Neil had opposed the superstore from the outset but had not played a highly visible role in the debate. It was difficult for him, as it was for other businessmen, to speak out publicly. "Lots of people wanted Wal-Mart," explains O'Neil. "Many businesses were afraid to offend their customers. I finally decided it was too important to stay quiet. The issue affected the entire community.''

O'Neil shared others' concerns about the loss of industrial land to large-scale commercial development and about the effects of a fourth commercial center on the three existing ones, but he also saw Greenfield's way of life at stake. ''If you want to preserve a town center—with its main street, its courthouse, its shops, insurance agencies, and banks—you've got to zone your town so these things can remain viable.'' But O'Neil found little support for this perspective during the first six months of the debate: ''Mine was a lonely voice.''

Between April and July, 1993, the coalition worked on persuading the Greenfield planning board and town council to vote against the rezoning, a vote now scheduled for July 21. The coalition put together and distributed a political advertisement. It also ran several ads. It turned people out for public hearings. Testifying wasn't always easy. In some cases, well-prepared presentations were met with scorn and hostility by local officials.

In the meantime, three probusiness organizations came out publicly against the superstore: the Franklin County Chamber of Commerce, the Greenfield Redevelopment Authority, and the Franklin County Community Development Corporation. The support of these prodevelopment organizations buoyed the spirits of the community preservationists. The momentum seemed now to swing in their favor.

Not for long. On July 21, the town council voted, 19 to 7, for the rezoning.[4] Coalition members felt devastated. Some were so dejected they decided to retreat from the debate altogether. What good would further opposition do?

But Cynthia Heslen, an attorney working with the coalition, saw the July 21 vote as a setback, not a defeat. Anticipating the outcome, she had done some important research before the vote. She had read Greenfield's town charter and learned that citizens could attempt to overturn the town council's decisions through a general referendum, and had drafted a properly worded petition seeking a referendum that would undo the rezoning. The petition first asked the board to rescind its decision. Failing that, it asked that the issue be put to the voters in the form of a binding referendum. Heslen brought seventy petition forms to the meeting, and after the vote, she gave them to people interested in giving their campaign one more shot. They had seven days to gather the necessary signatures.

Local reporters observed this activity and reported on it afterwards. The town council president, who had favored the rezoning, denounced the petition effort as something that would cost the town money. The local paper reported him as saying that petition sponsors should ''take responsibility for the petitions, so they are accountable for the money they may cost the town.''[5] The paper also reported the president as having made statements some people found intimidating: ''I have officially asked [organizations opposing the superstore] to make known the names of the coalition members, and they have not seen fit to do so. And this bothers me.''

Nonetheless, disheartened coalition members did nothing with the petition for several days.

Away on vacation during this period, Bete now returned to Greenfield, read the papers, and hit the ceiling. "I strongly disagreed with the suggestion that the [superstore] opponents should pay for the referendum. We set public funds aside for referenda. They are part of the democratic process," said Bete. He also observed that the town did not really have to go to the expense of holding a special vote; it could include the rezoning question in the next regular election.

When Ted Wirt, a teacher whose home abutted the Wal-Mart site, called Bete to ask for help gathering petition signatures, Bete said yes.

The following Monday, the local radio reported that coalition members would be down on the town common on Tuesday to collect petition signatures. Bete recalls the conditions under which this activity took place: "It was pouring rain. We stood under umbrellas and tarps. My pockets were full of water. People were driving up in this downpour to sign these petitions. We asked everybody to call their neighbors." He was impressed by Greenfielders' response: "This was obviously something people felt strongly about. These were people I knew and respected. They cared about their homes and neighborhoods, about the quality of life in Greenfield."

In the middle of this scene, the local cable TV station came down and asked Bete and others to appear on its call-in program: "Guerilla Television." Dripping wet, they went to the station to get their message out to the public.

By Wednesday, Bete and his allies had gathered 600 signatures, 100 more than needed. The town then scheduled the binding referendum vote for October 19. Round Three had begun. It would prove to be the most intensive phase in the entire campaign.

With the vote only eight weeks away, key players in this effort held a small meeting to discuss their next steps. Someone opposed to the superstore suggested they needed a better campaign strategy and recommended Al Norman to organize it.

A Greenfield resident, Norman is a lobbyist for a nonprofit organization that advocates for the elderly. He also has served area politicians as a media consultant. After interviewing Norman, Bete and the other activists hired him to formulate a strategy for winning the October 19 referendum.

Norman thought this assignment required a different approach from that used during the first two phases of the campaign. "I said, 'This is a political campaign, not a campaign to see how much you can educate people about economics. It's our job to appeal to people's hearts as well as minds.' "

Within a week, Norman laid out a comprehensive strategy for winning the October 19 vote. The campaign against the superstore would be run like a full-fledged political campaign: a media strategy, a grassroots organizing strategy, radio, ads, voter polling, a Get Out The Vote (GOTV) initiative, and poll watching. Norman also developed a timeline with hard deadlines for every task to be completed during the next eight weeks.

One of the first steps suggested by Norman was to give the new group of community organizers a new name. "We had a committee without a name collecting petition signatures," he said. "I suggested we call ourselves the 'We're Against the Wal' Committee." Everyone agreed and named Bete as the new group's chairman.

To give the new campaign visibility and momentum, Norman recommended getting 500 "Stop the Wal" bumper stickers made up and stuck on as many cars by August 30. He also suggested holding a press conference on the town common featuring a traveling "Wal." The committee invited townspeople to come down and record their views on the proposed superstore on a four-by-six-foot "community bulletin board." Letters from local residents and citizens in other communities fighting similar battles were tacked onto the "Wal." "We wanted a visible symbol of community opposition to the store," explains Norman. "We took 'The Wal' down to the town common every Saturday for eight weeks." By the campaign's end, people had filled three walls with letters of opposition. These "Wals" also traveled to Keene, New Hampshire, and Halifax, Massachusetts, where similar coalitions were battling superstores.

Norman also recommended reframing the debate, which until then had focused largely on what the superstore would do to downtown. "Many residents felt negatively toward the downtown and its short-comings," said Norman. "No one would fall on his sword for downtown Greenfield. We needed to shape the issue differently." Norman came up with a variety of ways to communicate one basic theme: Greenfield's small-town way of life was threatened by a superstore. As one of the ads he later produced put it: "There's one thing you can't buy at Wal-Mart: small town quality of life. Once you lose it, you can't get it back." The committee portrayed the electorate's vote on the referendum as a watershed event for the community, not just a decision about a single store: "We're not gaining a store," their ads said, "We're losing our community!"

The media strategy was another critical element, but this was tough to carry out because the local paper had editorialized twice in favor of the rezoning and had not reported information the committee wanted covered. For example, the committee had prepared an overlay drawing to illustrate visually the superstore's size relative to the downtown. The proposed development exceeded the square footage of the entire central business district and was, as the committee put it, the equivalent of three Fenway Parks (Boston's baseball stadium). But the paper did not print the overlay graphic.

Determined to deliver critical information to the voters, the committee raised money to pay for newspaper ads and radio spots. The committee also produced an ad in the form of a four-page, newsprint tabloid that summarized arguments against the superstore. The local paper included the "Retail News" tabloid, which looked like a real newspaper, as a special insert and distributed it to 6,000 regular newspaper subscribers. Five radio ads were produced, all using local opinion leaders. One radio spot, featuring the voice of a popular local super-market owner, aired fourteen times a day.

The committee also took advantage of "free" newspaper space by urging people to write letters to the editor. Norman's strategy called for getting no fewer than fifty people to submit letters by September 20. This goal was exceeded. The committee then copied and redistributed the letters in a packet used to educate people about the issues.

The committee needed to identify its base of voters, so Norman recommended a telephone survey of 1,000 voters to begin on August 23. A Greenfield-owned telemarketing company was hired to assist with a voter opinion poll. The company conducted 4,000 telephone interviews with local voters and produced a list of people for and against the store. The interviews also revealed how individual town precincts would probably vote on the referendum. Lists produced by the interviews proved invaluable the weekend before the referendum, when the volunteer committee members used them to call people leaning against the superstore and remind them to vote.

To show public support one week before the vote, the committee staged a "Main Street New England Walk Against Wal-Mart." A flier announcing this media event urged people to assemble on Main Street to hear speakers from several New England communities—including Westford, Massachusetts—that had opposed Wal-Mart. "Bring the children, grab a balloon, and walk with us, with our 'Wal' exhibits of letters, through the center of our community," read a promotional flier. "We are proud of the quality of life in our rural town, and we want to see industrial land used as it was intended—not wasted on X, Y, or Z marts. . . . Invite your friends to join us!" Steve Alves, a professional filmmaker on the committee, video-taped this march. The tape aired on local cable three times before the vote.

On the day of the referendum itself, the committee "poll-watched." As Norman explains: "You sit by the polling booths all day long and cross names off your list as supporters show up. At 5:00 P.M., with three hours left, you call your supporters who haven't yet voted and ask them to get out and do so."

As it turned out, the GOTV campaign, the poll-watching, the last-minute telephone calls, and the votes of individual citizens all made a difference. On October 19, 1993, voters rejected, by a nine-vote margin, the rezoning of the Wal-Mart site and the proposal to permit commercial stores exceeding 40,000 square feet in Greenfield.

Alves mused later: "The things that affect our daily lives are not well reported. It's hard to understand how community life can change, how relationships that used to be so fluid can be irrevocably altered by large-scale development. We were forced to examine the values of our small-town way of life, and then we voted to preserve them."

Postscript: *It was reported a few weeks later that Wal-Mart had spent $30,530 on advertising and other activities aimed at winning the Greenfield referendum, according to campaign finance reports. This was $13,000 more than the "We're Against the Wal" Committee had spent.*[6]

ORGANIZING TIPS FROM GREENFIELD

Al Norman, Political Campaign Consultant

- It isn't necessarily effective to appeal to people with just facts and figures. Some of that's okay, but you also need to appeal to people's emotions.
- Even if you lack zoning hooks, you have the power of public opinion. Large corporations can be very sensitive to this if you are able to get your story covered by the media.
- Some consultants recommend that local merchants adjust their product lines and carve out a special niche. That "accommodation" strategy is fine if you've lost the superstore battle. But we did not find that message particularly deep.

David L. Bete Sr., President, Bete Fog Nozzle, Inc.

- Organize quickly.
- If possible, tap the expertise of a professional political campaign consultant.
- Focus the campaign on the body that will make the key decision. If it's the planning board, focus on the planning board. If it's the town council, focus on the town council. If it's the voters, focus on the voters.

Cynthia Heslen, Esq., Environmental & Land Use Attorney, Anderson & Kreiger

- Have an understanding of the big picture. Any large development is likely to need a number of federal, state and local permits or approvals. Prepare a flow chart of those necessary approvals.
- Target your efforts and keep fighting.
- Remember: even though you may lose a vote before one permitting authority, you could win the next round.

NOTES

1. See *Fiscal and Economic Impact Assessment of the Proposed Wal-Mart Development,* by Land Use, Inc., of Hadley, Mass., and RKG Associates, Inc., of Durham, N.H. April 2, 1993.
2. This displacement would occur under a "high-impact" scenario.
3. Source: Campaign materials provided by the "We're Against the Wal Committee."
4. In June, the Greenfield planning board had approved the rezoning request and recommended its approval to the town council.
5. See *The [Greenfield] Recorder,* July 24, 1993.
6. See Ken Willis, "Wal-Mart to Target New Site," *The Recorder,* December 7, 1993.

CHAPTER 17

Reconceptualizing Work for the Twenty-first Century

Economic anxiety is likely to intensify and grow in the twenty-first century as increasing numbers of jobs are replaced by labor-saving technology. Unemployment and underemployment, already major problems for governments, are likely to increase in the future. As this happens, the social and spiritual costs to individuals and society will become more apparent. How governments and businesses react to these developments will become major political issues in the near future.

In the first reading, Jeremy Rifkin describes how and why this predicament is occurring. He also suggests some alternatives, such as a reduced workweek and strengthening the volunteer and nonprofit sector of American society as a means to address societal dilemmas.

In the second reading, the concept of ''new work,'' designed to connect individual freedom with self-sufficiency, is introduced. The reading suggests this can be accomplished by society rethinking and eventually synthesizing traditional boundaries of vocations and avocations with the unique talents of every citizen.

In what way are the solutions offered in these readings nonideological? What obstacles do American politics put in the way of solutions that do not fit neatly into traditional ideological categories? In particular, how would the two major political parties react to these ideas? How would the mass media report them?

WORK: A BLUEPRINT FOR SOCIAL HARMONY IN A WORLD WITHOUT JOBS

JEREMY RIFKIN

From the beginning, civilization—as well as people's daily lives—has been structured in large part around the concept of work. But now, for the first time in history, human labor is being systematically eliminated from the economic process. In the coming century employment, as we have come to know it, is likely to be phased out in most of the industrialized nations of the world. A new generation of sophisticated information and communication technologies is being introduced into a wide variety of work situations. These machines, together with new forms of business reorganization and management, are forcing millions of blue- and white-collar workers into temporary jobs and unemployment lines—or, worse, breadlines.

Our corporate leaders, economists, and politicians tell us that the rising unemployment figures represent only short-term "adjustments" that will be taken care of as the global economy advances into the Information Age. But millions of working people remain skeptical. In the United States alone, corporations are eliminating more than 2 million jobs annually. Although some new jobs are being created in the U.S. economy, they are for the most part in the low-paying sectors, and many are only temp jobs or part-time positions.

Men and women everywhere are worried about their future. The young are venting their frustration and rage in antisocial behavior ranging from drug abuse and gang violence in American ghettos to escalating attacks on foreigners in Europe. Older workers, feeling increasingly trapped by social forces over which they have little or no control, seem resigned. Some observers have attributed the victory of the Republicans' "traditional values" crusade in last year's U.S. elections to people's growing anxiety about the rapid pace of economic change all around them.

The hard reality that economists and politicians are reluctant to acknowledge is that manufacturing and much of the service sector are undergoing a transformation as profound as the one experienced by the agricultural sector at the beginning of the century, when machines boosted production, displacing millions of farmers. We are in the early stages of a long-term shift from "mass

labor" to a highly skilled "elite labor," accompanied by increasing automation
in the production of goods and the delivery of services. Workerless factories
and virtual companies loom on the horizon. While unemployment is still relatively low, it can be expected to climb steadily and inexorably over the next
four decades as the global economy makes the transition to the Information Age.

Reflecting on the significance of the transition taking place, Nobel-winning
economist Wassily Leontief has warned that with the introduction of increasingly sophisticated computers, "the role of humans as the most important factor
of production is bound to diminish in the same way that the role of horses in
agricultural production was first diminished and then eliminated by the introduction of tractors."

These developments do not have to mean a grim future. The gains from this
new technology revolution could be shared broadly among all the people with
a greatly reduced workweek and new opportunities to work on socially useful
projects outside the realm of the market economy. But before any such sweeping
reforms in the way we work can take place, it must be acknowledged that we
face a future where the traditional role of private-sector jobs as the centerpiece
of our economic and social life will be gone.

Nowhere is the effect of the computer revolution and re-engineering of the
workplace more pronounced than in the manufacturing sector. In the 1950s, 33
percent of all U.S. workers were employed in manufacturing. Today less than
17 percent of the workforce is engaged in blue-collar work. Management consultant Peter Drucker estimates that employment in manufacturing is going to
continue dropping to less than 12 percent of the U.S. workforce in the next
decade.

Although the number of blue-collar workers continues to decline, manufacturing productivity is soaring. From 1979 to 1992, productivity increased by 35
percent in the manufacturing sector while the workforce shrank by 15 percent.
For most of the 1980s it was fashionable to blame the loss of manufacturing
jobs in the United States on foreign competition and cheap labor markets abroad.
However, economists Paul Krugman of MIT and Robert Lawrence of Harvard
suggest, on the basis of extensive data, that "the concern, widely voiced
throughout the 1950s and 1960s, that industrial workers would lose their jobs
because of automation is closer to the truth than the current preoccupation with
a presumed loss of manufacturing jobs because of foreign competition."

William Winpisinger, past president of the International Association of Ma-
chinists, a union whose membership has shrunk nearly by half as a result of
advances in automation, cites a study by the International Metalworkers Federation in Geneva forecasting that within 30 years, as little as 2 percent of the
world's current labor force "will be needed to produce all the goods necessary
for total demand."

Many economists and elected officials continue to hold out hope that the
service sector and white-collar work will be able to provide jobs for the millions
of unemployed blue-collar laborers. Their hopes are likely to be dashed.

Andersen Consulting Company, one of the world's largest corporate restructuring firms, estimates that in just one service industry, commercial banking and thrift institutions, technological and management changes will eliminate 30 to 40 percent of the jobs over the next seven years. That translates into nearly 700,000 jobs. The number of banks in the United States is likely to decline by 25 percent by the year 2000, and this along with automatic teller machines and financial transactions over the information superhighway will significantly reduce the number of human employees.

The technological innovations taking place in the banking industry are indicative of the kinds of sweeping changes that are redefining every aspect of white-collar and service work. The nation's secretaries are among the first casualties of the electronic office revolution. The number of secretaries has been declining steadily as personal computers, electronic mail, and fax machines replace typewriters, paper files, and routine correspondence. There are fewer receptionists, too. Bellcore is currently developing an "electronic receptionist" that can answer calls, record messages, and even hunt down the party being phoned.

Changes have also been dramatic in the wholesale and retail sectors. Typical of the trend is retail giant Sears, Roebuck. Sears eliminated a staggering 50,000 jobs from its merchandising division in 1993, reducing employment by 14 percent. The cutbacks came in a year when Sears' sales revenues rose by more than 10 percent.

In most retail outlets, the use of electronic bar codes and scanners has greatly increased the efficiency of cashiers and thereby significantly reduced the number of positions available. Some fast-food drive-through restaurants are beginning to replace human order takers with touch sensitive menu screens. And many industry analysts are predicting that electronic home shopping will take over more and more of the nation's trillion-dollar-a-year retail market.

It's not just low-level jobs that are disappearing. A growing number of companies are deconstructing their organizational hierarchies and eliminating more and more middle management. They use computers to do the coordinating that people—often working in separate departments and locations within the company—used to do. Harvard business professor Gary Loveman points out that while better jobs are being created for a fortunate few at the top levels of management, the men and women in "garden-variety middle-management jobs" are "getting crucified" by corporate re-engineering and the introduction of sophisticated new information and communication technologies. Eastman Kodak, for example, has reduced its management levels from thirteen to four.

Intelligent machines are invading the professional disciplines and encroaching on education and the arts, long considered immune to the pressures of mechanization. A robot that will perform hip replacement surgery is being developed in California, and some firms now use a computerized hiring system to screen job applicants. Even in the arts, jobs are disappearing. Synthesizers—silicon musicians—are fast replacing human musicians in theaters, clubs, and even opera houses. The Washington Opera Company's recent production of *Don Carlo* had only the conductor, two pianists, and a synthesizer player in the pit.

Optimists counter with the argument that the new products and services of the high-technology revolution will generate additional employment, and they point to the fact that earlier in the century the automobile made the horse and buggy obsolete but created millions of new jobs. Although it is true that the Information Age is spawning a dizzying array of new products and services, they require far fewer workers to produce and operate them than the products and services they replace.

Many observers wonder how an increasingly underemployed and unemployed global workforce, displaced by new technologies, is going to be able to afford all of the products and services being turned out. While the optimists contend that the loosening up of trade barriers and the opening up of new global markets will stimulate pent-up consumer demand, others believe that soaring productivity will come up against weak consumer demand as growing numbers of workers are displaced by technology and lose their purchasing power.

It is also naive to believe that large numbers of unskilled and skilled blue-collar workers who lose their livelihoods will be retrained to assume the new jobs that are being created. The new professionals—the so-called symbolic analysts or knowledge workers—come from the fields of science, engineering, management, consulting, teaching, marketing, media, and entertainment. While their number will continue to grow, it will remain small compared to the number of workers displaced by the new generation of "thinking machines." Drucker says quite bluntly that "the disappearance of labor as a key factor of production" is going to emerge as the critical "unfinished business of capitalist society."

If no measures are taken to provide financial opportunities for millions of Americans in an era of diminishing jobs, then as the new industrial revolution spreads through the economy, crime, and especially violent crime, is going to increase. Trapped in a downward spiral, and with ever fewer safety nets to break their fall, a growing number of unemployed and unemployable Americans will find ways to take by force what is being denied them by the forces of the marketplace.

The violence taking place on the streets of America is already spreading to other industrialized nations. In Vauxen-Velin, a depressed working-class town near Lyon, France, hundreds of youths took to the streets, clashing with police and later riot troops, for more than three days. Although the riot was triggered by the death of a teenager who had been run over by a police car, local residents and government officials alike blamed increasing unemployment and poverty for the $120 million rampage.

French sociologist Loic Wacquant, who has studied urban rioting in First World cities, says that in almost every instance the communities that riot share a common sociological profile. Most are formerly working-class communities that have been caught up in and left behind by the transition from a manufacturing to an information-based society.

A growing number of right-wing politicians and political movements—especially in Europe—have been playing off the concerns of working-class and poor communities, exploiting their xenophobic fears that immigrants will take away precious jobs. In Austria and Germany, the neo-Nazi movement is growing. In Italy, the new fascist National Alliance Party won an unexpected 13.5 percent of the vote in national elections in March 1994. Political pollsters in Italy say that much of the party's support is coming from angry unemployed youth.

1950s—average unemployment for the decade stood at 4.5%

1960s—unemployment rose to 4.8%

1970s—rose again to 6.2%

1980s—rose to average of 7.3% for the decade

1990s—Wall Street analysts say unemployment should never dip below 6%

Nathan Gardels, editor of *New Perspectives Quarterly*, summed up the prevailing mood in terms remarkably similar to the arguments used to characterize the plight of America's urban underclass: "From the standpoint of the market, the ever swelling ranks of the [unemployed] face a fate worse than colonialism: economic irrelevance." The bottom line, argues Gardels, is that "we don't need what they have and they can't buy what we sell."

There is no question that we are being swept up into a powerful new technological revolution that will set off a great social transformation unlike any other in history. The negative effects on people and communities are beginning to be seen. Less clear is how this new high technology might benefit not just the high-level corporate executives, investors, and knowledge workers, but also the vast majority of people. For the first time in modern history, large numbers of human beings could be liberated from long hours of labor to pursue leisure and community activities.

It is time to prepare ourselves and our institutions for a world that will be phasing out mass employment. A fair and equitable distribution of the productivity gains from this new industrial revolution would require a shortening of the workweek in countries around the world and a concerted effort by central governments to provide alternative employment for workers whose labor is no longer required in the marketplace.

The call for the shorter workweek is spreading quickly through Europe, where unemployment has reached record postwar highs. At Hewlett Packard's plant in Grenoble, France, management instituted a four-day workweek for employees and a 24-hours-a-day, seven-days-a-week schedule for the plant. Employees are paid the same wages they received when they were working a 37.5-hour week, despite the fact that they are now working, on average, nearly six hours less.

The extra compensation is viewed by management as a tradeoff for the workers' willingness to accept flexible hours. Production has tripled as a result of the new plant schedule.

Still, in the United States, the argument persists that fewer hours at existing pay could put companies at a competitive disadvantage globally. A recent survey soliciting the support of 300 business leaders for a shorter week did not receive a single positive response. One Fortune 500 CEO wrote back, "My view of the world, our country, and our country's needs is dramatically opposite of yours, I cannot imagine a shorter workweek, I can imagine a longer one . . . if America is to be competitive in the first half of the next century."

One way to address this concern is the proposed solution being advocated in France. French business and labor leaders and politicians from several parties have embraced the idea of the government's taking over the employer's burden of paying for workers' compensation in return for an agreement by companies to shorten the workweek. French policy makers calculate that the hiring of additional workers will significantly reduce welfare and other relief payments, canceling out any additional costs the government might have to assume by absorbing the payroll tax for unemployment compensation.

American business leaders' opposition to a shorter workweek might also be overcome by extending generous tax credits to companies that shift to a shorter workweek and hire additional workers. The loss of government revenue up front, some argue, would be offset by the taxable revenue generated by more workers bringing home a paycheck. Finally, the government might consider granting additional tax credits to employers willing to introduce profit-sharing plans— along with the 30-hour workweek—to allow workers to participate more fully in the productivity gains.

The 30-hour workweek is likely to enjoy widespread support among Americans harried by the stress of their work schedules. A growing number say they would readily trade some income gains for increased time to attend to family responsibilities and personal needs. According to a 1993 survey conducted by the Families and Work Institute, employees said they are "less willing to make sacrifices for work" and "want to devote more time and energy to their personal lives."

Labor unions, civil rights organizations, women's groups, parenting organizations, social justice organizations, religious and fraternal organizations, and neighborhood civic and service associations—to name just a few—all share a vested interest in shortening the workweek. Together, these powerful constituencies could mount an effective grassroots campaign for the steady reduction of work hours in American society.

At the same time that the need for mass human labor is disappearing from the global economic system, the role of government is shrinking around the world. The clout of transnational corporations has begun to surpass the power of nations. The corporations have increasingly usurped the traditional role of the state and now exercise unparalleled control of global resources, labor pools, and markets.

While the political role of the nation-state is declining, so too is its role as employer of last resort. Governments hampered by mounting long-term debt and growing budget deficits are less willing to embark on ambitious public spending and public-works programs to create jobs.

With the commercial and public sectors less capable of providing fundamental economic security for millions of Americans, the public has little choice but to begin looking out for itself by re-establishing viable communities to serve as a buffer against both the ravages of transnational corporations and the decline in government services.

The foundation for a strong, community-based social force in American life already exists. The "Third Sector"—also known as civil society, the social economy, or the volunteer sector—is the realm where contractual arrangements give way to community bonds, and giving one's time to others takes the place of market relationships based on selling one's time. It also offers great potential as a source of work and livelihood for the millions who can't find employment in the traditional economic system. Voluntary organizations are serving millions of Americans in every neighborhood and community of the country. There are more than 1.4 million nonprofit organizations in the United States whose primary goal is to provide a service or advance a cause. They are financed, in part, by private donations and gifts, and the rest comes from fees and government grants.

Volunteers assist the elderly and the handicapped, the mentally ill, disadvantaged youth, the homeless and indigent. Volunteers renovate dilapidated apartments and build new low-income housing. Tens of thousands of Americans serve as foster parents, or as big brothers and sisters. A growing number volunteer in crisis centers, helping rape victims and victims of spouse and child abuse. People help each other in Alcoholics Anonymous and in drug rehabilitation programs. They participate in recycling activities, conservation programs, anti-pollution campaigns, and animal protection work. Others work to eliminate social injustice. Hundreds of thousands are involved in local theater groups, choirs, and orchestras. Many serve as volunteer firefighters and donate time to crime prevention work and disaster relief.

Nonprofit museums, libraries, and historical societies preserve traditions and open doors to intellectual experiences. The independent sector provides a place and time for spiritual exploration. Finally, the Third Sector is where people relax and play, and more fully experience the pleasures of life and nature.

The Third Sector now has assets that equal nearly half the assets of the federal government and has been growing at twice the rate at which the private and public sectors are growing. It already contributes more than 6 percent of the gross domestic product and is responsible for 10.5 percent of total national employment.

In the 1980s the Republicans rode into the White House in part on the strength of the volunteer theme. The Grand Old Party dominated the political landscape for more than a decade with the plea to "return government to the people." The Reagan forces realized early on the potential symbolic and emotional power of volunteer images and used them to their advantage. But for all their talk of redirecting the government to assist the Third Sector, neither President Reagan nor President Bush was willing to carry through on the pledge with concrete programs. In fact, the Reagan White House lobbied to change the Internal Revenue Service code governing tax-exempt work to further restrict the activities of nonprofit groups and narrow the kinds of deductions a taxpayer can claim for charitable contributions.

Criticism of the Reagan-Bush theme of renewed volunteerism was heard from many quarters. Some on the left charged that it was a cynical attempt to abdicate government responsibility to aid the poor and working people of the country. Now, however, a growing number of progressive thinkers are taking a second look. They are beginning to realize that the independent sector is the only remaining alternative now that the market economy's role as employer and the government's role as provider of last resort are diminishing. The jockeying between conservatives and liberals over how to enhance the profile of the Third Sector is going to be one of the most closely watched political issues of the coming decade.

The American people ought to consider making a direct investment in expanded job creation in the Third Sector, as an alternative to welfare, for the increasing number of jobless who find themselves locked out of the new high-tech global marketplace. The state and local governments could provide an income voucher for those permanently unemployed Americans willing to be retrained and placed in community-building jobs in the nonprofit sector. The government could also reward grants to nonprofit organizations to help them recruit and train the poor for jobs in their organizations.

An income voucher would allow millions of unemployed Americans, working through thousands of neighborhood organizations, the opportunity to help themselves. Providing "a social wage" in return for community-service work would also benefit both business and government. Reduced unemployment would mean that more people could afford to buy goods and services, which would spur more businesses to open up in poor neighborhoods, creating additional jobs. Greater employment would also generate more taxes for the local, state, and federal governments. A rise in employment would also cut the crime rate and lower the cost of maintaining law and order.

Paying for a social income and for re-education and training programs to prepare men and women for a career of community service would require significant government funds. Some of the money could come from savings brought about by gradually replacing many of the current welfare programs with direct payments to community-service workers. Government funds could also be freed up by discontinuing costly subsidies—tens of billions of dollars in 1993 in the form of direct payments and tax breaks—to transnational corporations that have outgrown their domestic commitments and now operate in countries around the world. Additional monies could be raised by cutting military expenditures and placing a value added tax (VAT) on all high-tech goods and services.

There are more than 1.4 million nonprofit organizations in the U.S. with total combined assets of more than $500 billion

In 1991, the average American household contributed $649, or 1.7 percent, of its income to volunteer organizations.

An average volunteer gives 4.2 hours of his or her time per week.

Although powerful vested interests are likely to resist the idea of providing a social wage in return for community service, the alternative—ignoring the problem of long-term technological unemployment—is even more onerous. A growing underclass of permanently unemployable Americans could lead to widespread social unrest, increased violence, and the further disintegration of American society.

It is not enough, however, simply to create more paid jobs at nonprofit organizations. With government programs diminishing and the social net shrinking, an increasing burden is going to be placed on the nonprofit sector to provide a range of basic needs and services. Nothing could be more important at this juncture in American history than to strengthen the role of the nonprofit world. We need to encourage more Americans to volunteer their time in neighborhood organizations.

More than 89 million Americans currently volunteer their time each year. Measured in dollar terms, their contributions would be worth $182 billion. Unfortunately, the number of people who volunteer, and the amount of time they give, has been dropping over the past five years, in large part because working Americans, anxious over diminishing wages and the loss of well-paying jobs, are spending more hours engaged in part-time work to bring in needed extra income.

One way to stanch the decline in volunteering would be to grant a tax credit for every hour a person volunteers to a nonprofit charitable organization that serves the local community. If we allow people to claim deductions when they give money, real estate, stocks, artwork, and other items of financial value to charities, then why don't we allow people to secure a tax break for donating their time to the same efforts and causes?

A tax credit would go a long way toward encouraging many more Americans to devote a greater share of their leisure time to volunteering. While a tax credit would mean a loss of tax revenue to the federal government, it would be compensated for by a diminished need for expensive government programs to cover needs and services best handled by volunteer efforts. By extending tax benefits directly to the volunteers donating their services and skills, the government bypasses much of the expense that goes into financing the layers of bureaucracy that are set up to administer public programs in local communities.

Some might argue that providing a tax credit for volunteering hours would undermine the spirit of volunteerism. The chances of that occurring are unlikely. After all, making charitable contributions tax deductible seems only to have encouraged the philanthropic spirit. With millions of beleaguered Americans attempting to both make ends meet and continue to volunteer time to worthwhile civic programs, a tax credit for volunteering time to nonprofit organizations could provide a much-needed stimulus to boost participation in charitable activities.

In the debate over how to divide up the benefits of productivity advances made possible by the new high-tech global economy, we must ultimately grapple with an elementary question of economic justice: Does every member of society, even the poorest among us, have a right to participate in and benefit from the productivity gains of the information and communication technology revolutions? If the answer is yes, then some form of compensation will have to be made to those whose labor is no longer needed in the new high-tech, automated world of the 21st century. Tying compensation to service in the community would aid the growth and development of the social economy and strengthen neighborhoods across the country.

By shortening the workweek to 30 hours, providing an income voucher for permanently unemployed Americans in return for retraining and service in the Third Sector, and extending a tax credit for volunteering time to neighborhood nonprofit organizations, we can begin to address some of the many structural issues facing a society in transition to a high-tech, automated future.

Up to now, the world has been so preoccupied with the workings of the market economy that the notion of focusing greater attention on the social economy has been virtually ignored by the public and by those who make public policy. This needs to change as we enter a new age of global markets and automated production. The road to a near-workerless economy is within sight; whether it leads to a safe haven or a terrible abyss will depend on how well civilization prepares for what is to come. The end of work could signal the death of civilization—or the beginning of a great social transformation. The future lies in our hands.

CAREER SEEN AS A CALLING, WITH MORE SATISFACTION IN WORK AND LIFE

JAMES RICCI

Many people dream of freedom from work. For fifteen years, University of Michigan philosopher Frithjof Bergmann has been dreaming of a new culture in which people are free to work.

In the vision, the boundaries between labor and living would be blurred in a way that satisfies the soul, liberates people to take care of themselves, their families and their communities, and promises greater economic efficiency for society at large.

Because of Bergmann, Michigan, which created the world's most lucrative and widespread industrial jobs system, might one day be known as the birthplace of a revolutionary alternative to that now-battered system.

New Work, a response to the problem of disappearing high-paying corporate jobs, is about to take tangible shape in the state, fifteen years after Bergmann began developing it as a body of thought. That view is supported by several recent developments:

- The Kalamazoo-based Fetzer Institute, a foundation established by late Detroit Tigers owner and communications pioneer John E. Fetzer, has agreed to underwrite an international New Work conference next month in Kalamazoo.

- A Center for New Work, seeded with private funds, has been established in Ann Arbor.

- Two prominent Michigan high-technology entrepreneurs, in consultation with Bergmann, are laying plans for a new manufacturing company based on New Work concepts.

- A New Work think tank of adult education teachers has formed within the Detroit public school system, and a new Detroit schools adult-ed center that will incorporate some New World activities is on the architect's drawing board.

- The Detroit Eastside Coalition of Churches just received a grant from the Mott Foundation to open an entrepreneurial center based on New Work principles; it's expected to be running within a month.

"It has certainly been a difficult and long and arduous task to get to where now it has reached a takeoff point," Bergmann says. "There is a sense of

From *The Detroit Free Press*, September 16, 1996.
Reprinted with permission.

convergence, a strong sense that a great number of different pieces are fitting together.''

An elusive concept, New Work is a notoriously difficult philosophy to summarize. Its core values are individual freedom and self-sufficiency, two virtues, Bergmann contends, the traditional jobs system has seldom nourished.

New Work holds that, for people to be truly free, they must discover and pursue work they truly want to do. It envisions a future in which people will spend something like a third of their customary work time at a job, a third pursuing a ''calling''—the work they deeply want to do, be it running a part-time business of their own, learning a foreign language or caring for elderly parents—and a third working at ''high-tech self-providing,'' to cut down on their personal expenses.

The cost of allowing people to pursue callings outside normal business contexts might be financed by a portion of the increased profits businesses will realize through the use of labor-saving technologies.

The philosophy emphasizes the importance of people acquiring such practical skills as computing, organizing personal finances, and home construction and maintenance. Such skills would better enable them to start their own businesses, work more effectively for existing ones, and reduce the kind of living costs that make people dependent on jobs they often dislike but live in terror of losing.

Bergmann, who spent time counseling laid-off autoworkers in Flint after the big wave of closings there in the 1980s, contends most people will choose to pursue callings that contribute to the well-being of their families and communities. Thus, New Work starts by making the individual happier and capable of a more meaningful and productive existence, and ends in happier and more prosperous communities.

''What New Work involves is not just a new way of working, but a gradual progression toward a new way of life,'' Bergmann says. ''It is a difficult concept for people to understand. Yet that's also one of its best aspects, because it means it cannot be reduced to a few slogans. Real progress happens only when people have to think and become subtle and complicated, and I think that's happening.''

Getting a foothold. The growing interest in New Work stems in part from its adaptability to various agendas, such as those of business people, educators, and religious leaders. ''Dr. Bergmann has been able to capture the imaginations of a broad cross-section of people who ordinarily wouldn't even sit down and talk to one another, except perhaps in an adversarial proceeding,'' says Arthur Carter, Detroit schools' deputy superintendent for governmental relations and community service.

The Fetzer Institute, which concentrates on issues of mental and physical health, and recently funded Bill Moyers' five-part public television series, ''Healing and the Mind,'' is ''in an exploratory phase of collaboration'' with New Work, says senior program director Arthur Zajonc.

Long-term and more substantial support could be forthcoming, he says, after the Institute sifts the evidence from the international conference it is underwriting with a grant of $60,000. The meeting will gather eminent "thinkers, foundation people, experimenters," from as far as Europe and India to pool their thinking on how human life can be improved in the face of an inevitable worldwide shortage of good-paying jobs.

"Issues around work and the future of work have never been more serious since the Industrial Revolution, at least," Zajonc says. "The impact of automation and technology will be unprecedented, and unless we find a way to reconnect human beings to work and vocations, we'll be in a very bad way in twenty to fifty years."

Zajonc says he identified Bergmann as one of "the most creative thinkers in the United States about the future of work. I'm very excited by his proposals to put meaning back into work, by his understanding that it's not just a job question but a moral and spiritual question: How does one connect one's purpose in life back into work? The thing that's unusual about him is that he goes from the idea of freedom to something eminently practical—now that you're free, how do you lead a life, create a future, which is a question of vocation."

Dwight Carlson, founder and vice chairman of Perceptron Inc., a high-tech supplier to the auto industry, sees in New Work the potential to unleash the creative passions of employees to the benefit of businesses. He says New Work's emphasis on encouraging people to think entrepreneurially may be the key.

"My sense is that the whole concept of self-reliance makes for a more whole person, and they become a much more productive worker as well as a happier human being," Carlson says. "If you can get people thinking entrepreneurially, I think they're better off at home and in the workplace. If you can get people to think creatively and give them the time-space in the workweek—you know, 'This is going to be your thinking time.'—our expectation is you're going to come up with some creative ideas and we're going to have a better company as a result.

"I think what Frithjof is saying is that what's good for the individual in his life is also good for the company and also good for the community and also good for America. If we change the workplace, we may find a lot of people will find their calling is, say, assembling world-class automobiles."

Carlson, who is helping to fund the start-up of a New Work Center in Ann Arbor, is partners with engineer Thomas Weber in a venture they hope will lead, within two years, to a manufacturing operation to be run according to New Work principles.

Weber, the former senior vice president and chief technical officer of industrialist Heinz Prechter's ASC Corp., turned to Bergmann for insight into how to change the in-house cultures that often keep manufacturing operations from being as successful as they could be.

"Culture can take a marginal technology and make it wildly successful, or it can take a highly successful technology and make sure it doesn't work," Weber says. "I understood the languages of business and industry, but I didn't understand culture. He understood culture."

Weber says he came to see that the way businesses are customarily run, workers have reason to be suspicious of technology, because they equate it with potential loss of their own jobs.

Weber believes a New Work environment, with ample time off for employees to pursue callings beyond the workplace, can be financed through rigorous elimination of waste.

"What I have come down to realize is this—less waste means more freedom," he says. "It's a matter of culture. As it stands now, what's the incentive for workers to try hard? They think, 'we're here to work our asses off to give more money to the shareholders?' No. Change the psychology to say, 'Less waste means more freedom. We're going to give you more freedom, more of what might make you happy.' Everybody wins. It's very rational. The most important part of this is its celebration of the individual. It's focused on what you as a person might be."

Help for inner cities. Detroit schools deputy superintendent Carter sees in New Work's emphasis on self-reliance and entrepreneurship the potential for economically revitalizing inner cities. He says adult education's traditional goals, such as helping people get their high-school equivalency degrees, are no longer sufficient to the task.

"The schools can't make it the way we are going," Carter says. "We have to link what we're doing in our curricula with the real world of work and jobs, and start to look to developing our own businesses. For blacks, that's absolutely imperative. There were more black-owned businesses in downtown Detroit in 1896 than there are today."

Carter, who grew up in a Detroit family that operated its own janitorial business, says teaching people the skills that enable them to fend for themselves economically can have broadly beneficial effects on communities. He suggests it can restore the social cohesion that marked African-American neighborhoods a generation ago.

"If a person acquires these entrepreneurial skills and sets up a business, it spirals into a lifestyle for his family and children. New Work is really very simple—teach people to create businesses where they are, then create networks so people can improve their skills and their businesses and get a window on the world so they can market beyond their community."

Carter says the Detroit schools' interest in New Work started after Bergmann addressed the system's adult education teachers more than a year ago. A New Work study group formed afterward and produced a dozen "disciples" who have been working hard to spread the New Work ethic among their colleagues.

The group had hoped to establish a clothing-manufacturing operation within the school system, but those plans had to be scuttled after the state legislature cut funding for adult education last year.

Still, Carter says, a new adult education center being designed for a site next to Redford High School, will include "a strip-mall concept in which students will be trained to make their own clothing, and run a shop selling it right there while they're working toward their GED. The idea is to include New Work directly in the curriculum.''

The Detroit Eastside Coalition of Churches similarly sees the entrepreneurial aspects of New Work as the key to resuscitating what the Reverend James Perkins, pastor of Greater Christ Baptist Church, calls "our redemptive turf." The newly received Mott Foundation grant of $80,000 will be used this fall to set up an entrepreneurial center along the lines of the New Work centers Bergmann's philosophy envisions, Perkins says.

The center will teach neighborhood residents computer skills, the business potential of the Internet, how to package and market an idea, and where to look for seed money. It will also maintain an idea bank for hopeful entrepreneurs searching for a focus.

Perkins says the coalition decided almost three years ago, after being addressed by Bergmann, to take a New Work approach to redeveloping the east side, rather than opting for a traditional development project.

"We thought his ideas were cutting edge," he says. "It was risky. This is new stuff. But it just felt better to us than going with a traditional developer who would be in it for profit, doesn't know the people in the area, and just puts up a project and leaves. This could allow people to transition from one phase of life to another—not just people being moved off welfare, but middle-class people being pushed out of the corporate world."

The potential impact on individuals is what made New Work especially attractive to church leaders, Perkins says. "It is part of the churches' role to help people find meaning in their lives. New Work is a kind of theology, too. It says that it doesn't matter who you are and where you are, you can contribute. You must ask yourself, 'what did God call me to do with myself?' To look inside at what God has given you and put that in the marketplace, and at the same time help rebuild the community.''

CHAPTER 18

A Concluding Speech from a True Believer

Pat Buchanan has been one of the main instigators of the ideological split which has plagued the Republican party since 1990. Running for president in 1992 and 1996, Buchanan severely weakened eventual nominees George Bush and Bob Dole by doing very well in the nation's first primary in New Hampshire. In 1993, he shocked the Republican establishment by winning almost 40 percent of the vote against Bush. In 1996, he upset the heavily favored Dole.

By publicly questioning policy stands, Buchanan fought for the ideological soul of the party. Specifically, he pressed social and cultural issues that made a lot of economic Republicans uncomfortable. This public battle allowed Bill Clinton and the Democrats to successfully appeal to the ample middle ground of American politics.

Buchanan sees himself as a conservative populist—hypernationalistic, uncompromising, and willing to defend heartfelt beliefs which he suspects a majority of Americans agree with him on. In this speech, he sums up his 1996 campaign. He describes and defends his positions on abortion, sovereignty, international trade, and immigration.

Many have argued that Buchanan appeals to the darkest part of Americans: intolerance, racism, and provincialism. In what ways is that true? False? Others have suggested that his appeal is directly related to an increased sense of powerlessness that many Americans feel. Is that true? Do Buchanan's views represent a majority of Republicans? What common ground does he share with Byron Dorgan, in Chapter 9?

THE CONSERVATISM OF THE HEART

PATRICK J. BUCHANAN

Why can't Dan Rather give us that kind of objective coverage?

Connie, Bay, my thanks for bringing together this wonderful crowd in the hall tonight. I'll take credit for the crowd outside.

Thank you, Dick Mountjoy and the committee, Phyllis, first lady of American conservatism, Rabbi Spero, Duncan Hunter, Cliff Stearns, Kelly Cash—and my old friend from White House Days, Ollie North.

But I want to pay special tribute to one who traveled with me tens of thousands of miles in the cars, vans, buses, and those tiny planes she loves so much, all the way from the Cook Inlet of Alaska to the Florida Keys: First Lady of my heart: Miss Shelley Buchanan.

I still think she'd make a great replacement for Hillary Clinton.

But we're not going to criticize Bill Clinton tonight. You really ought not to criticize someone while he's on active duty in the service of the United States.

But I do want tonight to talk about a "miracle campaign." This campaign came out of nowhere to set the agenda for the nation in 1996, to change the shape and direction of the Republican party, and to alter the course of American history.

I want to speak tonight about who we are, where we came from, where we are going.

When we declared, eighteen months ago, our campaign was a subject of bemusement to the Beltway élites. No one gave us a chance.

So, everyone was sweet to us—at first.

But, I will say, they sure made up for that later.

But, from the very beginning we had a dream. We had a plan. And we had a vision, a vision of a new conservatism of the heart, rooted in old and unchanging principles and values learned long ago in home, schools and churches—and grounded in the patriotism, the love of country, and the enduring ideas of our founding fathers.

We entered the primaries of 1996, to give voice to the voiceless: To the defenseless unborn—to the Forgotten Americans, left out and left behind in the raucous stampede toward a global economy—and a voice for those middle-class families, like the one I was raised in, for whom the American Dream has begun to vanish.

Delivered at the California Center for the Arts, Escondido, California, August 11, 1996.
Reprinted with permission.

We were taught to believe life is a gift of God. No man can take it away. This right to life is inalienable, Jefferson said.

When we began, some called this issue of life a losing issue.

If you want to win this nomination, they said, back off a bit, Pat.

But this is not an issue on which you can compromise, or split the difference. Because it is not simply a matter of "personal conscience." It is a matter of morality, of right and wrong. It is the defining issue of an age where the Culture of Life is locked in mortal struggle for the soul of America with a Culture of Death.

We simply must protect innocent human life, anywhere and everywhere, whether the unborn, the mentally disabled, or the terminally ill.

That is God's commandment.

So, we spoke up, and stood up, and good people came and stood by us. And, because we stayed in this race, right up through platform week, because we refused to fold our tents, Bay and Phyllis and Terry and Mary Summa and Sandy and Colleen were in San Diego—to fight on the ice.

Because the Buchanan Brigades would not compromise, and because we would not quit, the Republican party remains tonight a prolife party.

And our opponents' views have been placed in the appendix, which is where they belong.

Friends, we believe in tolerance of those with whom we disagree. But, I must tell the members of my party in all sincerity:

The day my party walks away from innocent unborn, that day it ceases to be my party.

What doth it profit a man, the Bible asks, if he gain the whole world, but suffer the loss of his soul. What is true of a man, is true of a party, and is true of a country.

We have forgotten that, as a nation and a people, we are under God's judgment. We are under God's law. We have forgotten that America is more than her gross national product. She is more than the world's largest economy. She is more than the sum of all we buy and sell. She is our country, our home.

We are not just "consumers." We Americans are citizens of a republic, sons and daughters of a great nation, brothers and sisters; and we have obligations and duties to one another.

In this campaign I have been critical of the conduct of these transnational corporations that show no loyalty to their workers, nor allegiance to any country.

I do so, because, no matter how rich and powerful they are, they do not represent what is right about American enterprise.

Let me tell you a story.

In the hours before the revolutionary war Thomas Nelson of Virginia stood in the House of Burgesses and declared, quote,

"I am a merchant of Yorktown, but I am a Virginian first. . . . Let my trade perish. I call to God to witness that if any British are landed in the County of

York, of which I am Lieutenant, I will wait no orders, but will . . . drive the invaders into the sea."

Seven years later the oath of Thomas Nelson was tested. He was governor of Virginia, with Washington's army, at Yorktown. As his soldiers shelled the British army inside the town, Nelson asked his men why they were not firing at all—on one sector of the city.

"[Out] of respect to you, sir," a soldier said.

Nelson's men did not want to fire on his home—in Yorktown. So, Thomas Nelson stepped up to the cannons, ordered the artillery turned around, and gave the signal to fire at his own home.

His home was destroyed. And Thomas Nelson died in poverty, trying to pay off his debts.

This is character; and that is patriotism, and that is what we need. "Ask not what your country can do for you, ask what you can do for your country," a young president said, thirty-six years ago.

Today, isn't it time we replace a corporate ethic of avarice and egotism, with that grand old ethic of patriotism, self-sacrifice, and spirit of community and country of Americans like Thomas Nelson?

Friends, what are we doing to our own people?

In the tiny town of Raine, Louisiana, I stood outside a Fruit of the Loom sewing plant, built in 1992. The women who worked there said nothing—as I spoke. After just three years in operation, their plant was suddenly shutting down.

The company was opening a new plant, just like it, in Mexico.

In Washington, the think-tank academics respond: So what, these are "dead end jobs"; these are "sunset industries." Let 'em go!

But, to the women of Raine, these are the best jobs they ever had, Those six-dollar-an-hour jobs were how they were raising their kids. When they lose these jobs, they're not going to be making computers. They'll be on unemployment; and they'll be on welfare.

Across America, company towns are becoming ghost towns. Families are being uprooted, forced to move out, to find new work. Young women who want to stay home with preschool children are being forced into the labor market to maintain the family standard of living.

If not families, neighborhoods, and communities, what is it we conservatives are trying to conserve?

Friends, either we Americans go forward together, or we're not going forward at all.

We must become one nation, and one people again.

Four years ago, I was up in Hayfork, high in the Trinity Alps of northern California. Loggers who had worked in that forest for generations had been cast onto the slag heap of society. A federal judge in Oregon had declared nine million acres off limits to logging.

I spoke from the back of a flatbed truck. When I finished, three shy little girls came up, about thirteen or fourteen, and politely asked for my autograph. As I was signing, one whispered,

"Mr. Buchanan, we all wish we were eighteen years old, so we could vote for you—'cause all our daddies are losing their jobs.''

What are we doing to our own people?

The economic security of our people is today being sacrificed, and America's national sovereignty is being surrendered.

Regularly, we read in the press that the IMF (International Monetary Fund) or World Bank has just made another multimillion dollar loan, backed by the full faith and credit of Americans, to a Chinese regimc that killed our men in Korea, or a Hanoi regime that killed our boys in Vietnam.

Soldier-patriots like Michael New are court martialed—for refusing to take orders of UN officers. A World Trade Organization, which did not exist two years ago, tells the United States to change its laws. European nations—that we defend—tell us we may not sanction Colonel Khadafi's regime that murdered our schoolkids on Pam Am 103. A UN Secretary-General roams the world, at our expense, campaigning to keep his job—in defiance of the nation that created the UN—and created his job.

Our servants are becoming our masters.

You have my word: As long as there is life in me, I will spend the rest of my days fighting to restore the lost sovereignty of the United States, and to rescue the Republic I love from the grip of their godless New World Orders.

Who will look out for America, if her own leaders will not?

Under NAFTA (North Amercian Free Trade Agreement) and GATT (General Agreement on Tariffs and Trade), the U.S. merchandise trade deficit has exploded to almost 200 billion dollars a year. That's four million lost jobs for America's working men and women—this year alone!

America is losing her industrial dynamism. She is becoming a dependent nation: Dependent on OPEC (Organization of Petroleum Exporting Countries) for oil, dependent on Japan to buy our debt. So dependent, that when a corrupt Mexican regime threatened not to pay its debts, we had to send it tens of billions of dollars, lest default by Mexico—bring America down.

Who did this to our country?

We need not look far:

Public officials who look on high office, not as a public trust, but a back door to personal wealth. Lobbyists who hire out to foreign interests, and buy and sell their own country. Politicians who cannot see beyond their next fund raiser. Diplomats who see themselves as "citizens of the world," rather than citizens of the United States.

Friends, the American people are crying for deliverance.

Let us join forces with men and women of all parties to clean up our politics. Let us put an end to all corporate contributions to political parties—and all PAC (political action committee) payoffs that have put America the Beautiful on an auction block—and corrupted the democratic politics of the greatest republic on earth.

Friends, I do not exaggerate: The issue of the new century will be whether America survives, as an independent republic, with her own defined borders, a common language, and a common culture.

A few miles south of here is a great country, with a great and good people, the Mexican people. But, robbed repeatedly by venal governments, the Mexican people are, by the millions, seeking their future in the United States. Desperate for work, they violate our borders and immigration laws to get here.

Our hearts go out to them.

But this land is our land. And this country is our country. And we have a duty to look out for America and Americans first.

Yet, our government seems paralyzed in enforcing its own laws and protecting our own national frontiers. Friends, if we can send an army halfway around the world—to defend the borders of Bosnia and the borders of Saudi Arabia—why can't we defend the borders of the United States of America?

As I said, my friends, we had a dream, and we had a plan:

Our dream was to capture this nomination, in a lightning series of upsets in the first primaries, before the Establishment woke up, to spend spring and summer unifying our party, and gathering the lost sheep of the Reform party and the U.S. Taxpayers party, then, leading a mighty populist and conservative coalition against President Clinton, and Prince Albert.

Our dream was to create a new Republican party of Main Street, not K Street, of the Union Hall, as well as the Legion Hall, of the bleachers, as well as the sky boxes.

It was not so wild a dream.

Had Lamar run second, instead of a narrow third, in New Hampshire, we now know, Senator Dole would have quit the race.

Had I worn a white hat, instead of a black hat, in Arizona, and hoisted fewer guns, friends say, we might have won Arizona—and the nomination. But, it was not to be.

But those were marvelous days. Shelley and I will cherish them all our lives.

There was Pioneer Day in Sholow, Arizona, out beyond the Apache Reservation. As we rumbled through the streets on a buckboard, behind high-school bands and rodeo riders, a fellow on the side of the road, peered at me, hoisted a long-necked bottle of beer, and called out,

"Hey, Pat, welcome to the United States of America!"

There was that night in central Louisiana, at an evangelical church, when I was to speak after the Christmas play. As I sat waiting forty-five minutes, I began to wonder: How long does this little play go on?

But when I entered the church I was astounded. Half of this huge congregation was on stage, dressed in authentic costumes. Cecil B. DeMille could not have put on a more magnificent scene. I was in Bethlehem, 2000 years ago. Joseph, Mary, and the Baby Jesus were at the center stage, surrounded by shepherds, wise men, and angels. I was so moved, I cut loose with a sermon Bill Sunday could not have matched.

When I finished, all Bethlehem was standing and cheering.

Even King Herod was on his feet, fist in the air, shouting, "Go, Pat, Go!"

Now, this miracle campaign is coming to an end.

Tonight, we are headed down to San Diego, to my eighth Republican national convention, and Shelley's tenth. Folks may not know it, but that pretty blonde receptionist, outside Richard Nixon's campaign suite in Chicago, in 1960, was Shelley Buchanan.

Yet, still some friends ask: Why even go, Pat, why even stay in a party some of whose leaders call us names, and who will not even let you speak at your own convention?

But, friends, this party is not just their party, it is our party, too.

Out in the heartland of America, it is a great party, full of spirit and soul. Out there, it remains Ronald Reagan's party: "Hopeful, big-hearted, idealistic—daring, decent and fair."

And, friends, if we walk, look who we leave behind.

We walk away from the wonderful people who came out that freezing night in January, to stand in the cold for hours, at polling places in Kenai and Ketchikan, Anchorage and Fairbanks, to give us our first great victory of 1996.

As long as I live, I will never forget being awakened at four in the morning, in a hotel room in some tiny Iowa town, to hear Bay's voice on the phone—with a backdrop of all this raucous yelling and partying back on Elm Street in McLean, and hear Bay say,

"Hey, Big Brother, you just won Alaska—by 170 votes."

One hundred seventy votes! King of the Klondike!

We can't walk away from these people.

We can't walk away from the men and women in those mills, factories, and plants who look to us for leadership and hope. We can't walk away from those folks who came out in the thousands, long after we had lost nomination—in Wisconsin, Michigan, California.

In late June of this year, friends, at that enormous Texas state convention, 15,000 people, no one got a warmer, wilder welcome.

These are our people. We can't walk away from them.

And we can't walk away from Peggy Glenny.

Days after she had her fourth baby, Peggy Glenny got into her car every morning at 5 A.M. and drove through the snow, from farm to farm across western New York state, to get signatures to get me on the ballot in New York—while the party bosses there did everything to keep us off.

Friends, if we walk away from Peggy Glenny, who does she turn to? No, they stood by us; now, we must stand by them.

America does not need a third party. America needs a fighting second party, a party that means what it says, and says what it means, that not only preaches, but practices, a conservatism of the heart—that looks out for all our people, but especially for those who have no one else to look out for them, and no one else to speak for them.

Friends, we are making the Republican party that kind of party again.

When no one else dared, back in 1991, we walked off a little TV show—and challenged a president of the United States. Yes, we lost. But the ideas we advanced were embraced in the platform of 1992; and those ideas gave us the great victory of 1994.

Read our party platform of 1996.

Whole sections—the stand for life, protecting our borders, immigration reform, economic patriotism, fair trade, equal justice under law, restoring our lost sovereignty, Putting America First, they are right out of the speeches we have been giving for eighteen months.

Friends, there is so much of ours in that platform, that we've decided to ask Haley Barbour for royalties.

Our rivals may be waving from the podium, but it is our ideas that now reflect the grass roots of this party, our ideas that are fixed firmly within the Republican Platform.

Before our eyes, this party is becoming a Buchanan party.

The old era is over; the old order is passing away. It may bristle, and it may resist, but, within this party, a new party is being born. God willing, we will be there at its birth, and one day, the stone the builders rejected, may yet become the cornerstone.

The other night, something came to me from the history books of my childhood.

In the Middle Ages, there was a time they called the Truce of God. During Lent, the warring nobles and knights suspended their battles with one another. No fighting during Lent.

Today, this disputatious party of ours needs such a truce, a Truce of San Diego. Let us—at least for the next ten weeks—nobles and knights—and, yes, even the peasants with pitchforks—suspend our battles with one another—and join together in common cause to defeat Bill Clinton and Prince Albert, and dispossess them of all their holdings east of the Potomac River.

It is time for a party truce, in the name of a Republican victory.

Let me say now a word to the young of the Buchanan Brigades.

I know how you feel. We fought it fair. We almost had it won.

Sure, it hurts. But life is like that for people who believe in ideas, causes, and one another. No triumph comes without tears.

My first cause was Barry Goldwater. Talk about a beating.

But, just one year later, I joined Richard Nixon and we began one of the great comebacks in history. We won the White House. Four years later, we won a forty-nine-state victory unlike any the nation had ever seen.

Then, Watergate struck.

I was at Mr. Nixon's side, as his presidency was destroyed. I said to myself: Now it is over. All we worked for, is gone.

But, two years later, Ronald Reagan rode out of the West, and we rode with him. Four years later, we had the White House; four years after that, another forty-nine-state landslide.

And, under Ronald Reagan, America won the Cold War.

The cause of my lifetime—triumphed.

So, now, you've had your first defeat. It's painful.

But I know in my heart this cause is going to prevail. This cause is going to triumph, because it is the cause of America.

And, even if I don't reach that promised land, you will be there.

And, through my remaining days, it will be the proudest honor of my life to have led the Buchanan Brigades.

CHAPTER 19

Postscript

In response to the 1996 Telecommunications Act, the TV industry created a rating system, which went into effect in 1997. The system rates programs like motion pictures (''G,'' ''PG,'' etc.). Critics point to surveys that show a majority of people wanting an alternative system; one where the level of sex, violence, and adult language is indicated, thus allowing the viewer to determine whether the show is acceptable for the audience intended.

The Communications Decency Act (CDA) was included in the telecommunications law. It would have restricted access of indecent material on the Internet. In 1997, the U.S. Supreme Court ruled it a violation of the First Amendment. A comprehensive resource guide to the CDA can be found on the Internet (http://velcome.iupui.edu/~droy1/cdaguide.html).

There are numerous books, stories, and commentaries that describe the relationship between American culture and aspects of the entertainment industry. On television: ''Why Parents Hate TV,'' by U.S. Senator Joseph Lieberman, *Policy Review* (May/June 1996). On the changes at the Disney Company: ''Walt Would Be Turning Over in His Cryogenic Chamber,'' by Julia Duin, *The Washington Times National Weekly Edition* (December 29, 1996). On the decision of Wal-Mart to not carry certain CDs which are deemed offensive: ''Wal-Mart Puts the Trash-Peddlers on Notice,'' Cal Thomas, *The Washington Times National Weekly Edition* (December 1, 1996). On the recent trend of commerce in breaking societal taboos: ''Photography View; Testing the Limits in a Culture of Excess,'' by Vicki Goldberg, *The New York Times* (October 29, 1995). In May 1997, President Clinton criticized the fashion industry as promoting a ''heroin chic'' which glamorizes the use of drugs. The conservative *World* magazine has an interesting article on drugs and American culture (http://www.worldmag.com/world/issue/11-09-96/cover__1.asp).

The Henry J. Kaiser Family Foundation (2400 Sand Hill Road, Menlo Park, Calif. 94025) and The Family Research Council (http://www.frc.org/) study the relationship between the mass media and the family. The American Family Association (601–844–5036) takes an activist approach to combating the negative influence of the mass media on the family while Robert J. Bork's *Slouching Towards Gomorrah* (HarperCollins, 1996) criticizes how the courts have contributed to this development.

The speech code at the University of Massachusetts has never been officially canceled, but it also has never been put into effect. Although most speech codes at universities have been ruled unconstitutional, Harvard Law School has recently adopted one. See "P. C. Gags Fair Harvard," by Harvey A. Silvergate, *The National Law Journal* (January 8, 1996). Two books that discuss political correctness and universities are Dinesh D'Souza's *Illiberal Education* (Vintage, 1992) and Lynne V. Cheney's *Telling the Truth* (Simon and Schuster, 1995).

1996 brought mixed results for legalized gambling. Although Michigan approved casino gambling for Detroit, Ohio rejected riverboat gambling. A recent article that describes contemporary trends is "No Dice: The Backlash Against Gambling," by Margot Hornblower, *Time* (April 1, 1996). An excellent book which describes the repercussions of the gambling boom is Robert Goodman's *The Luck Business* (The Free Press, 1995). One of the biggest interest groups against legalized gambling is the National Coalition Against Legalized Gambling (http://www.iquest.net/cpage/ncalg/).

In August 1997, the National Gambling Impact Study Commission began a two year study designed to study the relationship between gambling and political corruption, addiction, economic development, and government finance. The commission was created by Congress and has a $5 million budget.

The Cleveland Browns eventually moved to Maryland, where they became known as the Baltimore Ravens. After many legal moves, the NFL made a unique settlement with Browns fans and the city of Cleveland: The NFL would return to Cleveland by 1999, a new stadium would be built and the new team would be called the Browns and retain all the records of the original team. Although some Browns fans were satisfied, the problem of franchise instability remains in pro sports. Senator DeWine and Representative Hoke's bills were never passed by Congress. A comprehensive guide to what happened to the Cleveland Browns can be found on the world-wide-web (http://www.bright.net/~browns/browns.html).

The importance of personal seat licenses to pro-sports franchises is discussed in "Selling rights to tickets helps many owners hit paydirt," by Lorraine Woellert, *The Washington Times National Weekly Edition* (December 15, 1996). An organization devoted to fans taking back control of pro sports is FANS (P.O. Box 19312, Washington, D.C. 20036). A book of the same theme is Mike Lupica's *Mad As Hell: How Sports Got Away From the Fans and How We Get It Back* (Putnam, 1996). A more academic analysis is offered in *Major League*

Losers: What Governments and Taxpayers Need to Know, by Mark S. Rosentraub (Basic, 1997)

A recent article which describes the efforts of citizens to stop megastores from coming to their communities is Jonathan Walters's "Store Wars," *Governing Magazine* (January 1995). The Small Town Institute (509–925–1830) studies the challenges small towns face. Increasing citizen empowerment in the economic planning of communities is described in Jane Braxton Little's "Citizens Plan Their Futures," *The Progressive Populist* (September 1996). More information can be found by contacting the National Civic League (http://www.ncl.org/ncl).

In Context has an interesting interview with the creator of New Work, Frithjof Bergmann. It can be found on the world-wide web at http://www.context.org/ICLIB/IC37/Bergmann.htm.

Cultural populism will always have a certain appeal to a majority of Americans. Why? Because we enjoy tremendous freedoms. The positive aspects of comparatively unregulated economic markets and an almost totally free market for entertainment and ideas are well known and appreciated by our citizens. Markets bring out creativity and can reward entrepreneurship. The judicial branch, to a large extent, protects those freedoms. However, if a majority views these freedoms as being abused, and thus contributing to societal problems, then cultural populism will become more attractive.

CHAPTER 20

Contemporary Governmental Populism

"I'm mad as hell, and I'm not going to take it anymore!"

That famous line from the 1970s movie *Network* is how many Americans may feel about their government. The anger is directed at what populists sense is an élite-driven political system which is so deeply entrenched that genuine change is almost impossible. Populists fear that a political class is being created by the combination of an out-of-control campaign finance system and the persistence of career politicians in Washington. Chapter 21 describes why the influence of money must be curbed in elections. Chapter 22 outlines the need for states to call for a constitutional convention in order to pass congressional term limits.

Populists believe that the structure of our political system should reflect more faith in the ability of average citizens to exercise power. Some political scientists fear that opening up our two-party system will invite chaos and confusion into elections. However, for politics to remain relevant for a majority, it must reasonably resemble the diversity of American political thought. By expanding party choices, Chapter 23 highlights how our political system can be strengthened by encouraging diversity to be represented in elections.

The Sixth Amendment guarantees every American the right to a jury trial for criminal cases. How much does the legal system trust jurors? Chapter 24 makes a case that jurors should be given more responsibility during trials. Allowing them more freedom and flexibility could help democratize the judicial process.

Chapters 25 and 26 focus on personal and environmental responsibility. Recent legislation that would inject more personal responsibility into welfare programs is the subject of Chapter 25. Recognizing the relationship between environmental responsibility and religious values is the subject of Chapter 26.

If the American people are constantly being patronized by the Democrats and the Republicans, it is difficult to believe the major parties respect the views of U.S. citizens. Populists believe that respect comes by telling citizens about the major political challenges of the future and describing what needs to be done. That was the message of former Colorado governor Richard Lamm when he ran for president in 1996. Lamm's ideas are the subject of Chapter 27.

CHAPTER 21

How Money Corrupts Democracy: The Need for Campaign Finance Reform

There is widespread agreement among U.S. citizens that our system for financing campaigns needs major changes. Most experts agree that the election reforms of the 1970s have been judicially crippled and politically evaded. The Supreme Court's 1976 *Buckley v. Valeo* decision, which outlawed spending limits, opened the door to indirect and unlimited spending on campaigns. Although more than $1.5 billion was spent on the 1996 elections, voter turnout declined. Moreover, a majority of Americans continued to believe that campaign money buys too much influence in Washington.

In 1996, the bipartisan McCain-Feingold Bill was introduced in the U.S. Senate. The bill's most significant provisions were to ban political action committee (PAC) ''soft money'' and give candidates discounted mail and broadcast advertising rates in exchange for voluntarily accepting spending limits. In this reading, Senators Russell Feingold (D-Wis.), Paul Wellstone (D-Minn.), Robert Byrd (D-W.Va.) and Fred Thompson (R-Tenn.) speak to the need for the bill.

Populists believe that private wealth invested in our political system represents illegitimate power. They also believe that it structures public decision making towards élite interests, which seriously hinder the practice of equal political representation. How does money in politics effect accountability? Would a majority of Americans support public financing for congressional campaigns? Is a constitutional amendment necessary to control election spending?

CAMPAIGN FINANCE REFORM

SENATOR RUSS FEINGOLD (D-WIS.), SENATOR PAUL WELLSTONE (D-MINN.), SENATOR ROBERT BYRD (D-W.VA.), AND SENATOR FRED THOMPSON (R-TENN.).

FROM THE *CONGRESSIONAL RECORD*, JUNE 24, 1996 (SENATE)

MR. FEINGOLD. . . . The core of our proposal, the very heart of this legislation, is, for the first time, to provide qualified candidates who are not millionaires, and who are not able to amass colossal war chests and do not have access to the extensive net worth of well-heeled contributors with an opportunity to run a fair and competitive campaign for the U.S. Senate. That is what this bill tries to do. It tries to give most Americans, which includes those who are not multimillionaires, most Americans, a fighting chance to be a part of this process, that they were born and taught to believe was their right. That is what this effort is about.

Our current campaign system is heavily tilted in favor of a privileged few. If you have access to large amounts of campaign funds, then our current system is great for you; it accommodates you. If you are a millionaire and are able to contribute your own personal wealth to your campaign without having to participate in the endless cycle of attending fund raisers and soliciting contributions, then our current system is good for you, too.

But, Mr. President, if you are not an incumbent and you are not worth several millions of dollars, and even if you have a wealth of experience and ideas, and even a large base of grassroots support, the sad truth is that such candidates are automatically labeled long shots under the standards set forth under the current election system.

Why is this, Mr. President? Why is someone who may have served as a city council member, who may have been a police officer or a schoolteacher, who believes in public service and holds an ambition to represent their particular community, why is such a person in America automatically labeled a ''long shot,'' making it so very difficult to get credibility?

The answer is very simple, Mr. President. The answer, Mr. President, is money. Money has become the defining attribute of congressional candidates in this nation. If you have money, you are considered a serious contender; if you do not have money, you get stamped on your head the phrase ''automatic long shot.''

I tell you what happens when someone declares their candidacy for the Senate in this country. They are not asked about the issues very much. They are not asked that much about what level of support they have in their home states. Maybe at some point they will be asked that. Those are not the questions that first greet either a real candidacy or a planned candidacy. The question that they are greeted with has become the determining question in American politics. The determining question in American politics, Mr. President, is, "Hey, where are you going to get the money? How are you going to raise all the money? How much time will it take? How much do you have to raise every week in order to be a viable candidate?" Most of us have had these questions thrown at us when we first ran.

If you have the money, you are welcomed into our system with open arms. You are considered a credible candidate, and your pursuit of elected office is considered, right away, to be a tenable goal. But if you do not have the money, it is an entirely different reaction. Such candidates are usually shunned by the political establishment, labeled long shots, and entered into an electoral arena where chances of upsetting high finance candidates parallel their odds maybe of being struck by a lightning bolt or winning the Powerball lottery.

Our campaign should be a discourse between candidates of differing perspectives. Instead, we have a system that is the equivalent of a high-stakes poker game, where only those players with the ability to ante up are truly invited to sit at the table and join the game. It does not matter what sort of experience you have or what your positions are or what ideas you can bring with you. It is all about your ability to put up big money on the table and ante up. . . .

Mr. President, why does the public sense we absolutely have to move on campaign finance reform at this point? I think it is because people have finally realized that the number. One issue that we have to deal with in this country is getting the big money out of policy making that goes on in Washington. . . .

Just a few of the statistics that are very troubling: In a U.S. Senate race now, the average winner spent in 1994, $4.5 million. That is what the average winner needs. It is not good enough anymore just to be a millionaire. You better have a lot more than that. You better have about $10 million if you want to finance it yourself.

What about personal wealth contributions? They have gone up dramatically in the last few elections. In 1990, only 4 percent of the money that was spent on elections was from personal wealth, from individuals putting in their own money. The same in 1992. Suddenly, in 1994, 18 percent of all the money spent on U.S. Senate elections came from a dramatic increase in personal spending.

Mr. President, what about overall spending? In 1990, it was a lot of money— $494 million. In 1992, the spending in House and Senate races grew to $702 million. Just two years later, it jumped again to $784 million. The same thing goes with the trend on out-of-state contributions. After staying at 16 percent in 1990, in 1992, the percentage of money in Senate elections that comes from out of the state for a senator is now 23 percent, and growing. So these are not static concerns. These are not trends that have always been there or practices that have always been there. These are rapidly increasing trends in overall spending, out-of-state spending, and the huge infusion of personal money into campaigns. . . .

Mr. President, perhaps most disturbing, though, is not the issue of how can somebody finance their campaign, or even the issue of what happens when somebody is outgunned in a race, even though one person may be more qualified than the other. I think what the American public realizes more than anything else, and what really bothers them the most, is they know that this story does not end when the votes are counted. It is not just a question of who wins and who becomes a senator. They know that the very policies enacted in this Congress are altered in some way or another by the presence of all of this money in the process.

How does this happen? Well, one way it happens is that in this town there are, apparently, 13,500 people who are lobbyists. They help with this process. They are not inactive in connecting the campaign process to the policy process. Let me give you one example of what happens around here. I will omit the names of those involved, but it is just a sample so that nobody is confused or puzzled about how sometimes what we decide to do out here is somehow connected to what happens during the campaigns.

Here is an invitation:

During this year's congressional debate on dairy policy, representative "blank" has led the charge for dairy farmers and cooperatives by supporting efforts to maintain the milk marketing order program and expand export markets abroad.

To honor his leadership, we are hosting a fundraising breakfast for "blank" on Wednesday, December 6, 1995. To show your appreciation to "blank," please join us at Le Mistral Restaurant for an enjoyable breakfast with your dairy colleagues.

PAC's throughout the industry are asked to contribute $1,000. "Blank" would prefer that the checks be made to his leadership fund. If your PAC is unable to comply with this request, please make your PAC check to " 'blank' for Congress."

Thank you for your support of our industry's legislative campaign this year and your recognition of "blank's" important role toward achieving our objective.

Now, this is legal. I am not suggesting anyone here has done anything legally wrong. It is just what goes on in this town. A vote is taken, and a fund-raiser is held. I am not suggesting the opposite, which would be wrong. But, boy, it is a tight connection. That is what is going on in this town, and that is what the American people have come to realize.

Earlier this year, a report was issued by the Center for Responsive Politics. It does show a relationship—at least an arguable relationship—between campaign contributions and the congressional agenda. The list includes cattle and sheep interests contributing over $600,000 during the last election cycle, while fighting to protect federal grazing policies to give them access to federal lands at below-market prices. Mining interests spent over $1 million in 1993 and 1994 on campaign contributions to members of Congress while trying to prevent reform of the 1872 mining law. Oil and gas interests contributed over $6.1 million in the last election cycle pushing for the alternative minimum tax. That is a change that would cost the U.S. Treasury $15 billion.

So this problem affects everything, including our deficit problem. If special interest money can encourage us to spend more money, or create more tax loopholes, then it is part of the reason we cannot balance our budget. . . .

Let me conclude by saying what it means to me from the point of view of someone who grew up believing that everybody had a chance to run for Congress or the Senate if they really wanted to.

This summer, I will go to my twenty-fifth high school class reunion at Janesville Craig High School in Janesville. I am looking forward to it, and I am eager to see my former Democratic and Republican friends—there were more Republicans than Democrats in that town, which taught me the value of bipartisan cooperation. Recently, I had a chance, here in the halls of the Capitol, to meet with the political science students from another high school, our crosstown rival, Janesville Parker. They asked me what I was working on. As I looked at them, I realized something had changed from 1971 when I told people that maybe I would go into politics someday. You know, in 1971, nobody said, "First, Russ, you have to go out and raise about $5 million, or you better become so connected to the political structure in Washington, or you are never going to be a senator or a congressman." Nobody said that to me, and I have had the good fortune to be an exception to the rule here. But I could not tell those kids twenty-five years later that anyone of them had any reasonable expectation to ever be elected to this body, unless they become very, very wealthy, or very, very well connected.

To me, that is a little bit of a denial of the American dream.

MR. WELLSTONE. . . . This system right now does not meet the standard of real representative democracy, because the standard of a representative democracy in our country, or any other country, is that each person counts as one and no more than one. I dare any of my colleagues to, in this debate, come out here on the floor and say, given the system we have right now and the reliance on huge contributions—whether it be soft money, PAC money, or individual contributions—that, as a matter of fact, each and every citizen has the same influence over our political process. It is simply not true. And it is certainly not the perception that many have of our system.

This current system does very severe damage to the very essence of what representative democracy is supposed to be all about. . . .

I think all of us should want to change this system because I think, when we are involved in the fund-raising, the perception—and I do not accuse one colleague here of any individual corruption—but the perception of people is often that we are out there raising money from this person or that person or this PAC or that PAC, and people just simply lose confidence in the political process. All of us who care fiercely about public service, all of us who care fiercely about good politics, all of us who are proud to serve in the U.S. Senate ought to be concerned about the fact that people have lost confidence in this process.

So I argue the human realities are this: We need to pass this reform bill to restore some trust in this political process. That is what this is all about. I would say there is an A and a B part to this. The A part is this. I am wearing a political science hat, I am wearing a U.S.-Senator-from-Minnesota hat, and I am also wearing a citizen hat. People are not going to believe in the outcomes of this process unless they believe in the process itself. And as long as people believe that too few people, with so much wealth, power and say, dominate the political process and the vast majority of people feel left out, ripped off, underrepresented, not listened to, then I would say to everybody here we are not going to do well with the public.

People want to believe in this political process. They do not like the fact that big money dominates too much of politics in America. Regular people do not feel well represented within the current system. . . .

Now we come to the ethical issue of politics, I think, of our time, which is the way in which money has come to dominate politics: Who gets to run for office? Who is likely to win the election? Who is the best connected? Who are the heavy hitters? Which people have the most influence? What issues are on the agenda? What issues are off the agenda? How many people are out there in the anteroom, and whom do they represent? How do they secure access? What are their patterns of political giving? Political scientists and reformers have been asking these questions for years, and they've come up with some very telling answers.

And we see it here every day. We don't need anybody to point out what's going on. When it is a telecommunications bill or it is a health insurance reform bill, that anteroom is packed wall to wall with people. They represent the most powerful in America.

But when it comes to children's issues—Head Start, Title I, support for kids with disadvantaged backgrounds—I never see it wall-to-wall lobbyists.

This is the ethical issue of politics in our time. And, Mr. President, we are talking about a systemic problem, but not about the corruption of an individual officeholder. I do not believe that is the case. We are talking about systemic corruption when what happens is too few people have way too much power and say, and those are the people who can most affect our tenure in office and, unfortunately, in this system, those are the people who have the financial resources. We are trying to, through this legislation, take a significant step toward beginning to end that. . . .

If you believe that each person should count as one and no more than one, if you believe there should be some political equality, if you believe that citizens should have real input and real say and have the same opportunities to participate and be listened to and to be involved in public affairs and to run for office and to be elected for office, it is simply true—I do not want it to be true—but most of the people in the country know it to be true, that this is not what is happening in our country today, and big money mixed with politics has severely undercut the very ideal of representative democracy.

That is why people are so disenchanted. That is why people are so disengaged. . . .

I think many people have decided that we will never do deficit reduction on the basis of some standard of fairness. That is to say, yes, we will target a whole lot of deficit reduction on those citizens on the bottom economically who have the least political clout, but we do not do deficit reduction when it comes to the big military contractors or all those oil companies and coal companies, and tobacco companies and pharmaceutical companies that get all of their tax breaks.

I do not think people believe we will do deficit reduction with any standard of fairness. I do not think people believe that we are going to deal with the fundamental problem of making sure every child has a decent educational opportunity in our country; that we are going to resolve inner-city poverty; that we are going to make sure we have a clean environment, within our current system.

I do not think people believe that we are going to deal with the budget deficit or with the investment deficit, because I think people believe that this political process will not work, and the reason they think it will not work is because they think it is dominated by big money, because the citizens of the United States of America do not believe they exercise real power.

And guess what? In a democracy, the people ought to have the right to dominate their political process. They have the right to believe that the Capitol belongs to them. But it does not.

So we are at a critical juncture. Either we are going to go forward without a truly representative democracy, what some have called checkbook politics, or we are going to have a democratic renewal, and I mean democratic renewal not with a large "D," I mean with a small "d," where people have confidence in this process, where people feel like they are being listened to, where people feel like they can participate. That is what this is all about. . . .

Mr. President, it has only gone from bad to worse during the decade of the 1980s and the 1990s. It is just absolutely out of control, absolutely out of control, with the new twist being soft money. Much of it is just shifting to soft money. I mean, you have the individual contributions. And by the way, the people who make the large individual contributions represent a tiny slice of the American population. You have PAC money.

In addition, you have soft money that is supposed to be for party building or for issue-oriented ads. I know all about those ads in Minnesota. The sky is the limit. The parties are awash in this money. The attack ads do not add one bit of information to one citizen anywhere in the United States of America.

They do not contribute toward representative democracy. I have to smile when I hear the argument made, well, we ought to actually be spending more money. There are some people here that want to do that. On the House side they are talking about actually raising the limits. That is an interesting argument.

The argument goes like this. "Well, senators and representatives wouldn't have to make as many calls and do as much fund-raising if you could just raise it to larger chunks." That goes in exactly the opposite direction of having a representative democracy where there is some political equality and where citizens really count. . . .

FROM THE *CONGRESSIONAL RECORD*, JUNE 25, 1996 (SENATE)

MR. BYRD. . . . I believe that the primary problem in this body, the root problem plaguing the Senate today, is what I would term the "fractured attention"—the fractured attention of senators. Countless times, action on the Senate floor has been slowed or delayed because senators are not in Washington, or if they are, they are away from the Capitol. That absence is not because those senators are off on vacation or taking their leisure. They are not off somewhere lounging in the sun, neglecting their duties here. On the contrary, as each of us knows all too well, senators are often elsewhere because of the need to raise unthinkable sums of money—unthinkable sums—money essential for running for re-election.

Plato thanked the gods for having been born a man, and he thanked the gods for having been born a Greek. He also thanked the gods for having been born in the age of Sophocles. Sophocles said, "There's nothing in the world so demoralizing as money." Sophocles was not an American politician, but he knew what he was talking about.

I can say after fifty years in politics, there is nothing so demeaning, nothing so demeaning as having to go out with hat in hand, passing a tin cup around and saying, "Give me, give me, give me, give me." Not that old song, "Give me more and more of your kisses," but "Give me more and more of your money. Give me more and more of your money."

Sophocles said, "There's nothing in the world so demoralizing as money." And, indeed, in this Senate, the need for members to constantly focus on raising the huge sums necessary to stay in office has taken a heavy toll.

The incessant money chase is an insidious demand that takes away from the time we have to actually do our job here in Washington. It takes away from the time we have to study and to understand the issues, to meet with our constituents, to talk with other senators, and to be with our families and to work out solutions to the problems that face this nation.

Mr. President, consider this: According to data provided by the Congressional Research Service, the combined cost of all House and Senate races in the 1994 election cycle was $724 million, a sixfold increase from 1976. . . .

The money chase is like an unending circular marathon. Since the share of money coming from small contributors has declined while the share contributed by big political action committees has increased, candidates have to look more and more outside their home states to raise big bucks. The traveling, the time away from the Senate, the time away from talking with constituents, the time robbed from reading and reflection, the personal time stolen from wives, children, and grandchildren, the siphoning off of energies to the demands of collecting what has been called campaign grease is making us all less able to be good public servants. Ironically, we spend much time and raise huge sums of money in order to be re-elected to the Senate so we can serve our states and our country. Then, once here, we cripple our ability to serve our state and our country by spending an inordinate amount of our time on the money treadmill so we can come back for yet another try at serving our states and our country.

That kind of system sends the clear message to the American people that it is money, not ideas and not principles, that reigns supreme in our political system. No longer are potential candidates judged first and foremost on their positions on the issues, or by their experience and capabilities. No longer. Instead, potential senators are judged by their ability to raise the millions of dollars that are needed to run an effective campaign. Publilius Syrus said that ''a good reputation is more valuable than money.'' Senators should stop and reflect on that observation because our reputations and the feeling that we can be trusted by the American people are both in severe free-fall.

The American people believe that the key to gaining access and influence on Capitol Hill is money. Can anyone blame them for coming to that conclusion?

Now, Mr. President, if I were starting out in politics today, with a background like mine—working in a gas station, being a small grocer, a welder in a shipyard, a meatcutter, just common ordinary trades—I could not even hope to raise the sums of money needed for today's campaigns. In 1958, when Jennings Randolph and I ran together for the two Senate seats that were open—he ran for the short term, and I ran for the full six-year term—we ran on a combined war chest of something like $50,000 or less. When I first started out in politics, I would win a campaign for the House of Representatives and spend as much as $200, perhaps. Think of it. If I had been forced to raise $1 million, $2 million, $4 million, or $10 million the first time I ran for the Senate, in 1958, I would not have given it a second thought. In fact, I would not even have gotten past the first thought. I would not have been able to even contemplate running for office—a poor boy like myself.

The ever-spiraling cost of public office is not a healthy trend. The Congress could become the exclusive domain of the very wealthy. The common man, without the funds to wage a high-powered, media-intensive campaign could be removed from effectively competing in the political arena, reserving it for the exclusive use of the very wealthy and the well-connected.

That is why we must stop this madness. We must put an end to the seemingly limitless escalation of campaign costs. . . . The Bible says, ''The love of money is the root of all evil.'' In politics, the need for huge sums of money just to get elected is certainly at the root of most of what is wrong with the political system today. . . .

MR. THOMPSON. . . . I approach this from the standpoint of one who was recently a challenger and who is now an incumbent running for re-election in two years, having gotten the unexpired term of the vice president for a two-year term. I am now running as an incumbent for a full term. So I have seen it from both sides.

I also approach it from the standpoint of one who made a commitment to the people of Tennessee that I will try to change the system that we have now working in Washington and that I was dissatisfied with the process by which our legislation is enacted. But I think it is fundamentally the business of the U.S. Congress to address how we elect our public officials, how long they stay, and what their motivations are when they get here. So I am delighted to be a part of this effort.

The system now—let us take a look at the system that we have now. I believe I can be objective in describing it. Elections certainly cost more and more and more. We see Senate campaigns now that cost $10, $20, and $30 million. The combined expenditures in one Senate campaign were over $40 million. We have a system where more and more time is taken by members of Congress, at a time when technology and all the demands of modern campaigning require campaigns to cost more and more. More and more, we, the members of, supposedly, the world's greatest deliberative body, wind up having no time to deliberate anymore because of the fractured nature of our lives. For someone to run in a state such as mine, I have calculated that now it would be about $15,000 a week that I would have to raise, year in and year out, to run the kind of campaigns that would be traditionally raised in a state such as mine.

Mr. President, that is not why I came to the U.S. Senate. We have a system now where more and more of the perception is that contributions are tied to legislation. Perhaps that was not a problem when the amounts were smaller. But now we see larger and larger contributions, usually soft money contributions, with regard to larger and larger issues, millions of dollars being spent, billions of dollars being decided by massive pieces of legislation in the U.S. Congress.

We have a system where it is no longer ideological. The money does not flow to ideas. The money flows to power. Whoever is the incumbent party likes the system. Whoever is not the incumbent party plans on being the incumbent party. Democrats have killed this legislation for years, and now that the Republicans are in power, we are trying to return the favor. We have a system whereby, in individual cases, people are drawing closer and closer relationships with individual pieces of legislation and massive amounts of money that are being spent by the people affected by the legislation.

We constantly see news stories, day in and day out. There is a strong perception among the American people that any system that costs so much money and any system that requires us to go to such great lengths to get that money cannot be on the level. We see, day in and day out, editorials across the country. Common Cause has compiled 261 editorials from 161 newspapers and publications. What they say is not a pretty picture. It is not that I necessarily agree with the analysis made of these articles, but this is the perception among editorial writers across the country—liberal papers and conservative papers. The most conservative paper in my home state, in Tennessee, the *Chattanooga Free Press*, a Republican paper, has one of the editorials contained in this compilation. What they say, I think, is what is perceived by the American people. They say that neither party wants to end the abuses. One of the editorials says, "In Congress, Money Still Talks." Another says, "New Year's Sale on Votes." Another says, "Money Brings Votes." Another says, "Congressmen Admit Being Bought by Contributions." Another says, "Republican Reform; GOP Already Bought Off."

Mr. President, that hurts. The *Chattanooga Free Press* in Tennessee says in its article—it entitles it, "The Campaign Money Evil." Another article says, "Getting What It Paid For," talking about American industry. Another says, "Feeding Frenzy on the Hill," talking about us and our fund-raising activities. Another says, "Buying the Presidency." While we are not dealing with a presidential campaign, if I heard it correctly on the Brinkley show, now, apparently, for $50,000 you can sleep in the Lincoln bed at the White House. . . .

Another says, "Big Money Talks." Another says, "Taste of Money Corrupts Politics." This is from Texas. Another says, "The Great 'Unsecret' of Politics." That is the relationship between contributions and votes. Another says, "Legal Bribery Still Controls Congress." I do not believe that, but a lot of people believe that, and we have to ask ourselves why. Another says, "Campaigns up for Sale."

Mr. President, how much more of this can we stand as an institution? How can we go before the American people with the tough choices that we are going to have to be leading on, convincing the people, with no credibility? Ten percent of the people in this country have a great deal of confidence in Congress. Twelve percent have a great deal of confidence in the executive branch. Eighty percent of the people, at least, favor major change here. We always want to be responsive to the American people, until it comes to something that affects us and our livelihoods—whether it is term limits, campaign finance reform, or some other issue that affects us directly as politicians. Then we come up with all kinds of excuses why it will not work.

We have a system where soft money, of course, has completely made a sham of the reforms that were put in place in earlier years. We all know that. It is a bipartisan problem. Soft money now is up 100 percent—a 100-percent increase—with hundreds of thousands in contributions, in many cases that we see. So there has been a 100-percent increase since the last election cycle.

Now, that is the system, Mr. President. I do not think it is a very good one. I submit that it is not a good system. Some opponents of reform say there is not enough money in politics. It is not a question of too much; it is not enough; that $700 million spent in 1994 is not enough. They say that more money is spent on soap detergent advertisement, or whatever kinds of advertisement, than on political campaigning. I hope that that analogy will fall on its face without serious analysis, but a lot of people use that. Number 1, we are not in the soap-selling business. Number 2, if Procter & Gamble were advertising in a way that undermined the credibility of the company, they would not be doing it. Number 3, these businesses have only one goal, and that is profit. I would like to think that we have an additional goal in the U.S. Congress.

Other opponents say that it restricts freedom and the ability to participate. This is, of course, a voluntary system, Number 1, and number 2, we are not talking about Mom and Pop sitting around the kitchen table deciding how to distribute their $100 or $250 to a presidential campaign or a senatorial campaign. They can still do that any way they want to do it.

With regard to the PAC issue . . . it simply means that if this legislation were passed, instead of sending it to a political action committee, they would have to make a decision themselves as to which candidate they wanted to send it to. There is no restriction of freedom here on anyone except those in Washington who receive all those minicontributions from various people and make the political decision as to how to use that money. Their freedom will be restricted somewhat. There is no limit whatsoever in this legislation on anybody's ability to participate in the process. People need to understand that.

The current limitation we have is $1,000 on individual contributions. That is a limitation. That is the same limitation that we have here; no new limitation.

Many people say that certainly we want reform. Everybody knows we need reform. "It is a lousy system but not this reform. I would support it, if this particular feature was in, or out," or whatnot. I think that it is tempting to want to have it both ways; to be for reform but never be for a reform measure. Some people say it is an incumbent protection business. . . . I take a different view from that. . . . Under the system now . . . incumbents have substantial advantage. What this legislation would do is, let us say, at least place some limitation on the major incumbent advantage; and that is the ability to raise unlimited amounts of money. The incumbents are still going to have the advantages that they always had. But at least you are saying to that incumbent if he voluntarily chooses to participate that there will be some cap on the amount of money that you spend. You are an incumbent now. The money is going to come to you not because people believe in you in many, many cases any more but simply because you are an incumbent, and you have the power and authority at that point. They say, "Well, it restricts people from coming in and spending enough money to overcome the incumbent." How often does that happen in the real world? When it happens, it is somebody who is an extremely wealthy individual. And it happens then sometimes.

So you wind up with professional politicians on the one hand who are able to raise large sums of money because they are incumbents, and wealthy individuals on the other. That is what our system is becoming—those two classes of people and nobody else.

This legislation would level the playing field and let more people of average means participate. This bill is voluntary. Under it, campaigns will cost less. I think that is the crucial feature. A lot of us who support this legislation have different ideas about that. To me the PAC situation is not a crucial feature.

Opponents are certainly correct when they point out that the PACs were a reform measure in and of themselves in 1974 in the aftermath of Watergate. We thought that would substantially reform the process, and now PACs are an anathema to a lot of people.

The fact of the matter is—and both sides should understand and know this— that people, whether they be businesses or labor unions or whoever, individuals can still send money in. They can still contribute. They can still get together and decide that they want to individually send contributions in.

In my campaign, I ran against an individual that did not accept PAC money. He got all of the same kind of money that he wanted. It is a little more cumbersome. But we are not eliminating special interest money if we eliminate PACs.

So to me that is more of a symbolic measure than it is anything else. The real crucial measure is limiting the overall amounts of money—that $500 million that was spent in congressional races in the last election time. . . .

Mr. President, this is not a division any longer of business versus labor or of Democrats versus Republicans. It is a division of people who want to change the system and those who genuinely do not believe that we ought to have it. I would like to think that this is reform time. I would think that this would do more to assist in our attempt to balance the budget than anything else because much of the pressure that this process has within it is pressure to spend money. It would be a genuine reform measure. . . .

I do not think that we ought to get in a situation where we are for reform until it affects us individually and our livelihood when we are affecting everybody else's livelihood on a daily basis. I think it should not be viewed with suspicion among my Republican colleagues. I think too often that we are trying to figure out how this is going to benefit them, or us. The fact of the matter is we do not know. There is no way to figure it. There is no way to tell. It depends on swings. Sometimes we are going to be in. Sometimes we are going to be out. Sometimes a new scheme might hurt us. Sometimes it might help us. But the bottom line is that we should not be afraid of fundamental reform that the American people want, that we all know that we need, and we should get back to winning not on the basis of who can raise the most money but on the basis of the competition of ideas.

CHAPTER 22

Power to the People: Instigating Congressional Term Limits from the States

"Potomac Fever" and "Inside the Beltway" are two phrases that capture the incestuous nature of Washington, D.C. life. Too often the passage of time distorts idealistic representatives into apologists for the national political establishment, as they increasingly become preoccupied with how to stay in Washington.

Some people might feel that the ideal of the citizen-legislator has been lost as political professionals increasingly dominate our nation's capital. More and more Americans are realizing that the only way to hinder this dynamic is to put limits on Congressional terms.

This reading offers an alternative path for making term limits the law. Instead of relying on Congress, the method of calling a constitutional convention is discussed.

Critics of term limits argue that elections give citizens the chance to exercise term limits. Since so many incumbents are consistently returned to power, does that mean that Americans only want term limits for legislators that don't represent them? The Twenty-second Amendment limits presidents to a maximum of two terms. In what ways is the reasoning for this amendment similar to supporters of congressional term limits? In what ways does the reasoning differ? Is there a relationship between the need for campaign finance reform and the desire for term limits? What effect could term limits have on congressional expertise and power? Why do so many people fear calling a constitutional convention?

WHOSE GOVERNMENT IS IT, ANYWAY?

PAUL JACOB

Term limitation is a simple, straightforward concept, and one supported over-whelmingly by virtually every demographic grouping in the country save poli-ticians, lobbyists, senior government bureaucrats, and congressional staffers.[1] Perhaps put more simply, the people want term limits and the politicians do not.

Polls show the sweeping public support, as do election results. Twenty-three states enacted congressional term limits laws, all but two (New Hampshire and Utah) with a statewide vote of the people. Every state where the voters have been given an opportunity to enact congressional term limits has done so. Term limits are today the law for forty state governors, twenty-one state legislatures, and over 17,999 local elected officials.[2]

The people desire term limits for a host of reasons. Term limits are a catalyst for more candidates seeking office and improve the competitiveness of elections, thus bringing new people and new ideas into the political process.[3] Many voters believe term limits will reduce corruption—both in its overt and more subtle forms. Those members of Congress caught in the House Bank scandal and in criminal activity are disproportionally long-term incumbents.

But there is a more subtle corruption that occurs as members of Congress are removed from the community they represent and become part of the Washington community. Our greatest political leaders recognized this problem. Thomas Jef-ferson remarked, ''Whenever a man has cast a longing eye on them [offices], a rottenness begins in his conduct.''[4] Abraham Lincoln was even more dramatic in his analysis:

If our American society or the United States Government are overthrown, it will come from the voracious desire for office, this wriggle to live without toil, work, or labor—from which I am not free myself.[5]

Many political observers argue that term limits will have a positive effect on reducing deficit spending. Studies by the National Taxpayers Union show that members of Congress tend to support greater deficit spending after six to eight years in office, which is true for both conservative Republicans and liberal Dem-

From the *University of West Los Angeles Law Review*: Vol. 27 (1996) pp. 21–28.
Reprinted with permission.

ocrats.[6] A related concern is that representatives in Congress fail to understand the impact of their laws and regulations. As George Will wrote in *Restoration*:

Many Americans wish that a lot of legislators had a better sense of American life, and particularly of what it is like to be on the receiving end of the high-minded laws and regulations that gush like a cataract from Washington . . . term limits would increase the likelihood that people who come to Congress would anticipate returning to the careers in the private sector and therefore would, as they legislate, think about what it is like to live under the laws they make.[7]

Strict term limitation will also probably end the seniority system and, many supporters maintain, will open the system to other campaign reforms as term-limited legislators lose their incentive to block reforms that might otherwise shorten their career. Madeleine Kunin, the former Democratic governor of Vermont, points out, "Breaking the gridlock of incumbency could throw the doors wide open to new people and new ideas that would make politics rewarding, meaningful, even fun."[8]

That the American people want term limits for members of Congress is clear, but can the people overcome the resistance of the political class to enact the term limits they want? That question looms large at present. Another powerful question arises from it: If Congress and the political establishment can thwart the will of the vast majority of citizens for term limits, then the looming question is: Whose government is it, anyway?

On May 22, 1995, the U.S. Supreme Court handed down a ruling in the case *U.S. Term Limits v. Thornton* that amounted to "liberation day" for politicians in Congress. In the name of preserving "the relationship between the people of the Nation and their National Government," the Court struck down the work of 25 million voters who had enacted congressional term limit laws in twenty-three states.[9] The Court's close 5 to 4 decision says that to limit the terms of members of Congress requires amending the U.S. Constitution.

The movement for term limits now must focus on a constitutional amendment. Many suggest that the action therefore returns to Congress. But there are two methods established in Article V of the Constitution to propose amendments to our country's basic law, which must then be ratified by three-fourths of the states (thirty-eight states) to become part of the Constitution. One method is for two-thirds of both Houses of Congress to vote out a proposed amendment. The other method is for two-thirds of the states to force Congress to convene a convention to propose an amendment to the states for ratification.

WILL CONGRESS LIMIT ITSELF?

Members of Congress have a clear conflict of interest when it comes to proposing an amendment to limit their own terms. This conflict results in many members of Congress favoring limits twice as generous as most voters, that is, if they favor any limits at all. The present Congress has displayed its skill at political maneuvering on the issue.

Last March, the House of Representatives considered term limits, and far from representing their constituents, limits were defeated by outright opponents and "loved to death" by some questionable friends. Statutory approaches that could have passed were not permitted to come to a vote. When asked by Jill Zuckman of the *Boston Globe* why the House of Representatives leadership opted for a statute on the line-item veto, but refused to consider a statute on term limits, Representative John Boehner (R-Ohio) responded that with the line-item veto, unlike term limits, the GOP "was actually trying to get something passed."[10] A compromise was rejected that would have allowed the states to decide on term limits because Speaker of the House Newt Gingrich feared the states would opt for limits shorter than he desired.[11]

The three-term House limit enacted by most of the states and supported by gigantic percentages of voters was opposed by a majority of Republicans, as well as Democrats, with most long-time Republican incumbents wanting Congress to actually strike down shorter limits passed in the states. Only the freshman Republicans were generally in sync with the wishes of the American people—in itself demonstrating the benefit of regular rotation in office.

That term limits was the only plank in the *Contract With America* with two competing bills and that the number of measures was increased to four when term limits reached the House floor, was a sign that the leadership wanted lots of political cover, but nothing to pass. As Thomas Jipping of the Free Congress Foundation wrote in "Playing the Political Cover Game: The Real Meaning of the House Vote on Term Limits": "Regular observers of legislative politics know that introduction of several competing proposals on the same controversial issue often signals a round of the 'political cover' game. . . . [Members] want to claim they have voted a certain way on the issue, but do not want the status quo to change by actually passing legislation."[12]

The commitment of the House Republican leadership, especially Speaker Newt Gingrich, has been the subject of much doubt. Producer Brian Boyer, who spent a great deal of time with Gingrich recently while filming a documentary, said, "It was very surprising, and this was, remember, from very long conversations with Gingrich, to learn that he personally is not in favor of term limits."[13] Gingrich spokesman, Tony Blankley, told the *American Spectator* in July of 1994 that term limits was "something conceptually [Newt] doesn't like."[14] Columnist Robert D. Novak wrote in the *Washington Post*, "Republican leaders profess to want twelve years, but it is clear they prefer no limits at all."[15]

A number of Republicans in the leadership voted against every term limit bill as did five committee chairs. Only one member of the leadership, Majority Leader Dick Armey, and only one committee chair voted for the three-term House limit passed by most states. Yet while Mr. Armey said he would have stripped members of a committee chairmanship had they—like Senator Mark

Hatfield—voted against the Balanced Budget Amendment, there was no such pressure brought to bear for term limits.

Freshman Michael Forbes (R-N.Y.) told the *New York Times* after the failed March House vote, "Candidly, this leadership didn't want [term limits] anymore than the old leadership did."[16] But it appears that the American people were not fooled—a *Washington Post/ABC News* poll found that close to two-thirds believe neither Republicans nor Democrats in Congress really tried to pass term limits.[17]

In Congress, the danger for term limits is that, like the Balanced Budget Amendment, it becomes a powerful campaign issue while it remains forever one or more votes short of passage. Even an infusion of freshmen as large and as committed to term limits as those coming to Congress after the 1994 elections would not garner enough votes to pass a constitutional amendment through the House of Representatives.

Not surprisingly, most Americans believe Congress is unlikely to ever propose an amendment to limit its own terms.[18] The track record of this Congress, largely elected on a campaign of support for term limits, casts great doubt on the ability of voters to defeat enough incumbents to gain the two-thirds majority needed for Congress to propose a term limits amendment. Moreover, while House members face election every two years, and thus more directly risk defeat if they ignore their constituents' desire for term limits, the U.S. Senate is a considerably more difficult prospect because two-thirds of that body is not up for reelection at any given time. In October 1995, a sense of the Senate resolution for term limits was defeated 49 to 45.

The focus of the term limits movement must be on keeping the faith with the grassroots and not become over dependent on Congress. Congress doesn't hold all the cards; the voters do. President Dwight Eisenhower, a strong supporter of congressional term limits, warned decades ago, "... [A]n amendment of this kind could never achieve the blessing of Congress; it could be initiated only by the states."[19]

THE PEOPLE'S PATH

The framers of our Constitution had wisdom and foresight. They realized that over time Congress might usurp power and frustrate the will of the people. When the Constitution was debated, George Byron of Pennsylvania said, "We shall never find two-thirds of Congress voting for anything which shall derogate from their own authority and importance...."[20] That is why they provided another route to amend the Constitution, completely independent of Congress. A constitutional convention can be called by thirty-four states to propose an amendment for ratification.

As Abraham Lincoln believed, "the convention mode seems preferable, in that it allows amendments to originate with the people themselves...."[21] Nei-

ther this Congress nor future ones can thwart the will of the people forever—
if they do not act, the people will.

Already this path is being pursued by term limits activists across the nation.
Initiatives have been filed in Alaska, Colorado, Maine, North Dakota, Oklahoma,
and Oregon that supporters hope will lead to applications from these state legislatures to Congress to convene an Article V convention for term limits. More
initiatives are expected in other states, along with aggressive lobbying efforts in
states without the initiative process. At present, two state legislatures—South
Dakota and Utah—have issued calls to Congress for such a convention.

While it is impossible to predict whether term limits advocates will be successful in convening an Article V convention for the purpose of proposing a
term limits amendment, the issue has strong public support and sharply dem-
onstrates a need to bypass Congress. Still, there are those who strongly oppose
a convention including Phyllis Schlafly, the John Birch Society, and other usually conspiracy-theory groups. They fear the convention will rewrite the Constitution in ways which few, if any, Americans support.

However, these groups fail to understand Article V. A convention cannot
enact anything; it can only propose an amendment or amendments. Nothing can
become part of the Constitution without being first ratified by both Houses of
thirty-eight state legislatures. A ''runaway'' convention that proposed numerous
amendments not supported by a clear consensus of the people has no chance to
withstand this difficult ratification process. Mrs. Schlafly was instrumental in
blocking ratification of the Equal Rights Amendment—which though it was
conceptually supported by most Americans, worries over the implementation of
the amendment eroded support.

Opponents of an Article V convention claim to adore the Constitution and
see the Framers as inspired men. Yet, those same Framers put Article V in this
same Constitution. Regarding term limits, it would be a shame if we failed to
use the tool given to us by the Framers of the Constitution to preserve what
they established: true citizen government.

Some opponents may argue that while term limits are sound public policy,
we should not tinker with the Constitution regardless of the method. But where
would women and African-Americans be if previous generations had held such
an attitude? Our original Constitution gave neither group the right to vote and
it allowed slavery. Even our founders believed it necessary to amend the Constitution. Washington said in his farewell address, ''The basis of our political
systems is the right of the people to make and alter their constitutions of government.''[22]

While none of the twenty-seven amendments to the Constitution has been
enacted by way of a convention, many of them, including the Bill of Rights,
women's suffrage, and the direct elections of senators, came about because states
began the process of calling a convention and forced Congress's hand. The direct
election of senators is a compelling example. The public overwhelmingly supported a direct vote to elect senators, just as today they support term limits.

Opposition came almost entirely from the Senate—just as today for term limits it comes from the two Houses of Congress. States were beginning to develop systems to get around the constitutional prohibition of direct election and a constitutional amendment had five times passed the House, never to be even considered by the U.S. Senate. But then the forces in favor of direct election came within one state of forcing an Article V convention to propose the amendment, the Senate realized it could no longer block this movement and voted the amendment out to the states for ratification.[23]

Whether an amendment is proposed by our country's first convention under Article V, or by members of Congress finally surrendering to political pressure and realizing they cannot prevent the people from limiting their terms in office, is not important. What is important is that the U.S. Constitution, our governing compact, reflect the will of the American people for term limits to replace career politicians with citizen legislators. Whose government is it anyway? With term limits, it's ours.

NOTES

1. Polls have consistently put support for term limits on Congress at between 75 and 80 percent, with some polls showing support as high as 86 percent. Fabrizio, McLaughlin & Associates' poll commissioned by U.S. Term Limits—a survey of 1,000 adults conducted between May 20 and May 23, 1993, with accuracy of ± 3.1 percent at the 95 percent confidence interval. Bob Bernick, Jr., Most Utahns Favor Term Limits, *Deseret News*, August 29, 1993, p. 1—DESERET NEWS/KSL poll conducted by Dan Jones & Associates, August 3–5, 1993, of 600 adults with an error margin of ± 4 percent. National Taxpayers Union Foundation polls. *Capitol Ideas*, vol. 1, no. 1., Sept./Oct. 1992, p. 1. WALL STREET JOURNAL/NBC News poll; *Wall Street Journal*, April 17, 1992, A12. Gallup Poll, September 1992, "Attitudes Toward Proposed Policy Changes for Members of Congress," conducted by Center for Independent Thought, survey of lobbyists, congressional staffers, and senior government bureaucrats.

2. Danielle Fagre, "Microcosm of the Movement: Local Term Limits in the United States." U.S. Term Limits Foundation, *Outlook Series*, vol. 4, no. 2, August 1995, updated Dec. 1995, pp. 1–3.

3. John Armor, "Term Limits Work: Fifty Years in the Election of State Governors," U.S. Term Limits Foundation, *Outlook Series*, vol. 2, no. 4, October 1993, p. 22.

4. *The Oxford Dictionary of Quotations*, 3rd ed. (New York: Oxford University Press, 1979), 272—Letter to Tench Coxe, 1799.

5. Mike Klein, *Limiting Congressional Terms: An Historical Perspective*, Americans to Limit Congressional Terms, 1990, p. 6.

6. National Taxpayers Union Foundation, News Release, "The Longer They Stay, The More They Spend," September, 1994.

7. George F. Will, *Restoration: Congress, Term Limits and the Recovery of Deliberative Democracy* (1992), p. 200. New York: The Free Press.

8. Madeleine Kunin, "Term Limits Would Rejuvenate Politics," *Los Angeles Times*, September 13, 1991, B7.

9. *U.S. Term Limits v. Thornton*, U.S. Supreme Court, 1842, (1995) S. Ct. Affirmed 872 S.W.2d 349 (Ark. 1994).

10. Jill Zuckman, "House Opens Debate on Term Limits Amendment: Groups Give Little Chance of Passage to Proposals," *Boston Globe*, March 29, 1995.

11. Robert D. Novak, "Term Limits Turnaround," *Washington Post*, March 9, 1995, A25.

12. Thomas Jipping, "Playing the Political Cover Game: The Real Meaning of the House Vote on Term Limits," *Essays on our Times*, The Free Congress Foundation, April, 1995, #32, 5.

13. Ernie Freda, "The Real Deal on Term Limits," *Atlanta Constitution*, April 14, 1995.

14. Fred Barnes, "Me Too Republicans," *The American Spectator*, July 1994, 24.

15. Robert D. Novak, "Term Limit Turnaround," *Washington Post*, March 6, 1995, A25.

16. Melinda Henneberger, "Republican Is Warned: No Cheering," *New York Times*, April 17, 1995, B6.

17. Katharine Q. Seelye, "Gamble on Term Limits," *New York Times*, March 31, 1995.

18. Poll conducted by Fabrizio, McLaughlin & Associates for Term Limits Leadership Council, September, 1995. Sample of 1,000 respondents found 72.3 percent believed Congress unlikely to propose a term limits amendment.

19. Dwight D. Eisenhower, *Waging Peace* (1965) 643.

20. George Byron, "An Old Whig," *Independent Gazetter*, October 12, 1787. Reprinted in *The Debate on the Constitution*, vol. 1, edited by Bernard Bailyn, (1993) 123–124.

21. Abraham Lincoln, First Inaugural Address, March 4, 1861.

22. George Washington, Farewell Address, September 17, 1796.

23. Kris W. Kobach, "Rethinking Article V: Term Limits and the 17th and 19th Amendments," *Yale Law Journal* 103, 1972 (1994).

CHAPTER 23

Opening Up the Two-Party System: Reforming Ballot-Access Laws and the Presidential Debates

Many citizens mistakenly equate the two-party system with American democracy itself. However, the Constitution does not mention political parties. Increasingly, polls show that Americans are open to the idea of electing candidates from outside the two major parties. There are numerous alternative parties, but their influence has historically been very limited. Every president since 1860 has been either a Republican or Democrat, and there has been only token minor party representation in Congress.

There are major institutional obstacles for third parties to overcome if they are to become established and important players on the national political scene. One of them is gaining ballot access for elections, which is covered in the first reading.

Another barrier has been the exclusion of third-party candidates from most of the presidential debates which have occurred in recent years. The decision to bar Ross Perot from the 1996 debates is the subject of the second reading.

Liberalizing ballot laws and opening up the presidential debates are two ways to include new ideas and approaches to solving political problems in the twenty-first century. Would more Americans vote if there were strong third parties contesting elections? In what ways are the two major parties élitist?

THE IMPORTANCE OF BALLOT
ACCESS TO OUR POLITICAL SYSTEM

RICHARD WINGER

In December of 1992, Leon P. Baradat wrote an op-ed piece in *The San Diego Union-Tribune* entitled "Beware of Third Parties." In his piece, Professor Baradat asserted that the introduction of third parties into our political system would only exacerbate the existing problem of gridlock. Baradat concluded with an ominous warning to the American public: "Whether the parties in this country are Democratic or Republican, or something else, is not important. What is important is that there be only two major parties. . . . Beware of supporting third parties."

Professor Baradat's conclusion is only partially correct. Certainly, our "winner-take-all" electoral system ensures that we will have only two major parties, no matter how many political parties there may be. But American history shows that third parties *enhance* the positive consequences of a two-party system. Both gridlock and a low voter turnout, the usual signs of a two-party system that is not operating properly, have historically been associated with the restriction of new or third political parties.

In order to enjoy the benefits of a healthy two-party system, we must *encourage* the growth of new parties. And if we are ever to replace one of the two major parties with a new party (something that even Baradat acknowledges is possible, and something that we, the voters, ought to have a right to do), it will only be done if we lift the current ballot-access restrictions on third political parties.

THE MECHANICS OF A TWO-PARTY SYSTEM

In order to understand how new parties help a two-party system to function properly we need to understand our topic. "Two-party system" is a political science term that simply describes a political system in which two parties are much bigger than all the others. It does *not* refer to a system in which there are only two parties, as some would have us believe. Nor does it refer to a system where the government supports two established parties and tries to discourage the participation, or creation, of all others.

From *The Long Term View* (Massachusetts, School of Law at Andover), Vol. 2, No. 2, Spring 1994. Reprinted with permission.

Most political scientists agree that a two-party system comes into existence in any society in which elections are based on the "winner-take-all" system. If there are five candidates who represent five different policies, it will soon become apparent (via opinion polls and the media and public discourse) that two candidates enjoy more support than the others. Few people will want to "waste" their vote on a person who seems likely to finish third or fourth, and support will naturally coalesce around the two frontrunners. (Under proportional representation, a party that receives 5 percent of the vote would receive 5 percent of the legislative seats.)

In a healthy two-party system, the major parties are roughly equal in the size of their membership. Each is distinguished from the other by a clearly differentiated platform, and voters, for the most part, enthusiastically hold allegiance to one of the major parties. Subsidiary characteristics of this system include a high voter turnout and internal cohesion in each major party.

When these conditions exist, the two major parties will ideally protect the political system against tyranny and gridlock. The party in power, which voters usually place in control of both the legislature and the executive, will be able to implement its programs, but only as long as it retains the favor of the voters. Once a majority of the voters no longer approves of the ruling party's policies, it will vote that party out of office.

THIRD PARTIES IN THE NINETEENTH CENTURY

Using the criteria of high voter turnout, the absence of gridlock, and exchange of power between the two major parties, we can see that our two-party system was healthy in the 1870s, 1880s, and 1890s. During that time period, control of the House passed back and forth between the Democrats and the Republicans every four years or so. In addition, these two parties were clearly differentiated by their platforms. Republicans favored high tariffs, a rather interventionist foreign policy, more public works, and some civil rights for blacks, while Democrats were in favor of low tariffs, decreased federal spending, limited foreign intrigue, and states' rights. Further evidence of the good health of the party system in the late nineteenth century is the record of high voter turnout. According to Census Bureau figures, almost 80 percent of the eligible population went to the polls from 1876 to 1892.

Today, evidence of our stagnant two-party system abounds. Even though the 1992 voter turnout of 55 percent was 5 percent higher than that of 1988, it is dismal in comparison to the 1870s and 1880s. The GOP hasn't won control of the House since 1952, and the Democrats have lost seven of the last eleven presidential elections. Professor Baradat is absolutely correct when he labels our present system "frustrating and inadequate."

But the solution to our current dilemma does not lie in the further restriction of third parties, as Baradat also suggests. The times in U.S. history when the two-party system has worked best correspond with the times when the government did not interfere with the right of the voters to form new parties.

Throughout the late eighteenth and nineteenth century, our political system contained many vigorous and powerful third parties. Some of the best examples of this are the "farmers parties," such as the Greenback party, the Union Labor party, and the People's party, that existed from about 1874 to 1900. These groups forced the major political parties to pass significant anti-monopoly legislation as well as important labor legislation.

But these third parties did more than simply force the two major parties to adopt various policies. Third parties have always provided an "emotional bridge" for voters who are weary of supporting one major party but are not yet ready to vote for the other. George Wallace's 1968 third-party presidential campaign drew support from traditional southern Democrats who weren't emotionally prepared to vote as Republicans. In 1992, H. Ross Perot's support was based on voters who refused to continue supporting the Republicans but couldn't yet bring themselves to vote for the Democratic ticket. The presence of viable alternatives beyond the two major parties keeps Americans involved in our democratic process.

There is a final, crucial manner in which third parties help our political system. The emotional bridge that a third party provides does more than simply lure voters to the polls: it can also help to turn one of the major parties out of power. Without the third-party bridges, the party-in-power might never be defeated, a situation that could lead to stagnation and tyranny. Third parties performed this function in 1912 when Theodore Roosevelt's Progressive party helped the Democrats wrest the White House from twenty years of unchallenged Republican supremacy. To a lesser degree, this may also have occurred in 1992, as Ross Perot's candidacy probably hurt George Bush more than it hurt Bill Clinton.

In the nineteenth century, when new or third parties were very strong, the voters replaced one of the two major parties on three occasions. The Federalists were replaced in 1820 by the National Republican party (the party that ran John Quincy Adams for president in 1828 and Henry Clay in 1832). The National Republican party was in turn replaced by the Whig party, and the Whigs were replaced by the Republican party in 1854.

BALLOT RESTRICTIONS

Vigorous third parties existed in the last century because the election laws did not discriminate against them. People were free to form new parties, and the government treated all parties, new and old, equally. In 1854, the newly founded Republican party won more governor's seats, and sent more representatives to the House, than did any other party. It was able to do so because there were no ballot-access laws until 1888. Indeed, there were no *printed* ballots before that year: people simply prepared their own ballots and were free to vote for the qualified candidate of their choice. When the government began to print ballots in 1888, it acknowledged this freedom of an unrestricted vote and invariably left a write-in space on the ballots.

Furthermore, in the nineteenth century, there was no such thing as public financing of the two major parties, something that has plagued us since 1974. Today, the Democrats and Republicans have their campaigns for president financed by the taxpayers. Under the 1974 law, no third party has ever received general-election public funding, although a handful of third-party presidential candidates have received some primary season funds.

We no longer have vigorous and active third parties because Democratic and Republican state legislatures passed restrictive laws that make it exceedingly difficult for third parties to get on the ballot in many states. These laws usually require third parties to gather signatures for a petition to be on the state ballot, and they often place strict deadlines for gathering such signatures.

These restrictions did not emerge overnight. From 1888–1931, ballot-access laws were rather mild. In 1924, only 50,000 signatures on a petition were required to place a new party on the ballot in forty-eight states (a figure that represents .15 percent of the number of people who had voted in the previous election). During the 1930s, ballot-access laws became significantly restrictive, as they required new parties to gather more signatures and file for application earlier and earlier in the campaign year. Still, it was not until the 1960s that compliance with ballot-access laws became extremely difficult.

In 1994, a new party that wants to field a candidate in every race for the U.S. House of Representatives and have the party name appear on the ballot next to the candidate's name would need to register 1,593,763 members or gather an equal number of signatures. Yet the Democratic and Republican parties need not collect any signatures to assure themselves of a place on the ballot, and the number of signatures needed for individual Democratic candidates to place themselves on primary ballots in all 435 contests is 138,996 (the number would be slightly different for Republicans).

True, the severity of these ballot-access laws *does* vary from state to state. In Florida, one of the more restrictive states, a party is defined as one that has persuaded 5 percent of the state's voters to register with the new party. This may seem like an easy task, but not since the early 1900s has a third party in any state ever managed to register 5 percent of the voters. Even when people *vote* for a third party they don't want to register with it. The Conservative party of New York elected a U.S. Senator, James Buckley, in 1970, but they only persuaded 1.5 percent of the voters to register as Conservatives. Similarly, the Connecticut Party won the office of governor in 1990, but registered only 1 percent of the voters.

Florida does offer third parties an alternative: if the new party cannot register 5 percent of the voters, then it can get its statewide nominees on the ballot by submitting 196,000 valid signatures on a petition (a figure that is equal to 3 percent of all registered voters). Once again, this task is harder than it appears.

With a single exception, no third party has ever met a signature requirement greater than 110,000 signatures. In fact, Florida's laws are so stringent that no third party or independent candidate for governor has been on its ballot since 1920.

Admittedly, ballot-access laws are harsher for third-party congressional candidates than they are for third-party presidential candidates. No third party has managed to run candidates for the U.S. House in over *half* the nation's districts since 1920. By contrast, third-party presidential candidates get on the ballots in all fifty states every so often, which probably misleads the public into thinking that there is no significant ballot-access problem for third parties.

In reality, America's ballot-access laws are so stringent, and third parties are repressed to such a degree, that the United States is probably in violation of the Copenhagen Meeting Document, an international agreement the United States signed in 1990 that requires nations to

Respect the right of individuals and groups to establish, in full freedom, their own political organizations and provide such political parties and organizations with the necessary legal guarantees to enable them to compete with each other on the basis of equal treatment before the law and the authorities.

How does the United States violate this agreement? Suppose that a new party were founded in 1994, with popular support that equaled that of the Democratic or Republican party. In order to contest all the executive and legislative offices up for election on November 8th, 1994, it would need to collect over 4,454,579 valid signatures. And some of these signatures would need to be collected ten months prior to the election. By contrast, the Democratic and Republican parties would need not submit any signatures to get themselves on the ballots, and their candidates would need only to collect about 882,484 valid signatures to place themselves on the primary ballot.

The extreme disparity of the burdens placed on old, established parties versus new parties has no parallel in any other democratic nation in the world. Indeed, the number of signatures required for Democrats and Republicans to get on primary ballots is itself too high in some states, and as a result, about 25 percent of all state legislative races present the voter with only one candidate on the general-election ballot.

In Britain, the political science model of a healthy two-party system, every candidate for Parliament faces the same ballot-access hurdle—a simple filing fee. Candidates, regardless of their party affiliation, are granted two free mailings to all the voters, and every candidate gets an equal amount of free TV and radio time. There exists perfect legal equality between all the parties. Yet Britain has a healthy two-party system, as did America in the nineteenth century.

There have been attempts to rectify the inequality in America between established and new parties. A pending bill in Georgia would lower the number of signatures needed for third-party and independent candidates for the House of

Representatives from 14,000 to 5,000. A similar bill was recently introduced in Illinois to lower the number of signatures needed for third-party candidates for the House from 12,000 to 1,000. Sadly, neither bill is expected to pass.

Perhaps one of the best remedies currently available is H.R. 1755, Minnesota Congressman Tim Penny's bill, which would establish a federal standard of one-tenth of 1 percent of the last vote cast as the number of signatures required to place a candidate's name for statewide federal office on the ballot. One-half of 1 percent would be required to get on the ballot for the House.

Unfortunately, the U.S. Supreme Court has a rather erratic record when it comes to decisions regarding the constitutionality of ballot-access laws. While the Court has, on occasion, upheld the challenges to restrictive requirements, it has at other times ignored these same decisions. In the 1968 case of *Williams v. Rhodes*, the Court struck down Ohio state laws that made it virtually impossible for a new political party, even one that had hundreds of thousands of supporters, to gain access to the state's presidential ballot. But in 1971, *Jenness v. Fortson* upheld Georgia's ballot-access laws, even though these laws were somewhat more restrictive than those of Ohio. (Ohio's laws, though ruled unconstitutional, had actually placed *more* independent candidates on the ballot than had Georgia.)

The logic of the Court, while varying from decision to decision, can also be sloppy within the context of a single case. In a 1974 case, *American Party of Texas v. White*, the Court upheld a Texas law that barred voters who had voted in a partisan primary from signing a petition to place a new party on the state-wide ballot. It was rational, according to the Court, to limit voters to a single nominating act. But voters who signed the petition weren't *nominating* any candidates—the Texas petition for a new party did not even carry the names of any candidates. Signing the petition simply indicated the voter's belief that the third party deserved a place on the ballot.

Despite the importance of third and new parties to our political system, the topic of restrictive ballot-access laws gets very little scholarly attention. Groups that are harmed the most by ballot-access laws tend to lack the political and financial clout required to command media attention. What media coverage there is of the topic is often muddled or misleading. E. J. Dionne, a well-known writer on politics, stated in the May 21st, 1992, edition of *The Washington Post* that it is "easier than ever for third-party presidential candidates to qualify for state ballots." Even though the complete inaccuracy of this statement was brought to his attention, no correction was made. Scholarly works are often no better. *Third Parties in America*, a well-respected book published in 1984 by Princeton University Press, states on page 23 that "Ballot-access laws are now as lenient as they have ever been in this century." But as was mentioned earlier in this article, the 1924 ballot-access laws were far less rigid than they are today.

The fact remains that active and vigorous third parties play a vital role in maintaining the health of our two-party system. We need third parties today, more than ever, if we are to change the "frustrating and inadequate" political system that Leon Baradat spoke of. Yet if Professor Baradat and others like him had their way, public financing and ballot-access laws would be made even *more* discriminatory toward third parties. The federal government would artificially extend the Democratic and Republican parties far beyond their natural life cycle, thus condemning us to ever greater levels of stagnation and voter apathy. In order to keep our political system healthy, we must once again allow people the freedom to vote for the qualified candidate of their choice. Such freedom is not only essential to the health of our government, but it is also our right as citizens of the United States.

LET PEROT DEBATE

ANTHONY CORRADO

In an election process dominated by attack ads and eight-second soundbites on the evening news, nothing has been as valuable to voters as the advent of presidential candidate debates. No other campaign activity provides voters with a comparable opportunity to see the candidates discuss their views in a face-to-face setting before a national audience. And no other event commands as much public attention. In 1992, the presidential debates were the most widely watched political event in history, with an average audience of 90 million viewers. More than 40 percent of those who went to the polls indicated that the debates played a significant role in their concern for candidates and voters alike.

Debate participation is determined by the bipartisan Commission on Presidential Debates, which was formed before the 1988 election and has served as the debate sponsor ever since. The commission makes its decisions based on the recommendations of an advisory board that has been established to review prospective participants. This board assesses each candidate on the basis of a set of selection criteria, which include estimates of a candidate's organizational strength, level of public support, and "newsworthiness and competitiveness." In implementing these criteria, the commission has adopted a restrictive view of who should qualify. The operative principle is that the purpose of debates is not to introduce candidates to the electorate or provide non-major-party candidates with a forum for sharing their views. Instead, the commission believes that the purpose of these events is to encourage voters to confront a final choice; it is to present to the electorate the individuals likely to win the election. The commission thus invites only those candidates who are thought to have a "realistic" or "more than theoretical" chance of winning the election. Consequently, in 1996, the commission argued that Ross Perot did not have a "realistic chance" of winning the election and did not invite him to take part in the debates.

While the purpose of the debates should be to provide the public with a chance to learn more about the individuals who are likely to be the next president and vice president, it is important to protect the legitimacy of the process by guarding against the exclusion of a candidate who generates substantial pub-

January 1997.
Reprinted with permission.
Anthony Corrado is an associate professor of government at Colby College and served as executive director of the Twentieth Century Fund's Task Force on Presidential Debates.

lic interest, even if that candidate is thought to have no realistic chance of winning. Consequently, any candidate who has broad public support and might have a substantial impact on the outcome of the election should be invited to participate. Such an approach ensures that the candidates the public expects to see in the debates will be included, without minimizing the value of debates to voters by opening them up to five or six or more minor party candidates. Given this standard for candidate participation, there is little doubt that Perot should have been invited to participate in the 1996 debates.

Perot should have been included based on his strong showing in the 1992 election and the support he generated in 1996. He qualified for the ballot in all fifty states and his party had more than 1.3 million registered members. By capturing 19 percent of the vote in 1992, Perot qualified for close to $30 million in public funding, making him the first non-major-party general election candidate to receive public money in advance of an election since the public funding program was established twenty years ago. Because his campaign was financed in large part through taxpayer monies, the public had a right to see him included in the debates.

Even though most preelection polls showed Perot with only 5–6 percent of the vote, his level of support was broad enough to justify inclusion in the debates. Perot was not a regional or "favorite son" candidate; he drew support from all parts of the country. Although his standing in the polls was well below his standing in comparable surveys conducted in 1992, he received substantial media coverage during the course of the campaign and spent tens of millions of dollars on his campaign. Even though his level of support in preelection surveys was low, it might have proven substantial enough to determine the outcome in a number of states. Moreover, if he did earn only 5–6 percent of the vote, his performance would have been adequate enough to qualify the Reform Party for federal funding again in the presidential election of 2000 should the party decide to nominate candidates for the presidential ticket.

Finally, there was a widespread expectation among voters that Perot would be invited to debate. He was not a relatively unknown minor party contender trying to gain national attention or to impose himself on an unwilling electorate. Predebate polls indicated that a significant share of the public, including a significant percentage of those who did not support Perot, thought he should be included in these forums. By failing to acknowledge this opinion, the commission denied the voters their role in the process. The commission should take public opinion into account when deciding who to invite to these historic events.

No other minor party candidate running for president in 1996 had the resources, public support, or media attention that Perot did. No other was likely to have a comparable impact on the outcome of the election. No other had demonstrated the level of organizational strength and public support adequate for an invitation to debate. Including Perot would not have opened the door to three or four other candidates and turned the debates into a multicandidate press conference.

If the debates are to continue to be a valuable tool for voters, the process must ensure that all candidates are treated fairly and that the public's interest is well served. A first step towards achieving these objectives would be for the commission to exercise greater flexibility in the implementation of its guidelines. The commission should ensure that its selection process does not exclude candidates who enjoy broad support and may have a significant influence on the outcome of the race, even though they have little chance of winning the election. Another step would be to change the structure of the commission to include members who do not specifically represent the two major parties. The addition of "independent" members will help ensure balanced decision making in the future and guard against the possibility of the process only serving the major parties' interests. Such actions will promote the legitimacy of the debate process, and ensure that it does become a vehicle for important political views in the future.

CHAPTER 24

Empowering Jurists: Democratizing the Judicial System

In the last several years, many people have disagreed with the outcomes of high-profile court cases that were covered by the media. The most famous case is O. J. Simpson's criminal trial. Many Americans, having closely watched the proceedings on television, were outraged that the jury found him not guilty. Numerous observers directed their blame squarely on the citizens on the jury. It was not unusual to hear questions like: "Who are these people?" and "What trial were they watching?"

Instead of blaming the jurors, some critics of the legal system want to empower them. This is the primary focus of the next reading. Akhil and Vikram Amar argue that a sense of duty needs to be reinstilled in citizens. This can be accomplished by giving jurors more responsibility and independence in determining verdicts. Specific reforms could include allowing juries to take notes, giving them reasonable pay for their efforts, restricting peremptory challenges, and legalizing nonunanimous verdicts. In the authors' opinions, freeing the process of justice from overly rigid rules could produce more faith and trust in the legal system, a primary goal of strengthening democracy.

In what ways are trials élitist? Why are some legal professionals hesitant to give jurors more responsibility? Are nonunanimous verdicts just?

UNLOCKING THE JURY BOX

AKHIL REED AMAR and VIKRAM DAVID AMAR

The founders of our nation understood that no idea was more central to our Bill of Rights—indeed, to government of the people, by the people, and for the people—than the citizen jury. It was cherished not only as a bulwark against tyranny but also as an essential means of educating Americans in the habits and duties of citizenship. By enacting the Fifth, Sixth, and Seventh Amendments to the Constitution, the framers sought to install the right to trial by jury as a cornerstone of a free society.

Today that cornerstone is crumbling. In recent years, a parade of notorious criminal trials has called into question the value of citizen juries. The prosecutions of Oliver North, O. J. Simpson, William Kennedy Smith, the Menendez brothers, and the assailants of Rodney King and Reginald Denny have made armchair jurors of millions of Americans. Now the failings of the system seem obvious to anyone with a television:

- In search of "impartial" jurors, the selection process seems stacked against the educated, the perceptive, and the well informed in favor of those more easily manipulated by lawyers and judges. Attorneys exercising their rights to strike candidates from the pool cynically and slyly seek to exclude jurors on the basis of race, gender, and other supposed indicators of bias.

- Courts subject citizens to repeated summonses, intrusive personal questioning, and long and inefficient trials. Unsurprisingly, many citizens avoid jury duty.

- In court, jurors serve a passive role dictated by rules that presume jurors are incapable of impartial deliberation and that provide little help in understanding points of law or evaluating testimony.

- The public perceives that the scales of justice tip in favor of rich defendants with high-priced counsel.

More than a million Americans serve as jurors on state courts each year. Jury service offers these Americans an unequaled opportunity to participate democratically in the administration of justice. But on its present course, this vital egalitarian institution may shrivel up, avoided by citizens, manipulated by lawyers and litigants, and ridiculed by the general public. To be sure, the system has inherent limitations; "correct" verdicts cannot be guaranteed. But given the

From *Policy Review*, May/June 1996.
Reprinted with permission.

jury's present form, society is bearing the costs of a jury system's vices without enjoying a jury system's virtues. Our task is to demonstrate why the citizen jury is worth defending, and to propose a number of specific reforms designed to restore the jury to its rightful status in a democracy under law.

A CORNERSTONE OF DEMOCRACY

The Framers of the Constitution felt that juries—because they were composed of ordinary citizens and because they owned no financial allegiance to the government—were indispensable to thwarting the excesses of powerful and over-zealous government officials. The jury trial was the only right explicitly included in each of the state constitutions penned between 1776 and 1789. And the criminal jury was one of few rights explicitly mentioned in the original federal constitution proposed by the Philadelphia Convention. Antifederalists complained that the proposed constitution did not go far enough in protecting juries, and federalists eventually responded by enacting three constitutional amendments guaranteeing grand, petit, and civil juries.

The need for juries was especially acute in criminal cases: A grand jury could block any prosecution it deemed unfounded or malicious, and a petit jury could likewise interpose itself on behalf of a defendant charged unfairly. The famous Zenger case in the 1730s dramatized the libertarian advantages of juries. When New York's royal government sought to stifle its newspaper critics through criminal prosecution, New York grand juries refused to indict, and a petit jury famously refused to convict.

But the Founders' vision of the jury went far beyond merely protecting defendants. The jury's democratic role was intertwined with other ideas enshrined in the Bill of Rights, including free speech and citizen militias. The jury was an essential democratic institution because it was a means by which citizens could engage in self-government. Nowhere else—not even in the voting booth—must Americans come together in person to deliberate over fundamental matters of justice. Jurors face a solemn obligation to overlook personal differences and prejudices to fairly administer the law and do justice.

As the great historian of antifederalist thought, Herbert Storing, put it, "The question was not fundamentally whether the lack of adequate provision for jury trial would weaken a traditional bulwark of individual rights (although that was also involved) but whether it would fatally weaken the role of the people in the administration of government."

Perhaps most important was the jury's educational mission. Through the jury, citizens would learn self-government by doing it. In the words of Alexis de Tocqueville, "The jury is both the most effective way of establishing the people's rule and the most effective way of teaching them how to rule." This learning, of course, would carry over to other political activity. As Tocqueville explained:

Juries, especially civil juries, instill some of the habits of the judicial mind into every citizen, and just those habits are the very best way of preparing people to be free. . . . They make all men feel that they have duties toward society and that they take a share in its government. By making men pay more attention to things other than their own affairs, they combat that individual selfishness which is like rust in society. . . . [The jury] should be regarded as a free school which is always open and in which each juror learns his rights. . . . I think that the main reason for the . . . political good sense of the Americans is their long experience with juries in civil cases.

Once we see how juries serve as major avenues for popular education and political participation, the connections early American observers drew between jury service and other means of political participation—especially voting—make more sense. Tocqueville keenly understood these linkages:

The jury system as understood in America seems to me to be as direct and extreme a consequence of the sovereignty of the people as universal suffrage. They are both equally powerful means of making the majority prevail. . . . The jury is above all a political institution [and] should be made to harmonize with the other laws establishing the sovereignty. . . . For society to be governed in a settled and uniform manner, it is essential that the jury lists should expand or shrink with the lists of voters. . . .
    [In general] in America all citizens who are electors have the right to be jurors.

We have come to think of voting as the quintessential act of democratic participation. Historically, the role of the people in serving on juries was often likened to the role of voters selecting legislative bodies, and even to the role of legislators themselves. Indeed, the jury's place in the judicial framework was closely related to the idea of bicameralism: Just as the legislature comprised two equal branches, an upper and a lower, juries and judges constituted the lower and upper branches, respectively, of the judicial department.

The Supreme Court has reinforced the linkage of jury service and voting as part of a "package" of political rights. For example, in a 1991 case challenging race-based exclusions in jury selection, Justice Anthony Kennedy observed in his majority opinion that "with the exception of voting, for most citizens the honor and privilege of jury duty is their most significant opportunity to participate in the democratic process. . . . Whether jury service may be deemed a right, a privilege or a duty, the State may no more extend it to some of its citizens and deny it to others on racial grounds than it may invidiously discriminate in the offering and withholding of the elective franchise."

Later, in the same term, Justice Kennedy again invoked the similarity between jury service and voting, observing that just as government cannot escape from constitutional constraints by farming out the tasks of administering elections and registering voters, neither can it evade constitutional norms by giving private parties the power to pick jurors.

The link between jury service and other rights of political participation, such as voting, was also recognized and embraced by the drafters of the Reconstruction amendments and implementing legislation, and still later by authors of various twentieth-century voting amendments. For example, the framers of the Fifteenth Amendment, which prohibited race-based discrimination in voting, understood well that the voting they were protecting included voting on juries. That amendment, drafted and ratified in the 1860s, proved to be a template for later amendments protecting women, the poor, and the young from voting discrimination.

JUSTICE'S WEAK LINK?

The weaknesses of jury trials are sometimes ascribed to the mediocre capacity of ordinary citizens to adjudicate matters of law and fact in an increasingly complex society. It is true that jurors will not always decide "correctly" any more than voters will always choose the most qualified candidates for public office. But the real problem is not that we rely too much on men and women of ordinary intelligence and common sense to decide questions of fact and value in the courtroom. The problem is that we rely too little. The jury is crippled by constraints imposed by the court professionals.

In the era of the founders, the jury was no more egalitarian than was suffrage, limited by race and sex and by tests of personal traits thought necessary for judging cases. Over two centuries, even as the right of jury service was gradually extended to all citizens of voting age, the freedom of jurors to participate in the finding of fact in the courtroom was constricted. Contrary to the spirit in which the jury trial was woven into our constitutional fabric, judges and lawyers have aggrandized their own roles in litigation at the expense of the jury.

The deepest constitutional function of the jury is to serve not the parties but the people—by involving them in the administration of justice and the grand project of democratic self-government. Alas, over the years, the search for adversarial advantage by attorneys won out over the values of public education and participation.

Judges, charged with protecting these enduring constitutional values, have at times done just the opposite in order to maintain their control over trials. The jury was to check the judge—much as the legislature was to check the executive, the House of Representatives to check the Senate, and the states to check the national government.

It is not surprising that we—as jurors, as citizens—have not fought off these creeping assaults. The benefits of jury service are widely dispersed—they redound to fellow citizens as well as the individual jurors. But the individual juror bears all of the cost—the hassle, the inconvenience, the foregone wages—of jury service.

If the jury service is to remain a central institution of democracy and citizenship, it must be refined. Jury trials must attract engaged and thoughtful citizens; the rulers of the courts must treat jurors as sovereign, self-governing citizens rather than as children. To this end, we suggest a number of reforms. In many instances, these changes would require no new laws, but merely a willingness on the part of the courts to unleash the common sense of the ordinary citizen.

I. Respect jurors

First, we must try to design the system to welcome jurors. All too often they are mistreated by the trial process, forced to wait in cramped and uncomfortable quarters while the judge and lawyers question jury candidates, who are often dismissed from selection without explanation. We should use juries to reconnect citizens with each other and with their government. After serving on a jury, a citizen should, in general, feel better—less cynical, more public-regarding— about our system.

II. Make juries more representative

Earlier in the nation's history, juries were impaneled under the élitist principle that only the propertied or the highly educated possessed the habits of citizenship needed to serve well. Now that we know better, it is perverse that professional and literate citizens often are exempted or struck from the jury pool. When juries produce stupid verdicts, it is often because we let interested parties pick stupid jurors in stupid ways. It is a scandal that only those who had never heard of Oliver North were permitted to judge him. Now that we have ceded so much control over trials to the court regulars, this shouldn't come as a surprise—it is akin to letting lobbyists handpick candidates for office.

A juror should have an open mind but not an empty mind. We must empower juries in ways that make them more representative and less vulnerable to encroachments of the judicial professionals, without turning them into professionals themselves.

Limit peremptory challenges. By and large, the first twelve persons picked by lottery should form the jury. The jury—and not just the jury pool summoned for each case—should be as representative of the entire community as possible. Peremptory challenges (a device that allows lawyers to remove a specified number of jurors from the panel without having to show "cause") should be eliminated; they allow prosecutors and defense attorneys to manipulate demographics and chisel an unrepresentative panel out of a representative pool. Juries should represent the people, not the parties.

Consider the analogies outlined earlier. Our society does not let an individual defendant handpick the legislature to fashion the norms governing his conduct; or the prosecutor who pursues him; or the grand jury that indicts him; or the judge who tries him; or the appellate court that reviews his case. We do not set out—and we'll resist the temptation to wisecrack—to pick the most stupid people imaginable to populate our legislatures or our judiciary. And we are especially uneasy about depriving citizens of the right to vote on the basis of discretionary criteria that may mask racial or sexual stereotyping.

Some major arguments have been advanced to support peremptories. First is the idea of legitimacy: the parties will respect a decision reached by a body they helped to select. But what about the legitimacy of verdicts for the rest of society—We, the people, whom the jury system is supposed to serve? After all, the parties regard the trial judge, the appellate court, the legislature, and the grand jury as legitimate, even though the defendant didn't personally select any of them or exercise any peremptory challenges. In the name of principle, the court professionals are merely disguising a power grab at the expense of the jury.

Second, some argue that peremptories allow counsel to probe jurors with incisive questions during the selection process to unearth "cause" to remove particular jurors. Lawyers need peremptories to vigorously exercise this right, the argument goes, lest they offend a juror for whom no provable grounds exist for a "for cause" dismissal. Our response to this is that "for cause" dismissals should be limited; jurors should not have to recuse themselves by different criteria than do judges. If "for cause" challenges are restricted, the prophylactic argument for peremptories collapses.

The Supreme Court has made clear that no constitutional right to peremptories exists: They are a relic of an imperfectly democratic past. At the founding, we suspect, peremptories were exercised mainly as a polite way of dismissing folks with personal knowledge of the parties. In a homogeneous jury pool, peremptory challenges would rarely skew the demographics of the eventual jury. But to vindicate the Fifteenth and Nineteenth Amendments, we must close off attempts by lawyers to exploit race and gender in jury selection in a way that deprives some citizens of their right to participate as democratic equals.

Jury pay. We should pay jurors for their time. Payment at a fair, flat rate will permit a broad cross section of society to serve. Our analogy to a bicameral legislature suggests that payment is appropriate, for judges and legislators are paid for their time. To decline to compensate citizens for their sacrifice—or to pay them a token $5 per day as is done in many California courts—is in effect to impose a functionally regressive poll tax that penalizes the working poor who want to serve on juries, but who cannot afford the loss of a week's pay. Payment should come from the government, not private employers. All jurors are equal as jurors, and should be paid equally: One person, one vote, one paycheck.

III. Restore the notion of duty

Jury service is not only a right, but also a duty. Few of us have militantly insisted that we perform this obligation, just as few of us insisted in the last thirty years that we pay our fair share of the intergenerational tax burden. *The Economist* reports that half of all Californians called for jury duty in the state's criminal courts ignore the summons. Citizens should not escape so easily.

Few exemptions. Exemptions from service should be extremely limited: If you are the brother-in-law of the plaintiff, you may be excused; but you may not be excused merely because you happen to read the newspaper or work in a profession. The idea of the jury is rooted in equality; just as all defendants are treated equally before the law, all jurors have equal claims as well as obligations to play a part in the administration of justice. This measure would expand the size of the jury pool, enforce the universality of required service, and raise the average education level of juries.

Yearly service. The Swiss defend their country with a citizen militia that regularly requires a citizen to serve a periodic stint of active service. Similarly, we should ask each citizen to devote, say, one week a year to jury service, depending on the needs of his or her jurisdiction. Each citizen could register in advance for the week that is most convenient, and except for genuine emergencies, citizens should then be obliged to serve when their turn comes. Courts should be willing to provide professional day care or day-care vouchers to enable homemakers to take their turns in this project in collective self-governance.

Enforcing the duty. And how should this obligation be enforced? Progressive fines are probably the best option. If you miss your week, you should pay two weeks' salary. (Flat fines, by contrast, would be functionally regressive and create incentives for highly paid citizens to dodge service.) If for some reason fines didn't work, perhaps we could consider a more radical recoupling of jury service with voting: If you want to opt out of the responsibilities of collective self-government, fine—but you may not then exercise any of its rights. You may choose to be a citizen, with democratic rights and duties, or a subject, ruled by others. On this view, you are not entitled to vote outside juries if you are unwilling to serve and vote inside juries. If you are not willing to engage in regular focused deliberation with a random cross section of fellow voters, you should not be governing the polity, just as you may not vote in the Iowa presidential caucuses unless you attend and hear the arguments of your peers.

Serial jurors. Each jury, once constituted, should be able to try several cases in a row. If you can hear four quick cases in your week a year, so much the better. The grand jury reviews more than one indictment, the judge sits on more than one case, and the legislature may decide more than one issue in a session. The quality of deliberations is likely to improve with practice. The burden of jury service will be more evenly distributed—one week for everyone—and more trials can take place if we get rid of all the wasteful preliminaries like elaborate jury questioning and peremptories. Indeed, perhaps a jury should hear both civil and criminal cases in its week. One week a year will not turn citizens into government bureaucrats, though it will give them regular practice in the art of deliberation and self-government.

IV. Free jurors to do their jobs

Juries today are often criticized for reaching foolish decisions. But it's not all their fault. Nothing is more important to fulfilling the democratic aims of jury service—including just outcomes—than active participation by the jurors. Over the years, the court professionals have conspired to strip jurors of their ability to evaluate the facts. Running the courtroom to maximize their own convenience, they have often slighted the jury's legitimate needs to understand its role, the law, and the facts. The bicameral analogy is instructive: Would we expect the House of Representatives to perform its duties competently if its access to information and ideas were entirely determined by the Senate?

Taking notes. Many judges do not allow jurors to take notes. This is idiocy. Judges take notes, grand jurors take notes, legislators take notes—what's going on here? This prohibition is based on the misguided beliefs that note-taking distracts jurors from the testimony and that deliberation would be unfairly dominated by jurors with extensive records. Neither fear outweighs the benefit of giving jurors the means to highlight key evidence and keep track of their impressions, particularly in long trials.

Plain-English instructions. Judges should give the panel, at the *outset* of a case, the basic elements of the charged offenses—in English, not legalese—so jurors can consider them and check them off in their notebooks as the trial unfolds.

Questioning of witnesses. Jurors should be allowed to question witnesses by passing queries to the judge. This allows jurors to pierce the selective presentation of facts offered by counsel, and it also keeps jurors more attentive to proceedings. Best of all, it would expose any lingering confusion about testimony in the minds of the jurors, giving prosecutors and defense counsel the chance to address these concerns. Consider, for example, the possibility that each of the jurors in the O. J. Simpson trial had a different pet theory of police conspiracy. If each juror could submit questions, prosecutors would have had an opportunity to understand, address, and debunk many of these mutually inconsistent and factually insupportable theories.

Discussion among jurors prior to deliberation. A ban on such discussion assumes that jurors are superhumanly capable of suspending all judgment for days or weeks and that conversation can only contaminate their faculties. Common sense suggests that it is human nature to form provisional judgments; at least by discussing a case prior to deliberation, jurors can test each other's impressions of the evidence and begin to hone their understandings of key points before these points are lost in the rush of the proceedings. Such a reform must, of course, be accompanied by reminders from the judge that jurors may not reach final conclusions about guilt or innocence until they have heard all the evidence.

Support staff. We should allow juries to hire support staff when it is necessary. In a world of increasing complexity and specialization of labor, few can do an important job well without such help. If legislators and judges can have staffs, why not grand juries? We trivialize jurors when we insist that they alone remain trapped in the eighteenth-century world of generalists. Perhaps every court should hire a permanent staff with undivided loyalty to the jury itself, and subject to ''term limits'' to prevent the staff from entrenching itself and using the jury to advance its own agenda.

V. Avoid hung juries

When hung juries occur, mistrials waste the time and resources of all concerned. They even harm defendants in cases where the jury was leaning toward acquittal, because a mistrial allows a vindictive prosecutor a second bite at the apple. All this brings us to another controversial—and we admit extremely tentative—suggestion. Perhaps, just perhaps, we should move, even in criminal cases, away from unanimity toward majority or supermajority rule on juries. Founding history is relatively clear—a criminal jury had to be unanimous. But this clear understanding was not explicitly inscribed into the Constitution, and the modern Supreme Court had upheld state rules permitting convictions on 10-2 votes. (England today also permits 10–2 verdicts in criminal cases.)

Three arguments support our suggestion that nonunanimous verdicts should be upheld. First, at the founding, unanimity may have drawn its strength from certain metaphysical and religious ideas about Truth that are no longer plausible: to wit, that all real truths would command universal assent. Second, most of our analogies tug toward majority rule—used by legislatures, appellate benches, voters, and grand juries—or supermajority rule: In impeachment proceedings, for example, a two-thirds vote in the Senate is required for conviction.

Last, and most important, all our other suggestions lead the modern American jury system away from its historical reliance on unanimity. At the founding of our nation, unanimity *within* a jury was nestled in a cluster of other rules that now must fall. In early days, blacks, women, the poor, and the young were excluded from voting and jury service. Peremptory challenges probably made juries even more homogenous. But now that all adult citizens may serve on juries, and we have eliminated all the old undemocratic barriers, preserving unanimity might also be undemocratic, for it would create an extreme minority veto unknown to the Founders.

Even at the founding, unanimous jury verdicts may have existed in the shadow of a custom of majority or supermajority rule. Jurors would discuss the case and vote on guilt; and even if the minority were unconvinced about the verdict, they would in the end vote with the majority after they had been persuaded that the majority had listened to their arguments in good faith. This custom bears some resemblance to legislative "unanimous consent" rules. A single lawmaker may often slow down proceedings—force her colleagues to deliberate more carefully on something that matters to her—but in the end she may not prevent the majority from implementing its judgment. Perhaps the same should hold true for juries.

In allowing juries to depart from unanimity, we must try to preserve the ideal of jury deliberation and self-education. Jurors should communicate with each other seriously and with respect. Fans of unanimity argue that it promotes serious deliberation—everyone's vote is necessary, so everyone is seriously listened to. But unanimity cannot guarantee *mutual* tolerance: What about an eccentric holdout who refuses to listen to, or even try to persuade, others?

Nonunanimous schemes can be devised to promote serious discussion. Jurors should be told that their job is to communicate with others who have different ideas, views, and backgrounds. Judges could also advise jurors that their early deliberations should focus on the evidence and not jurors' tentative leanings or votes, and that they should take no straw polls until each juror had a chance to talk about the evidence on both sides.

We suggest a scheme in which a jury must be unanimous to convict on the first day of deliberations, but on day two, 11–1 would suffice; on day three, 10-2; and so on, until we hit our bedrock limit of, say, two-thirds (for conviction) or simple majority (for acquittal).

VI. Educate the people

Once we start thinking about the jury from the perspective of democracy rather than adjudication—from the viewpoint of the citizenry rather than the litigants—other possibilities open up. Recall Tocqueville's description of the jury as a "free school . . . always open" to educate the people in citizenship. If this is the big idea, why not take advantage of new video technology to advance it? Think of how C-SPAN broadcasts of legislative debates and hearings have contributed to the education of the public. The courts could likewise tape jury deliberations for use as high-school teaching materials about democracy in action (perhaps delaying the release of sensitive cases). Of course, we would have to ensure that these records would not be used to impeach jury verdicts.

LET THE CHANGES BEGIN

The vision we have sketched is a demanding one. Yet many states are already taking up the challenge, enacting reforms by statute or by court policy. The court system of New York state is mulling over reforms to make the experience of serving more efficient and convenient for citizens, and many states already have a one-day, one-trial policy. New Jersey and New York last year joined the twenty-five or so states that eliminate exemptions based on profession. Arizona is the leader in endorsing proposals, such as note-taking and questioning witnesses, to increase jurors' participation in the process. Oregon and Louisiana allow nonunanimous verdicts in some cases, and Arizona allows a jury to ask the lawyers to explain evidence again if it has reached an impasse in deliberations.

But much more needs to be done. Until America's state and federal judicial systems live up to the ideals embedded in their founding documents and learn to trust the capacity of ordinary citizens to dispense justice, a cornerstone of democracy will continue to crumble.

CHAPTER 25

Welfare Reform: The Importance of Responsibility, Work, and States' Rights

For many years, there has been growing criticism of the modern welfare system. One of the most controversial was the Aid to Families with Dependent Children (AFDC) program. AFDC was designed by the Roosevelt administration as a partial response to the Great Depression. Its focus was to give relief to families including females, children, and unemployed fathers. Liberals, like President Lyndon Johnson, expanded AFDC and created other programs out of the ideological faith in rationalism: the federal government could not only create, but successfully administer, many different programs designed to eliminate poverty.

Critics opposed the welfare programs for many reasons. Fundamentally, they contended that they encouraged a culture of dependence, making it more difficult for individuals to accept responsibility. They also thought that welfare discouraged the work ethic, threatened the coherence of the family unit, and illegitimately expanded the power of the federal government.

In the summer of 1996, Congress passed and President Clinton signed the Personal Responsibility and Work Opportunity Reconciliation Act. The law is the most significant reform of welfare policy since the 1930s. The controversial legislation ends the federal entitlement of AFDC for the poor by placing time limits on eligibility, mandating work in exchange for benefits, giving increased responsibility to the states, discouraging illegitimacy, increasing child support enforcement, and eliminating welfare programs for felons and noncitizens.

In the reading, Representatives Dave Weldon (R-Fla.), Marge Roukema (R-N.J.), Steny Hoyer (D-Md.) and John Kasich (R-Ohio) describe why they support the legislation.

Encouraging responsibility, whether it is at the individual or state level, is a principal goal of populist reform efforts. Will states adequately take up the responsibility for welfare? In what ways has the responsibility for employment and income maintenance been shifted to the private sector? Will time limits on eligibility be an effective tool for reducing welfare?

CONFERENCE REPORT ON H.R. 3734, PERSONAL RESPONSIBILITY AND WORK OPPORTUNITY RECONCILIATION ACT OF 1996

REPRESENTATIVE DAVE WELDON (R-FLA.), REPRESENTATIVE MARGE ROUKEMA (R-N.J.), REPRESENTATIVE STENY HOYER (D-MD.), AND REPRESENTATIVE JOHN KASICH (R-OHIO).

MR. WELDON of Florida. Mr. Speaker, I thank the distinguished gentleman for yielding, and it has been a pleasure for me to be here and advocate for the people in my district, who have been calling out for welfare reform for many years.

Mr. Chairman, they know that the current welfare system is broken. The people in my district know that the rate of poverty has not decreased since welfare has been enacted. The average stay on welfare is thirteen years, and today illegitimacy rates among many welfare families approach 50 percent. . . .

It did not take a Republican Congress to end welfare as we know it. This bill makes welfare a helping hand, not a lifetime handout. It places five-year limits on collecting AFDC benefits. For hardship cases states can exempt 20 percent of their case load from the five-year limit, and able-bodied people must work after two years or lose their benefits.

It cuts taxpayer-financed welfare for noncitizens and felons. It returns power and flexibility to the states. It ends numerous redundancies within the welfare system by giving block grants to the states and rewards states for moving families from welfare to work.

It seeks to halt the rising illegitimacy rates. Moms are encouraged for the first time to identify the father or risk losing benefits by as much as 25 percent. It increases efforts to make deadbeat dads pay child support. And these, of course, are men who father children but then have shirked their financial responsibility for caring for them.

It gives cash rewards to the top five states who [sic] make the most successful improvement in reducing illegitimacy. As we know, fatherlessness is linked to high juvenile crime rates, high drug abuse rates, and declining educational performance. . . .

This historic welfare reform bill will end welfare as we know it. During the

From the *Congressional Record*: July 31, 1996 (House).

past thirty years, taxpayers have spent $5 trillion on failed welfare programs. What kind of return have the taxpayers received on their investment? The rate of poverty has not decreased at all. Furthermore, the average length of stay on welfare is thirteen years. Today's illegitimacy rate among welfare families is almost 50 percent and crime continues to run rampant. Current programs have encouraged dependency, trapped people in unsafe housing, and saddled the poor with rules that are antiwork and antifamily. Clearly, those trapped in poverty and the taxpayers deserve better.

This bill overhauls our broken welfare system. This plan makes sure welfare is not a way of life; stresses work not welfare; stops welfare to felons and most noncitizens; restores power and flexibility to the states; and offers states incentives to halt the rise in illegitimacy.

By imposing a five-year lifetime limit for collecting AFDC, this bill guarantees that welfare is a helping hand, not a lifetime handout. Recognizing the need for helping true hardship cases, states would be allowed to exempt up to 20 percent of their caseload from the five-year limit. In addition, H.R. 3734 for the first time ever requires able-bodied welfare recipients to work for their benefits. Those who can work must do so within two years or lose benefits. States will be required to have at least 50 percent of their welfare recipients working by 2002. To help families make the transition from welfare to work, the legislation provides $4.5 billion more than current law for child care.

Under this bill, future entrants into this country will no longer be eligible for most welfare programs during their first five years in the United States. Felons will not be eligible for welfare benefits, and state and local jails will be given incentives to report felons who are skirting the rules and receiving welfare benefits.

Our current system has proven that the one-size-fits-all welfare system does not work. H.R. 3734 will give more power and flexibility to the states by ending the entitlement status of numerous welfare programs by block granting the money to the states. No longer will states spend countless hours filling out the required bureaucratic forms hoping to receive a waiver from Washington to implement their welfare program. States will also be rewarded for moving families from welfare to work.

Finally, this bill addresses the problem of illegitimacy in several ways. H.R. 3734 authorizes a cash reward for the five states most successful in reducing illegitimacy. It also strengthens child support enforcement provisions and requires states to reduce assistance by 25 percent to individuals who do not cooperate in establishing paternity. Lastly, this bill mandates an appropriation grant of $50 million annually to fund abstinence education programs combating teenage pregnancy and illegitimacy.

The sad state of our current welfare system and the cycles of poverty and hopelessness it perpetuates are of great concern to me. I believe this bill goes to the heart of reforming the welfare system by encouraging and helping individuals in need become responsible for themselves and their family. I wholeheartedly support this bill because it makes welfare a helping hand in times of trouble, not a handout that becomes a way of life. I truly believe that this reform will give taxpayers a better return on their investment in helping those in need.

MRS. ROUKEMA. Mr. Speaker, as someone who has advocated a "tough love" approach to welfare reform legislation, this goes a long way toward reforming our broken welfare system as we return the system to its original purpose—a temporary safety net, not a way of life.

Furthermore, as a pioneer in the battle to also reform our child support enforcement system, I am very pleased to see that the reforms I have been pushing for almost four years now—which represent the heart and soul of the U.S. Interstate Commission on Child Support's final report—have been included in the package before us today.

Ensuring that these child support enforcement reforms were included in this bill acknowledges what I've been saying for years: effective reform of our interstate child support enforcement laws must be an integral component of any welfare reform plan that the 104th Congress sent to President Clinton.

Research has found that somewhere between 25 and 40 percent of welfare costs go to support mothers and children who fall onto the welfare rolls precisely because these mothers are not receiving the legal, court-ordered support payments to which they are rightfully entitled.

With the current system spending such a large portion of funding on these mothers, children are the first victims, and the taxpayers who have to support these families are the last victims.

The plan before us also puts teeth into the laws that require unwed mothers to establish paternity of their children at the hospital, thereby laying the groundwork for claiming responsibility for their actions and families.

The core of the welfare reforms incorporated into this bill are clearly defined work requirements for welfare beneficiaries—which is essential to moving people off of the welfare rolls—strict time limits—thereby giving welfare recipients a strong incentive to find a job—and more flexibility for states to design welfare programs that fit the needs of their people.

In addition, this welfare reform plan protects the safety net for children by including a rainy day fund to help the families in states suffering from recession or economic downturns.

The enhanced flexibility that states will receive under this plan is meritorious, provided that the safety net is maintained in order to protect families who truly need temporary assistance—not a lifetime of handouts generation after generation. . . .

Additionally, this legislation does take a modest step in the right direction by allowing states to use their own money, or social services block grant funds—to provide families on welfare with vouchers—instead of cash benefits—to pay for essential services needed by the family, that is, medicine, baby food, diapers, school supplies—if a state has terminated the family's cash benefits as part of its sanction program.

This is the right thing to do because even if a welfare recipient is playing by all of the rules and has not found a job when the time limits become effective, the use of vouchers for services plays an important role in helping the family and its children keep their head above the waterline.

There should be no question that we must enact strong welfare reform legislation this year. The American people are correctly demanding that we restore the notion of individual responsibility and self-reliance to a system that has run amok over the past twenty years.

Although I have strongly supported some welfare reforms that have been described as ''tough love'' measures for several years now, I want to reiterate that my goal has always been to require self-reliance and responsibility, while ensuring that innocent children do not go hungry and homeless as a result of any federal action. . . .

Mr. Speaker, this bill is not perfect. But it represents the first major reform of our broken-down welfare system in generations. We have been given a historic opportunity that I hope and trust we will not squander. We owe no less to our children. . . .

MR. HOYER. Mr. Speaker, I rise in support of the bill.

America's welfare system is at odds with the core values Americans believe in: responsibility, work, opportunity, and family. Instead of rewarding and encouraging work, it does little to help people find jobs, and penalizes those who go to work. Instead of strengthening families and instilling personal responsibility, the system penalizes two-parent families, and lets too many absent parents off the hook.

Instead of promoting self-sufficiency, the culture of welfare offices seems to create an expectation of dependence rather than independence. And the very ones who hate being on welfare are desperately trying to escape it.

As a society we cannot afford a social welfare system without obligations. In order for welfare reform to be successful, individuals must accept the responsibility of working and providing for their families. In the instances where benefits are provided, they must be tied to obligations. We must invest our resources on those who value work and responsibility. Moreover, we must support strict requirements which move people from dependence to independence. Granting rights without demanding responsibility is unacceptable.

The current system undermines personal responsibility, destroys self-respect and initiative, and fails to move able-bodied people from welfare to work. Therefore, a complete overhaul of the welfare system is long overdue. We must create a different kind of social safety net which will uphold the values our current system destroys. It must require work, and it must demand responsibility. . . .

Like many Americans, I continue to have concerns about some of the provisions in this bill. We must be certain that both the federal and state governments live up to their responsibilities to protect children who may lose assistance through no fault of their own. We must make sure that legal immigrants, who have paid taxes and, in some cases, defended the United States in our armed services, are not abandoned in their hour of need. And it is not enough to move people off of welfare—we must move them into jobs that make them self-sufficient and contributing members of society.

This bill supports the American values of work and personal responsibility. . . .

MR. KASICH. . . . As my colleagues know, it was pretty amazing today to watch the president of the United States come on television and say that he was going, in fact, to sign this welfare bill. The reason why it is so amazing today is that because the American people, during all of my adult lifetime, have said that they want a system that will help people who cannot help themselves, but they want a system that is going to ask the able-bodied to get out and begin to work themselves. This has been delayed and put off, with a million excuses as to why we could not get it done.

I just want to suggest to my friends who are in opposition, and I respect their opposition; many of them just did not talk; many of them were not able to talk, as they were beaten in the civil rights protests in this country. I respect their opposition. But the simple fact of the matter is that this program was losing public support.

Mr. Speaker, the cynicism connected to this program from the folks who get up and go to work every day for a living, and I do not mean the most fortunate, I mean those mothers and fathers who have had to struggle for an entire lifetime to make ends meet, they have never asked for food stamps, they have never asked for welfare, they have never asked for housing, and they are struggling. They are counting their nickels. They do not take the bus transfer because it costs a little extra money, and they walk instead so they can save some more money to educate their children. These people were becoming cynical, they were being poisoned in regard to this system, and they were demanding change.

Mr. Speaker, we all know here, as we have watched the Congress, the history of Congress over the decades, that when the American people speak, we must deliver to them what they want. They said they wanted the Vietnam War over. It took a decade, but they got it, and public cynicism and lack of support was rising against this program. It was necessary to give the people a program they could support.

But I also want to say that the American people have never, if I could be so bold as to represent a point of view, have never said that those who cannot help themselves should not be helped. That is Judeo-Christianity, something that we all know has to be rekindled. Our souls must once again become attached to one another, and the people of this country and Judeo-Christianity said it is a sin not to help somebody who needs help, but it is equally a sin to help somebody who needs to learn how to help themselves.

But I say to my friends who oppose this bill:

This is about the best of us. This is about having hopes and dreams. After forty or fifty years of not trusting one another in our neighborhoods and having to vacate our power and our authority to the central government, to the Washington bureaucrats, this is now about reclaiming our power, it is about reclaiming our money, it is about reclaiming our authority, it is about rebuilding our community, it is about rebuilding our families, it is about cementing our neighborhoods, and it is about believing that all of us can march to that state capitol, that all of us can go into the community organizations and we can demand excellence, we can demand compassion, and that we can do it better.

We marched thirty, forty years ago because we thought people were not being treated fairly, and we march today for the very same reason. What I would say, and maybe let me take it back and say many of my friends marched. I was too young, but I watched, and I respect it. What I would suggest at the end of the day, however, is that we all are going to have to stand up for those who get neglected in reform, but frankly this system is going to provide far more benefits, far more hope, restore the confidence in the American people that we have a system that will help those that cannot help themselves and at the same time demand something from able-bodied people who can. It will benefit their children; it will help the children of those who go to work.

America is a winner in this. The president of the United States has recognized that. He has joined with this Congress, and I think we have a bipartisan effort here to move America down the road towards reclaiming our neighborhoods and helping America.

And I would say to my friends, we will be bold enough and humble enough when we see that mistakes are being made, to be able to come back and fix them; but let us not let these obstacles stand in the way of rebuilding this program based on fundamental American values.

CHAPTER 26

Environmental Protection and Religion

Populism's roots are deeply based in the spirit of faith and renewal. Protecting the environment is a central conviction of that faith. The moral responsibility of protecting our natural heritage and the duty of religious leaders to speak to that is the focus of this reading. In addition, U.S. Interior Secretary Bruce Babbitt describes some grassroots actions by communities across the nation that bind the practices of religious values with environmental protection efforts.

If your religious values conflicted with an economic opportunity, which would you choose? Why? Does your generation have a responsibility to pass on to the next an environment as clean as the one you inherited? What responsibility does private business owe to the environment?

LEADING AMERICA CLOSER TO THE PROMISE OF GOD'S COVENANT

U.S. SECRETARY OF THE INTERIOR BRUCE BABBITT

I'd like to start today by telling you two interrelated stories from my life: one as a father, one as a Cabinet Secretary.

For arriving in Mesa reminds me of a time, just over a decade ago, when I took my son hiking into the White Mountains of western Arizona. I remember, in particular, my son asking a child's question: "Dad, are there wolves living here?" As a partial answer, I later read him the moving Arizona passage in *A Sand County Almanac* where the author, like other federal agents at that time, had shot one of the last remaining packs of wolves. It was part of a national eradication policy, based on the assumption that "because fewer wolves meant more deer, that no wolves would mean a hunters' paradise." But Aldo Leopold experienced a conversion after he

reached the wolf in time to watch a fierce green fire dying in her eyes. I realized then, and have known ever since, that there was something new to me in those eyes, something known only to her and to the mountain . . . I now suspect that just as a deer herd lives in mortal fear of its wolves, so does a mountain live in mortal fear of its deer.

The second story began one morning in January 1995 in the heart of Yellowstone National Park, where I stood knee deep in a layer of deep snow that blanketed the first protected landscape in America. For as Interior Secretary I was helping to carry the first gray wolves back into that landscape. Through conservation laws, I was there to restore the natural cycle, to help make Yellowstone complete. The first wolf was an Alpha female, and after I set her down in the transition area, where she would later mate and bear wild pups, I looked through the grate into the eyes of this magnificent creature; I saw the green fire flare up again, a fire brought back by America's conservation laws, with the power to help restore God's creation.

Between those two events, separated by nearly a century, there awoke in America a profound new sense of national stewardship, a shift that has been embodied in our most important conservation law: the landmark 1973 Endangered Species Act.

I then returned to Washington where a newly elected Congress was armed

The keynote address of the Associated Church Press 1996 Annual Convention, Mesa, Arizona, April 11, 1996.

with an agenda that was both hostile to God's creation and determined to dismantle the very legal tools—especially the Endangered Species Act—that allow us to restore it.

These legislators claim that God gave Adam and his descendants "dominion" over Creation with instructions to "subdue" it as they see fit. Thus absolved of responsibility, leaders in Congress maintain that DDT "should not have been banned" because it "drove up the cost of doing business"; that "one hundred and fifty national parks of the some 368 need to be dropped"; and that the Environmental Protection Agency is "the Gestapo of government." Whereupon they quietly proceed to introduce bills that dismantle laws like the Endangered Species Act and 1972 Clean Water Act.

Whatever our differences on specific matters of policy, many of these leaders show a deep and pervasive hostility not only to the environment, but to the values expressed by America's religious leaders, both those in the church hierarchy and those speaking from the back pews.

For example, last October five leaders from the Presbyterian, Methodist, Evangelical Lutheran, Jewish, and Mennonite faiths, representing tens of millions of churchgoers, all wrote different letters opposing a bill to cripple the Endangered Species Act. They opposed it not for technical or scientific or agricultural or medicinal reasons, but for spiritual reasons.

These letters were submitted to be entered in the *Congressional Record*, a routine and invariably honored request. But the committee chairman at first refused to admit them; only after protest over their exclusion were the letters begrudgingly allowed. Why? What was so politically dangerous about the letters? To find out, I obtained copies, and read each one.

One wrote: "Contemporary moral issues are related to our understanding of nature and humanity's place in them." Another: "Our tradition teaches us that the earth and all of its creatures are the work and the possessions of the Creator." A third: "We need to hear and obey the command of our Creator who instructed us to be stewards of God's creation."

It seems only if religious leaders support legislation can they speak with authority and deliberation. For in January, after the Evangelical Environmental Network unveiled a nationwide campaign to support the Endangered Species Act as "the Noah's ark of our day" and warn that a bill in Congress may well "sink" it, they were suddenly rebuked as less than honest. Accusing them in an open letter of "using the pulpit to mislead people," House leaders criticized them: "As religious people, you have a high obligation to seek the truth, even in the political arena."

But even if Congress keeps you off Capitol Hill, even if they force you to wait behind a long line of corporate lobbyists clutching their due bills after financing the last election, you may find, as I did, that the only political arena that matters is out here on the American landscape, far from Washington.

For example, one year ago I traveled beyond the beltway to see how the rest of America felt about bills to close national parks, repeal stormwater treatment, and permit extinction. Here's what I found:

- At a Los Angeles "Eco-Expo" last April, hundreds of children were invited to write down their answers to the basic question: "Why save endangered species?"
  One child, Gabriel, answered, "Because God gave us the animals."
  Travis and Gina wrote, "Because we love them."
  A third answered, "Because we'll be lonely without them."
  Still another wrote, "Because they're a part of our life. If we didn't have them, it would not be a complete world. The Lord put them on earth to be enjoyed, not destroyed."

- On the banks of the St. Johns River in Jacksonville, Florida, a fisherman said we need to restore the river for recreation, a civic scientist said we need to have drinkable water, an environmentalist said we need clean streams for waterfowl and wildlife, and a restaurateur said we need a clear waterfront as a magnet to draw people and business. But then a minister rose and said, beyond all those reasons, we need to restore the river because God gave us clean rivers and to allow it to become fouled was simply, unequivocally, "wrong."

- On the banks of the Kentucky River in Frankfort, a group of local doctors, parents, teachers, and scientists had "Come to the waters" just as you have today. But whatever their unique line of work, they all shared the same emphasis: We have a moral obligation as stewards to the land. When I noted the unity of their voices, answering on religious grounds, a woman chimed in, "Well, Mr. Secretary, you are in the Bible Belt!" If so, that belt encompasses the entire nation. For in each city I traveled to, North, South, East, or West, I heard a familiar spiritual answer.

- I joined a Wednesday night interfaith meeting at the Peachtree Presbyterian Church in Atlanta. There, the minister read us Psalm 24 that proclaims, "The earth is the Lord's and the fullness thereof, the world and those who dwell therein; for he has founded it upon the seas, and established it upon the rivers."

- Upon one of those rivers, on a cloudy, windswept morning in Portland, religious groups helped us plant native willow and Oregon grape to restore the streambank of Fanno Creek.

- At the New Waverly Baptist Church in West Dallas, congregants discovered the disastrous health effects on neighborhood families from a nearby lead smelting plant. They succeeded in having the plant closed and have convinced the city to establish a health clinic in the church basement.

- At the Full Circle House of Prayer in Port Huron, Michigan, nuns brought together members of the community to learn how to control invasive pests in order to protect local wetlands.

- Children from the Mainline Reform Temple in Wynnewood, Pennsylvania, have painted fish on sewers to discourage dumping where it threatens the purity of local waters.

- And just three Sundays ago, Pope John Paul II reminded the world that while the scripture allows humans to have a "privileged position" on Earth, "this is not authority to lord over it, even less to devastate it." The season of Lent, he said, offers us a "profound lesson to respect the environment. Among the negative outcomes of this culture of domination is a distorted use of nature that disfigures its face and jeopardizes the equilibrium. And it does not slow even with the threat of ecological disaster."

During the course of my travels, and watching America's environmental awakening unfold in cities and towns everywhere, I turned back to reread Genesis, in light of the comments I had heard in so many communities.

We all remember the Deluge as an account of sin and punishment, of destruction followed by hope and renewal. But upon reading it once again, I saw still more meaning.

Noah was, of course, commanded to take into the ark two by two and seven by seven every living thing in creation, the clean and the unclean. Our Creator did not specify that Noah should limit the ark to two charismatic species, two good for hunting, two species that might provide some cure down the road, and, say, two that draw crowds to the city zoo.

No, He specified the whole of creation. And when the waters receded, and the dove flew off to dry land, God set all the creatures free, commanding them to multiply upon the earth. Then, in the words of His covenant with Noah, "when the rainbow appears in the clouds, I will see it and remember the everlasting covenant between me and all living things on earth."

Why is this relevant in the modern political arena, as the religious community speaks to and from the pulpit? Because today, we are still living between the flood and the rainbow: between threats to creation on the one side and God's covenant to protect life on the other; between the incomplete landscape I grew up with and the full restoration of wolves that my son will know.

Only two things stand between these two visions. The first is our secular conservation laws, laws which preserve habitat, protect national parks, and restore our lakes, rivers, and shores so that, when they are clean, we can indeed "Come to the waters." But the second is something less visible and more fundamental than the laws themselves. It is the spiritual and moral values that are embodied in those laws. Without those values we cannot develop as responsible stewards of the land. And so I conclude here by asking you who speak to our religious leaders and to our congregations: How can we work together—in our respective callings—to protect God's creation?

We can continue to awaken others to our stewardship of the land. For America's religious community—convinced of scientific evidence and consensus, and acting across a remarkable spectrum of faith groups—is arraying its ancient and authoritative teachings for action in response to the crisis of planetary environment.

We can assert and amplify our values, whether or not Congress wants to hear them.

We can listen when the Bishops of the Catholic Church declare: "As individuals, as institutions, as a people, we need a change of heart to preserve and protect the planet for our children and for generations yet unborn,'' and we can answer, ''Amen.''

We can endorse the hundreds of evangelical Christian scholars and national agency executives who have signed and distributed an ''Evangelical Environmental Declaration.''

We can praise the leaders of American Judaism who collectively state that ''The ecological crisis hovers over all Jewish concerns, for the threat is global, advancing, and ultimately jeopardizes ecological balance and the quality of life.''

We can actively support the Protestant communions, acting within the National Council of Churches of Christ, who have brought together as no national environmental organization has, constituencies opposing racism as well as pollution.

Finally, we can remember that conservation did not begin as a partisan, or even a political issue. Nor did it begin on Earth Day. It began in that time between the flood and the rainbow, a time that begins with the break of each new day. You can help by asking your leaders, your congregations, and yourselves to transcend the narrow partisan differences, which can only drive us back toward destruction, and instead uphold our moral obligation as stewards of God's creation, which can only to bring us closer to the hope and renewal that was and is the promise of His covenant.

Thank you.

CHAPTER 27

A Concluding Speech from a True Believer

Many people compared former Colorado governor Richard Lamm to Don Quixote when he challenged Ross Perot for the Reform party's presidential nomination in the summer of 1996. Not only was beating Perot nearly impossible, but the issues that brought him into the race were some of the most controversial in contemporary American politics. He characterized those issues as orphans. These orphan issues are financial responsibility, election and campaign reform, immigration reform, rehabilitating our public institutions, and a renewed commitment to values.

Neither Bill Clinton nor Bob Dole was willing to honestly and fully debate them because of the party cleavages they would expose. Lamm thought the nation needed a political agenda that directly confronted those societal dilemmas.

Lamm is squarely within the populist tradition because of his trust in the ability of most Americans to accept difficult truths. He believes that both major political parties have been captured by elite interests. Lamm emphasized the need to speak to long-term societal trends and manage them responsibly for the interests of the majority of Americans.

Are a majority of Americans willing to accept difficult truths from their politicians? What are the consequences for the United States if controversial issues continue to be evaded? Can a system structured around frequent elections responsibly act to solve long-term problems?

THE NEW AGENDA

RICHARD D. LAMM

Thank you for honoring me with this invitation to speak. Thank you for being you—for not giving up on the political process—for not throwing out the concept of democracy with the political bath water that badly needs changing. Thank you for still caring—and still hoping—and still believing in America. If Rosa Parks could change the world by refusing to move to the back of the bus, just think what your combined talent and dedication can do. This is still a nation worth saving. People are still the ultimate power—especially if they are indignant. The Constitution of our nation guaranteed us the "pursuit of happiness," but as Ben Franklin cautioned, "It only guarantees the pursuit; we have to catch up with it ourselves."

I shall probably offend a number of you—but I am going to show you some dirty pictures—starting out with two obscene pictures that you will not want your children or grandchildren to see. If you are below the age of forty-five, close your eyes because here they come.

In my thirty years of public policy, this is the most terrifying and obscene public policy document I have ever seen. It will not only impact our future, but our fundamental views on politics and ethics. It signals a change in American public policy as large as the New Deal or the end of the Cold War. But where the New Deal meant additional programs and benefits, the inevitable implications of this chart will require sacrifice, belt tightening, and political realism. It will require a massive rethinking about existing retirement policy, the role and scope of government, medical ethics, safety nets, and compassion. It will require a new political language because we cannot get very far into the future within the existing political dialogue. It will require a new maturity in the American public. It will require people like you.

Simply put, this chart shows that in sixteen years—by the year 2012—the current tax structure applied to the revenue anticipated in 2012 will only fund entitlements and interest on the national debt. No defense department, no national parks, no judiciary, no executive branch of government. This is only four presidential elections into our future. Then, in 2029, the current tax structure applied to anticipated revenue will only fund four programs: Social Security, Medicare, Medicaid, and federal retirement. Nothing else! The status quo in

A speech delivered to the Reform Party of California State Conference, Los Angeles Convention Center, Los Angeles, CA, June 1, 1996.

American public policy is not an option. We do not have the luxury of "standing pat."

The New Deal has become a "raw deal" for our children and our grand children. Not because it wasn't appropriate for the time—it was. But demography has turned against many of its most important programs. Our Social Security has become our children's and grandchildren's "social insecurity" (as Pete Peterson put it). We can only honor the spirit of the New Deal by amending it. It is well-meaning, but unsustainable. It worked in the past, but will not work in the future without substantial amendment.

Second dirty picture: Here is a chart of the federal debt. It is not $5 trillion as our politicians tell us—it is between $14 and $17 trillion. Never has a generation of politicians so prespent its children's money.

These two charts show that my generation is guilty of "generational malpractice." Without genuine, fundamental—yes, let's not be afraid to say it without unpopular reforms, without a grassroots renewal of American politics, the future of the American experiment stands in grave jeopardy. Never before in American history have our democratic institutions evidenced such desperate need of political repair. For a dozen generations, American mothers and fathers raised children better educated than themselves. For a dozen generations, we left our children a more competitive economy and greater wealth than was enjoyed by their parents and grandparents. Despite the blessings of peace and an abundance of natural resources—both physical and human—America arrives at the dawn of a new millennium as a nation profoundly at risk—a nation whose problems are rapidly outrunning its solutions. We have become a country that borrows, rather than saves. A country that spends, rather than invests. A country that is blindly, thoughtlessly consuming not only our own share, but an inexcusable part of our children's and grandchildren's share of America's resources.

It is a time for alarm—a time to ride through the streets alerting our neighbors to the failures of will—the failures of greed and grievance—the failures of integrity and simple humanity that now imperil our democracy. Ross Perot has been doing this—but not enough of the rest of us have. The hour is late and we have a country to save. The existing political parties are treating Americans as children to be bribed with political candy rather than as mature adults who can be trusted with the truth. Like Tweedle-Dee and Tweedle-Dum, the Democratic and Republican parties look into the past for their guideposts to our future.

If we are not to become a nation accused by our children of "generational malpractice," we must act now to reform our government, our elections, and our personal lives. We must accept limits on what we can afford, personally and collectively. Otherwise, we may well be remembered in a few short years as the last comfortable Americans—a selfish, short-sighted generation willing and eager to consume more than it produced—and then, only too ready to pass along the tab for its excesses to posterity. And in doing so, risks everything we have built up over 200 years.

When I graduated from high school, the national debt took seven cents out of every tax dollar that I paid. It is now nineteen cents; and almost certainly my children will have to spend twenty-five cents out of every tax dollar they pay just to service the debt that my generation imposed upon them. That is more than "generational malpractice"—that is "fiscal child abuse."

Where there is every reason to understand why my parents ran up debt (fighting the Depression and Hitler), there is no justification for my generation running up a debt. Simply put, mine is the first generation (not at war) in America's history not to pay its own way. We inherited a small federal debt, and we are leaving an albatross of debt to the next generation—a nation-threatening albatross of debt.

There comes a time in the history of every great nation where its citizens must reassert their control, must shake up institutions and political parties grown corrupt, inefficient, and lazy.

There comes a time in the history of every great nation when they have to change the emphasis from "rights and privileges" to "duties and responsibilities."

There comes a time in the history of every great nation when they have to change from "borrowing and spending" to "savings and investment."

There comes a time in the history of every great nation when they have to re-explore the concept of "stewardship." When was the last time you heard a politician talk about "posterity"? When was the last time any politician reminded you that you had an obligation to your country?

Some Americans seem to want democracy on the cheap—as if you can always run a great country by constantly bribing people. But I do not think they are a majority.

Democracy is a fragile flower. No great nation can go through its history without having to make hard choices. FDR said it so well, "Of some generations, much is given. Of other generations, much is asked. This generation has a rendezvous with destiny." Truly, we have a rendezvous with destiny. We must have the maturity to face our problems realistically. There comes a time when every generation must be accountable.

America is not facing up to its problems. Mayor Tom McEnery says it so well. Our issues "only reach the front burner when they are burning." America needs a new agenda—a future-oriented agenda that is equal to the nation's problems. It needs new leadership. It needs a new challenge.

We need a "Decade of Renewal and Reform"—an agenda that makes no promises except that we will be honest and tell the truth to get America ready for the next 100 years. An agenda that challenges the best in the American character rather than pandering to the worst. An agenda that has the generational honesty not to try to cut taxes by adding debt onto its children.

What would the men who fought that winter at Valley Forge—who left their blood in the snow—say about a political system that cut the gas taxes until next

January? Or about giving ourselves tax relief when we still face gargantuan deficits?

They would rise out of the grave and cry, "SHAME."

What would the soldiers who died (on both sides) at Gettysburg say about the negative campaigning that has already dominated this year? Or the process whereby we raise the funds to run for office?

They would say, "SHAME. THAT IS NOT WHAT WE GAVE OUR LIVES FOR."

What would those who fought on Normandy or Guadalcanal say to calling a 7 percent increase in Medicare—in an attempt to put it in shape so that it will be there beyond the year 2002—a "cut in Medicare"?

They would cry, "SHAME."

The North Star for America for the next decade must be to leave a better world for our children. We should take no special interest money and do no negative campaigning. We will not only pledge to balance the budget in a decade, but we must—absolutely must—show how we are going to do so—which will require stepping on many toes.

America needs an agenda that should not try to please all the people. Perhaps it should only try to win a plurality. America could be saved by a "principled plurality." An agenda that rallies a farsighted and patriotic 40 percent. An agenda that does not try to win the Radical Right and the Eagle Forum, or those who want to give tax relief in a time of unprecedented spending. An agenda that does not try to win the support of the trial lawyers and the open border liberals, or those who want to buy votes by adding to our children's debt. An agenda that is open and honest with the American public.

America's most difficult problems are "orphan issues." Neither existing party wants to take responsibility for them.

Financial responsibility is an orphan issue. The Republicans should be given credit. I believe they sincerely tried to balance the budget within the existing political system. But under the most conservative Republican agenda, we still add $1.8 trillion over the next seven years to our children's debt. President Clinton should be given credit for reducing the yearly deficit. But neither party has solutions equal to the magnitude of the problem. Debt is "economic cocaine." We are so addicted to putting our needs on our children's credit cards that we call a seven-year $1.8 trillion increase in the national debt "fiscal responsibility."

Everything in the federal budget must be on the table. You cannot make sense out of America's future unless you take on entitlements—unless you take on all the sacred cows in the federal budget.

Pete Peterson said it so well: "Trying to balance the budget without taking on entitlements is like trying to clean the garage without moving the Winnebago." That's the kind of straight talk we need.

America must get ready to retire the baby boomers. To do that we must,

- Raise the retirement age to qualify for Social Security.
- Reduce the cost-of-living adjustments (COLAs) to more realistically reflect real inflation.
- Slowly allow people to self-direct some of their Social Security money into self-directed pension plans.

I wish I could stop there—but that alone will not balance the budget. We must look at federal civil service pensions; we must look at military retirement; we must look at whether we really need 175 Veterans Administration hospitals; and we must look at farm subsidies, and sugar and tobacco price supports. We must crawl out into the political ''no man's land'' where everyone is firing at you—because that is where many of the solutions are to be found.

The second orphan issue is campaign and election reforms. At the hour of our greatest need, our political process stands in self-inflicted disrepute. A ''FOR SALE'' sign hangs over the American political system. The greatest correlation to getting elected in America is how much special interest money you pry from the system. America faces a looming crisis and cannot count on the normal political process to save it. Hypocrisy has become a way of life in our nation's capital. A national tragedy is about to take place. I use my words judiciously. It is nothing short of a tragedy. We are about to go through a whole election process and not have America's most pressing issues raised and debated. The tragedy is not that we are not going to come up with all of the solutions to America's problems, but that we are not even going to adequately discuss them.

Our campaigns are legalized briberies and our elections have become bidding contests, pandering to the public. But I suggest that the Republican and Democratic parties are never, of themselves, going to reform the election system. History shows us that institutions don't reform themselves. They need an outside force—like those of you here. When Gingrich and Clinton shook hands a few months ago in New Hampshire, pledging to enact real campaign finance reform, it was a hideous overblown metaphor made up of equal measures of hypocrisy and hype. Both they and their parties like the present bloated and corrupt system. They reject reform because they believe they can manipulate the existing system—and they can.

We need to find ways to take the money out of politics or, in the alternative, to find ways to get more citizens to support campaigns. We could give some tax credits to encourage small contributions from citizens to expand the financial base of campaigns. We should restrict all or part of a candidate's campaign funds to people in their districts. We should put further restrictions on special interest money. We should pass legislation granting candidates free TV and radio time. We should set limits on campaign contributions and spending. Most important, we must not only talk the talk, we must walk the walk.

Immigration is an orphan issue. America is rapidly developing a second underclass when it has not solved the problems of its first underclass. We cannot accept all the world's huddled masses. The Statue of Liberty has been hijacked by well-meaning, but mistaken, people. The Statue of Liberty stands for liberty. That is why the French government gave it to the United States. America has to make a choice—either it is going to give its first priority to its own poor, or are we going to give our first priority to the world's poor?

Emma Lazarus was poetic, but incorrect, when she asked for an unending stream of newcomers. Why do we want an America of 500 million people? I suggest that we, at a minimum, need to adopt the recommendations of the late Barbara Jordan Commission and stop illegal immigration and cut legal immigration at least in half.

The fourth orphan issue is to reform all America's public institutions. It is not only the election process that needs reforming. So does our legal system, our education system, and our health care system. America has developed dysfunctional institutions that must be reformed and renewed. We have too many lawyers and not enough justice; we spend too much on health care, but don't buy enough health.

The fifth issue—but perhaps one which subsumes all others—is the issue of values. For too long, this subject has been the polarized domain of zealots on one fringe or the other. It is time for the responsible, moderate mainstream of this country to engage this issue and recognize that it is central to our national crisis.

It is not enough to deal with our fiscal bottom line, though restoring fiscal sanity is a must. It is not enough to reform our institutions, though making them work again is vital. America is more than a ledger sheet. America is a people, a culture, a society, and we must regain our moral bearings and cultural integrity if we are to continue to nurture, to prosper, and to have our fortunes burn bright. A "Decade of Renewal and Reform" must begin with a rebirth of values.

A society which cannot delay gratification—which rewards consumption instead of savings—is not a society which can sustain itself.

A society seemingly unable to dissuade children from having children generation after generation is not a society which can remain successful.

A society in which children carry weapons along with their school books (or instead of their school books) is not a society in good moral health.

A society built on honoring fatherhood—which allows millions of fathers to financially and emotionally abandon their children—is not a society with an appropriate sense of shame.

A society which fosters dependency and raises victimhood to some exalted status is not a society with a lasting claim to greatness.

A society where the depiction of violence and promiscuity is the surest way to an entertainment hit is not a society on sound moral footing.

A society in which political discourse grows increasingly negative and trivial, and in which culture and human interactions grow increasingly coarse, is not a society which holds out the promise of a better tomorrow.

A society addicted to borrowing for today's indulgence and to putting the tab on its children's credit card is not a society with its values straight.

America needs a new agenda that

- is free of the special interests;
- educates but does not pander to the public; and
- calls upon people to give their best rather than appealing to their worst.

We need, in short, a no "BS" agenda.

There is no problem facing America that cannot be solved; no issue that cannot be made substantially better. We need an agenda which stresses patriotism, realism, restraint, common sense, and compassion. We need to go back to our historical roots. Historian Stephen Ambrose notes that history today "cheats children out of their heritage. Their legacy has been stolen—they look at the hole and not the donut." We need a positive agenda that

- is compassionate, caring—but realistic;
- is fiscally responsible and socially progressive;
- does not back down from telling the public the truth;
- believes and acts on the basic "political golden rule" that every generation must pay its own way;
- states we have a moral responsibility not only to pay our own way, but to leave a better America for our children;
- states citizens have not only rights and privileges, but duties and responsibilities;
- makes Americans understand that God is not an American who will protect us no matter how irresponsible, hedonistic or profligate we become.

We need a party that tells America what it needs to remain a great nation—not what it wants to hear so they can win the next election; and

- has an audacious belief in themselves. If we believe we can make a difference—then we may make a difference.

There comes a time in the history of all great nations when we have to ask, in the great words of John F. Kennedy, "What can we do for our country"— where citizens take personal responsibility and have a personal commitment.

I end as I began—with the entitlement problem. America must ask itself: Does either party have an agenda equal to the magnitude of this problem? Is either political party courageous and honest enough to solve this problem? Is either party free enough of special interests to solve this problem—or any of America's real problems? If the answer is no—then America needs a new political party.

CHAPTER 28

Postscript

Although over $1.5 billion was spent on the 1996 elections, voter turnout for federal elections declined by 6 percent compared to 1992. There were almost 100 million nonvoters in 1996. Voter turnout was the second lowest since 1824. An excellent source for federal election information is the Federal Election Commission (http://www.fec.gov/index.html). Curtis Gans of the Committee for the Study of the American Electorate (http://tap.epn.org/csae) says the downturn is related to citizen dissatisfaction over the use of campaign consultants and attack ads, *The Washington Times National Weekly Edition* (November 17, 1996).

There has been renewed pressure on Congress to pass campaign finance reform in 1997. Part of the pressure is related to revelations of illegal campaign fund-raising practices by the Democratic National Committee on behalf of President Clinton's re-election. An excellent article which chronicles how élites frame our political agenda through campaign contributions is "The Country Club," *Common Cause Magazine* (Spring/Summer 1996, 1250 Connecticut Avenue, NW, Washington, D.C. 20036). A comprehensive source for campaign finance reform is the Electronic Policy Network (http://epn.org/camfinre.html). For an excellent on-line discussion of the relationship between money and American politics see the Brookings Working Group on Campaign Finance Reform (http://www.brook.edu/GS/CAMPAIGN/home2.htm). Several states passed campaign finance referendums in 1996, including California, Colorado, Montana, Nevada, and Maine.

The Center for Responsive Politics (http://www.crp.org), the Working Group on Electoral Democracy (70 Washington St., Brattleboro, Vermont 05301), *The Buying of the President*, Charles Lewis (Avon, 1996), and *Dirty Little Secrets*, Larry Sabato (Times Books, 1996) are excellent sources on the relationship between money and American politics.

The movement for term limits continues at the state level. In 1996, nine states passed laws that would change ballots to include the identity of officeholders who refused to support term limits. These states were Alaska, Colorado, Idaho, Maine, Missouri, Nebraska, Nevada, and South Dakota. U.S. Term Limits (http://www.termlimits.org) is an excellent source of information about the movement.

One of the best sources of information on third parties is Richard Winger, who is the editor of *Ballot Access News* (Box 470296, San Francisco, California 94147). Although Ross Perot only received 8 percent of the presidential vote in 1996, his Reform party is eligible to receive public funds for the 2000 presidential contest. (http://www.reformparty.org). An interesting biography of Ross Perot is *Citizen Perot* by Gerald Posner (Random House, 1996).

Welfare reform continues to be vigorously debated at both the federal and state levels of government. A particularly controversial provision of the 1996 law is the cutoff of federal disability and food stamps benefits to legal immigrants. Another significant change is that states can now encourage faith-based groups to get involved in administering welfare services.

In 1997, $12 billion was restored to welfare programs. Many disabled legal immigrants and children were given welfare coverage which had been taken away from them in the 1996 legislation.

Wisconsin has been a leader in welfare reform at the state level. Andrew Bush of the Hudson Institute analyzes Wisconsin's efforts in "Replacing Welfare in Wisconsin" (http://www.hudson.org/Hudson). James Q. Wilson and Kathleen Sylvester critique past welfare policy and describe possible alternative policies in "No More Home Alone," *Policy Review* (March/April 1996). Workfare in Iowa is described in "Will Workfare Work?" *Governing* (April 1996). The Urban Institute (http://www.urban.org) provides a liberal analysis of welfare policies. Two books that criticize modern welfare policy are *Losing Ground* by Charles Murray (Basic, 1994) and *The Tragedy of American Compassion* by Marvin Olasky (Eagle, 1995). U.S. Senator Daniel Patrick Moynihan (D-N.Y.) opposed the 1996 welfare reform law. He writes about his efforts on welfare policy over the years in *Miles To Go* (Harvard University Press, 1996).

The National Religious Partnership for the Environment (http://www.nrpe.org) is an organization that seeks to connect faith and justice with environmental policy. The Sierra Club (http://www.sierraclub.org), Rachel's Environment and Health Weekly (erf@rachel.clark.net) and Friends of the Earth (http://www.foe.org) are excellent sources of information on the environment.

The same general type of reforms that Dick Lamm pushed in his presidential run can be found in speeches by the late Paul Tsongas and Tim Penny which were delivered to the International Conference Foundation in Minneapolis, Minnesota, *Vital Speeches* (February 1, 1996). The Concord Coalition is devoted to many of the principles that Dick Lamm stands for (http://sunsite.unc.edu/concord). You can investigate for yourself where our public debt stands from official figures from the Treasury Department (http://www.ustreas.gov/treasury/bureaus/pubdebt/penny.html).

Because of a strong economy, the federal deficit for fiscal year 1997 was projected to be under $40 billion. Although this is remarkable progress from the early 1990s, the deficit could start going up again after the turn of the century unless significant entitlement reforms are made.

There are many other organizations that are attempting to revitalize American democracy. One group is the American Initiative Committee (1320 Old Chain Bridge Road, Suite 220, McLean, Virginia 22101), which wants to allow voters the power to oppose and propose legislation directly through a national initiative. Another is Democracy 2000 (http://www.democracy2000.org), which promotes accountability in American politics. They have developed an idea called "interactive representation" which would energize citizens into increased and more effective political participation. In particular, congressional districts, voting procedures, and internal congressional rules would be reformed with the aim of making articulated priorities the focal point for all decision making. In this way, reaching consensus becomes the goal and standard operating procedure of Congress. The book that describes the theory is *Reinventing Congress for the Twenty-first Century* (MIT-Harvard Public Disputes Program, 1997).

Selected Bibliography

Bell, Jeffrey. *Populism & Elitism*. Washington, D.C.: Regnery, 1992.

Berry, Wendell. *Sex, Economy, Freedom and Community*. New York: Pantheon, 1993.

Boyte, Harry C., and Frank Riessman. *The New Populism*. Philadelphia: Temple University Press, 1986.

Brinkley, Alan. *Voices of Protest*. New York: Knopf, 1982.

Dionne, E. J. Jr. *Why Americans Hate Politics*. New York: Simon and Schuster, 1991.

Domhoff, G. William. *The Higher Circles*. New York: Vintage, 1971.

———. *The Powers That Be*. New York: Vintage, 1979.

Dugger, Ronnie. "Real Populists Please Stand Up." *The Nation*, August 1995, 14–21.

Edsall, Thomas Byrne, and Mary D. Edsall. *Chain Reaction*. New York: W. W. Norton, 1991.

Fallows, James. *Breaking the News*. New York: Pantheon, 1996.

Federici, Michael P. *The Challenge of Populism*. Westport, Conn.: Praeger, 1991.

Goodwyn, Lawrence. *Democratic Promise*. New York: Oxford University Press, 1976.

———. *The Populist Moment*. New York: Oxford University Press, 1978.

Greider, William. *Who Will Tell the People*. New York: Simon and Schuster, 1992.

Harris, Fred. *The New Populism*. New York: Saturday Review Press, 1973.

Hertzke, Allen D. *Echoes of Discontent*. Washington, D.C.: CQ Press, 1993.

Holmes, William F., ed. *American Populism*. Lexington, Mass.: D.C. Heath and Company. 1994.

Kazin, Michael. *The Populist Persuasion*. New York: Basic, 1995.

Lasch, Christopher. *The True and Only Heaven: Progress and its Critics*. New York: W. W. Norton, 1991.

———. *The Revolt of the Elites and the Betrayal of Democracy*. New York: W. W. Norton, 1996.

Lemann, Nicholas. "A Cartoon Elite." *The Atlantic Monthly*, November 1996, page 109.

Lerner, Michael. "Buchanan, Meaning, and the Economy." *Tikkun*, March-April 1996, page 9.

Lesher, Stephan. *George Wallace: American Populist*. Reading, Mass.: Addison-Wesley, 1994.

Lipset, Seymour Martin, and Earl Raab. *The Politics of Unreason*, 2d ed. Chicago: University of Chicago Press, 1978.

Mansfield, Harvey C. "Democracy and Populism." *Society*. July-August 1995, page 30.

McGuigan, Jim. *Cultural Populism*. New York: Routledge, 1992.

McKenna, George, ed. *American Populism*. New York: Putnam, 1974.

McMath, Robert C. Jr. *American Populism: A Social History, 1877–1898*. New York: Hill and Wang, 1993.

Menand, Louis. "The Trashing of Professionalism." *New York Times*. March 5, 1995, section 6 page 41.

Mills, C. Wright. *The Power Elite*. New York: Oxford University Press, 1957.

Perot, Ross. Foreword to *Preparing Our Country for the 21st Century*. New York: Harper Perennial, 1995.

Phillips, Kevin P. *Arrogant Capital*. Boston: Little, Brown, 1994.

———. *The Politics of Rich and Poor*. New York: Harper Perennial, 1991.

Pollack, Norman. *The Just Polity*. Urbana, Ill.: University of Illinois Press, 1987.

Populism: An Annotated Bibliography. New York: Gordon Press, 1994.

The Progressive Populist. January 1997. Special Report. Speeches from the founding convention of The Alliance.

Reich, Charles. *Opposing the System*. New York: Crown, 1995.

Riker, William. *Liberalism Against Populism*. Prospect Heights, Ill.: Waveland Press, 1988.

Wilentz, Sean. "Populism Redux." *Dissent*. Spring 1995, page 149.

Wilson, Clyde. "Up at the Fork of the Creek: In Search of American Populism." *Telos* 104. Summer 1995, page 77.

Zinn, Howard. *A People's History of the United States*. New York: HarperCollins, 1995.

Index

Abortion. *See* Right to life

Addiction. *See* Gamblers, problems of

Agricultural price instability, winners and losers from, 19

Aid to Families with Dependent Children (AFDC), 207, 209–10

The Alliance, xv, 82

Alliances, business, 23

Alves, Steve, 132

Ambrose, Stephen, 228

American Party of Texas v. White, 191

Americans with Disabilities Act (ADA): ambiguity of, 30; as amended by the 1991 Civil Rights Act, 29; benefits of, 36–37; costs of compliance, 33–34; lobbyists for, 29; original definition of, 28; possible reform of, 37; use of, 35

Antitrust laws, 119–20

Archer, Bill, 55–56

Archer Daniels Midland Co. (ADM), 19, 58

Atlantis/ADAPT. *See* Auberger, Mike

Auberger, Mike, 32–33

Bank of North Dakota, 73–74

Banking industry, 137

Baradat, Leon P., 186, 187, 192

Barbara Jordan Commission, 227

Beer II decision. *See* General Agreement on Tariffs and Trade

Bentsen, Lloyd, 55

Bergmann, Frithjof, 145–46

Berry, Wendell, 123–24

Bete, David L., Sr., 128, 130; organizing tips of, 133

Bible, 69, 152, 172; Genesis, 219; Psalm 24, 218

Bipartisan commission, on corporate welfare, 58–59

Blinder, Alan, 49

Blue-collar. *See* Manufacturing

Boehner, John, 180

Boxer, Barbara, 56–57

Braveheart, 93

Buchanan, Patrick J., xiv, 150–58; and Richard Nixon, 157; and the Republican party, 155–57

Byron, George, 181

Campaign finance. *See* Money

Canton, Mark, 89–90

Carlson, Dwight, 147

Carter, Arthur, 146, 148

Cato Institute, 53–55, 57

Center for Media Education, 24

Center for Responsive Politics, 24

CEOs. *See* Corporate executives
Chattanooga Free Press, 174
Chicago Board of Trade. *See* Futures, agricultural
Children: and gambling, 112; and health care, 67; and the national debt, 224; and popular culture, 88–89, 93, 96–97; and welfare, 211–12
Choice Care, 65
Citizens for Responsible Development (CRD), 126–27
Class system, 124, 162, 175, 179
Clearwater, Andree, 126–27
Cleveland Browns, 115–18, 160; community support of, 116
Clinton, Hillary Rodham, 17
Columbia Journalism Review, 45–46, 49
Commission on Presidential Debates, 193–95
Committees, "We're Against the Wal" strategy and tactics, 131–32
Communications Decency Act (CDA), 159
Communities, 70, 102, 120–21, 131–32, 141–43, 146, 149, 153, 218
Confidence, in governmental institutions, 174
Connecticut Party, 189
Conservative Party, 189
Constitutional convention, 179, 181; as a pressure tool, 182–83; and term limits, 182
Copenhagen Meeting Document, 190
Copper market. *See* Sumitomo Corporation
Corporate executives, 74, 77, 88–89, 140
Corporate welfare: and campaign finance, 58; cost to government, 53; definition, 52, 55; groups supporting cuts in, 55; non-partisan aspect of, 54; and President Bill Clinton, 55–57; and professional sports, 115–16, 119
Cost-benefit analysis, as applied to the ADA, 38
Cost-of-living adjustments (COLAs), 226
Cronin, Frank, 35–36
Cultural populism, xv, 84–85, 151–58, 161

deMeuers, Christine, 62, 64–65
Democratic Party: and corporate welfare, 55–57, and cowardice, 228
Department of Justice (DOJ), 31–32
Dionne, E. J., 191
Disabilities, types of, 35
Dorgan, Byron, 72–79
Drucker, Peter, 136, 138

Economic insecurity. *See* Unemployment
Economic justice, 144
Economic populism, xv, 1–2, 74–79, 82–83
Edwards, Ada, 99
Eisenhower, Dwight, 181
Endangered Species Act, 216–17
Entitlements, 222, 225, 228
Environmental protection: and Congressional opposition, 216–17; and religious support, 217–20
Equal Credit Opportunity Act (ECOA), 48–49
Establishment, 73, 155
Evangelical Environmental Network, 217
Export Enhancement Program, 54
Extortion, of cities, 121

Family values, and popular culture, 86–89, 92–94, 227
Fan Freedom and Community Protection Act of 1995, 119–21
Fans Rights Act of 1995, 115–18
Farmers, 18–20, 78
Farmers parties, 188
Federal Open Market Committee (FOMC), 42–44; secrecy of meetings, 44–45
Federal Reserve: and consumer issues, 47–49; fear of inflation, 41–42, 77–78; and growth rate of the economy, 41, 77–78; independence of, 43–44; and interest rates, 41, 44, 77; potential waste in, 46–47; power of, 42; relationship with banks, 43, 49; self-financing nature of, 46
Federal Trade Commission (FTC), 48
Federalist party, 188
Fetzer Institute, 145–46

Fields, Jack, 24
Fifteenth Amendment, 200
Forbes, Michael, 181
France. *See* Shorter workweek
Franchise relocation: financial incentives for, 116, 120; methods to minimize, 120–21
Franklin, Benjamin, 222
Free trade, 3, 74, 153–54
Freedom, 88–89, 91–92, 192, 199; academic, 100; and campaign finance reform, 175; and work, 146, 148
Freedom-to-farm bill, 78
Futures: agricultural, 16–20; copper, 13

Gag clauses, 65, 82
Gamblers: and families, 111–12; problems of, 107–9, 111–13; teen, 107–9, 113; treatment programs for, 110
Gambling: growth of, 109–10; and Iowa, 110; and Minnesota, 107, 110; and Mississippi, 112; and the work ethic, 109
Gardels, Nathan, 139
General Agreement on Tariffs and Trade (GATT), 5–7, 154; impact on states, 7–11; nontariff barriers of, 7
Geto Boys. *See* Willie D
Gingrich, Newt, 180
Glenny, Peggy, 156
Gonzalez, Henry B., 45, 47
Governmental populism (general), xv, 222–28
Graduate Employee Organization (GEO), 101
Grain companies, large, 19, 78
Greed, 123–24
Greenfield Community Preservation Coalition, 128–29
Greenfield, Massachusetts: and referendums, 127, 129–30, 132; and town council, 126, 129; and Wal-Mart, 126–28
Greenspan, Alan, 40–41, 77; involvement with savings and loans, 50; and the media, 45–46

Handicapped: mentally, 35–36; wheelchair, 35

Health Insurance Reform Act, 66–68
Health Maintenance Organization (HMO): definition, 63; and fee-for-service, 63; need for regulation of, 65, 82; practices of, 63–65
Health Net, 62, 64
Hedging. *See* Speculation
Heslen, Cynthia, 129; organizing tips of, 133
Hollywood. *See* family values
Honesty, 224–25, 228

Illegitimacy, 209–10
Immigration, 226–27
Incumbents, 173, 175, 180–81
Information superhighway, 25
Institutions, reform of, 223, 227
Internet. *See* Information superhighway
Interscope Records. *See* Time-Warner

Jacobs, Durand, 107–8, 111–12
Jefferson, Thomas, 1, 178
Jenness v. Fortson, 191
Jipping, Thomas, 180
Job Accommodation Network, 34
Juries: and citizenship, 197–98, 201, 203; and duty, 202–3; and the founding fathers, 198; and judges, 200; and reforms, 201–6; and states, 206; and voting, 199–200

K—Dog, 98
Kasich, John R., 53, 55–56
Kassebaum-Kennedy Bill. *See* Health Insurance Reform Act
Kennedy, Anthony, 199
Kennedy, Edward, 54, 56–58
Kennedy, John F., 153, 228
Kerrey, Bob, 24
Koslowski, Joe, 107
Kristol, William, 72–73
Kubach, Robert, 30
Kunin, Madeleine, 179

La Follette, Robert, 79
Lamm, Richard, 221–28
Lang, Herbert, 64

Lasch, Christopher, 84
Leontief, Wassily, 136
Limits, 223
Lincoln, Abraham, 178, 181
Lobbyists, 154, 167, 169
Lori L. Vande Zande v. State of Wisconsin Department of Administration, 38
Luxury boxes, 117

Manufacturing, 5, 136
Market Promotion Program, 54, 56–57
McCain, John, 56, 58–59
McCain-Feingold Bill, 164
McEnery, Tom, 224
Medicare, 225
Mergers, 23, 49, 65, 115
Mexico: and economic assistance, 154; and illegal immigration, 155
Money: and duties of legislators, 171–73; and electoral viability, 165–66, 168, 172, 226; and political equality, 169, 171; and the political process, 168–70, 226; and representative democracy, 168, 170–71; spent on elections, 164–66, 171–76, 229; and systemic corruption, 169, 226
Monopolies, 119
Moynihan, Daniel Patrick, 102–3
Munnell, Alicia, 49
Murdoch, Rupert, 23

National Conference of State Legislators (NCSL), 8–9
National debt and generational responsibility, 223–25
National Organization on Disabilities, 36
National Republican party (historical), 188
Negative campaigning, 225
Nelson, Thomas, 152–53
New Deal, 222–23
New Jersey Council on Compulsive Gambling, 108
New Work: definition, 146; and entrepreneurship, 147–49; and inner cities, 148–49
Newspaper editorials, 174

Non-profit organizations. *See* Volunteer organizations
Nonunanimous verdicts, 205–6
Norman, Al, 130–31; organizing tips of, 133

O'Neil, Kevin, 128–29
Organization of Petroleum Exporting Countries (OPEC), 154

Patriotism, 153, 224–25
Penny, Tim, 191
Peremptory challenges, 201–2, 205
Perkins, James, 149
Perot, H. Ross, 188, 193–94, 221, 223
Personal Responsibility and Work Opportunity Reconciliation Act of 1996, 207, 209–14
Peterson, Pete, 223, 225
Pfaff, William, 124
Political action committees (PACs), 154, 167–68, 171, 175–76; and legislation, 167–68
Pope John Paul II, 218–19
Popik, William, 62
Populism (general): as both liberal and conservative, xiv; definition, xiii; difficulties as an unified political movement, xv; expression of, xiii–xiv. *See also* Dorgan, Byron
The Populist Persuasion, xiv
Posner, Richard. *See Lori L. Vande Zande v. State of Wisconsin Department of Administration*
Power, xiii–xvi, 26, 92–94, 169–70, 173, 179, 183, 214, 222
Presidential debates, importance of, 193–95
Pressler, Larry, 24
Production: and computers, 136; and Hewlett Packard, 139–40; as a part of the economy, 75–76
Professionals, criticism of, xv, 153, 200, 202–4
Progressive Policy Institute, 55, 58

Raine, Louisiana, 153
Ranchers, 19

Reagan, Ronald, 158
The Recorder (Greenfield, Massachusetts), 126–27, 129, 131–32
Reform Party, 194, 228
Rehabilitation Act of 1973, 28
Reich, Robert B., 53–55, 58
Republican Party: and capitalism, 124–25; and corporate welfare, 55–56; and cowardice, 228; as a new party, 188; and populism, 72–73; and term limits, 180–81; and volunteerism, 142
Responsibility: and fathers, 99, 209, 211, 227; financial, 225; and Hollywood, 88, 92; and unemployment, 75–76
Right to life, 152; and Republicans, 152
RKG Associates, 127–28
Robber barons, 15; modern, 22; perception of, 25; personal wealth of, 23; political influence of, 24; potential reaction against, 26
Rohatyn, Felix, 49
Rollerblades, 76–77
Roosevelt, Franklin Delano (FDR), 224
Roosevelt, Theodore, 188
Rubin, Robert E., 55
Ruess, Henry, 47

St. Johns River, 218
Salvation Army, 69–70
A Sand County Almanac, 216
Sarbanes, Paul, 44
Schilling, Don, 47
Schlafly, Phyllis, 182
Sex. *See* Family values
Shaffer, Howard, 108
Shame, 89, 225, 227
Shorter workweek, 139–40
Simpson, O. J., trial, 196–97, 204
Social security, 222–23, 226
Soft money, 170, 173–74
Sophocles, 171
Speculation, 13–14, 16–20
Speech code: definition, 102; how it would operate, 103–4; unintended consequences of, 103
Sports Broadcasting Act of 1961, 119
Statue of Liberty, 227

Stewardship: and environmental protection, 219–20; and political reform, 224
Storing, Herbert, 198
Storming the Gates, xiv
Striptease, 93
Sugar industry, 57
Sumitomo Corporation, 13–15
Supply and demand, distortion of, 18

Talk shows, 96–97
Taylor, Blair, 31–32, 38
Telecommunications Act of 1996, 21, 23–24; possible effect on consumers, 24–25; possible effect on creators, 25; possible effect on jobs, 24–25
Television rating system, 159
Term limits: and Congress, 178–81; and public support, 178, 183; and states, 230
Third parties: and Florida, 189–90; importance of, 186–88, 191–92; and public financing, 189, 194
Third Parties in America, 191
Third sector. *See* volunteer organizations
Time Warner, 89
Tocqueville, Alexis de, 198–99, 206
Trade deficit, 75, 154
Transnational corporations, 75–76, 140–41, 152
Two-party system: characteristics, 186–87; and Britain, 190

Unemployment: and consumer demand, 138; and government, 141; and immigrants, 139; and the logging industry, 153–54; and the retail sector, 137; and technology, 135–38, 148; and violence, 138–39
United Nations (UN), 154
University of Massachusetts (UMass), and administration, 101–2, 104–5
University of Pennsylvania, 104
Uruguay Round. *See* General Agreement on Tariffs and Trade
United States Trade Representative (USTR), 9–10
U.S. Term Limits v. Thornton, 179

Values: and reform, 227; and welfare, 212–14

Violence. *See* family values

Volunteer organizations, 141–43; and income vouchers, 142; numbers participating in, 143; and tax credits, 143

Voter turnout, 187, 229

Vouchers, 211–12

Wacquant, Loic, 138–39

Wallace, George, 188

Walt Disney Corporation, 23

Washington, George, 182

Weber, Thomas, 147–48

Welfare, 99, 209; and child care, 210; and child support, 210–11; and felons, 210; and Judeo-Christianity, 213; and legal immigrants, 212–13; and public support, 213; and states, 210–11; and work, 210–11

Whig party, 188

Will, George, 179

Williams v. Rhodes, 191

Willie D, 98–99

Winner-take-all electoral system. *See* Two-party system

Winpisinger, William, 136

Wolves, 216

WTO (World Trade Organization), 3, 80, 154; enforcement power, 7

Yellowstone National Park, 216

Zajonc, Arthur, 146–47

Zenger case, 198

About the Editor and Contributors

KARL G. TRAUTMAN, editor, currently teaches political science in Michigan at Lansing Community College and Washtenaw Community College.

Akhil Reed Amar is Southmayd Professor of Law at Yale Law School.

Vikram David Amar is Acting Professor of Law at the University of California at Davis.

Bruce Babbitt is the U.S. Secretary of the Interior.

Constance E. Beaumont works for the National Trust for Historic Preservation in Washington, D.C.

Joe Biden is a Democratic U.S. Senator from Delaware.

Patrick J. Buchanan was a candidate for the Republican presidential nomination in 1992 and 1996.

Robert Byrd is a Democratic U.S. Senator from West Virginia.

Anthony Corrado is an associate professor of government at Colby College.

Robert M. Costrell is a professor of economics at the University of Massachusetts at Amherst.

Mike DeWine is a Republican U.S. Senator from Ohio.

Brian Doherty is assistant editor of *Reason Magazine*.

Bob Dole was a U.S. Senator from Kansas and Republican presidential nominee in 1996.

Byron Dorgan is a Democratic U.S. Senator from North Dakota.

Russ Feingold is a Democratic U.S. Senator from Wisconsin.

Suzanne Fields is a columnist for *The Washington Times*.

Michael Gray is a graduate of Western Michigan University.

Howell Heflin was a Democratic U.S. Senator from Alabama.

Martin R. Hoke was a Republican U.S. Representative from the 10th District of Ohio.

Steny Hoyer is a Democratic U.S. Representative from the 5th District of Maryland.

Paul Jacob is the executive director of U.S. Term Limits.

John Kasich is a Republican U.S. Representative from the 12th District of Ohio.

John Kerry is a Democratic U.S. Senator from Massachusetts.

A. V. Krebs is director of the Corporate Agribusiness Research Project in Everett, Washington.

Paul R. Krugman is a professor of economics at the Massachusetts Institute of Technology.

Richard D. Lamm unsuccessfully ran for the Reform party's presidential nomination in 1996 and is the director of the Center for Public Policy & Contemporary Issues at the University of Denver.

Ralph Nader is a consumer advocate in Washington, D.C.

Julia Raiskin is a student at Harvard University.

Ronald A. Reno is a research associate in the public policy division of Focus on the Family, based in Colorado Springs, Colorado.

Joan Retsinas is a sociologist who writes about health care in Providence, Rhode Island.

James Ricci was a staff writer for *The Detroit Free Press*.

Jeremy Rifkin is president of the Foundation on Economic Trends in Washington, D.C.

Marge Roukema is a Republican U.S. Representative from the 5th District of New Jersey.

Charles M. Sennott is a staff writer for *The Boston Globe*.

Jonathan Tasini is a writer in New York and president of the National Writers Union.

Cynthia Thomas is a staff writer for the *Houston Chronicle*.

Fred Thompson is a Republican U.S. Senator from Tennessee.

William T. Waren works for the National Council of State Legislatures in Washington, D.C. where he serves as a federal affairs counsel.

Dave Weldon is a Republican U.S. Representative from the 15th District of Florida

Paul Wellstone is a Democratic U.S. Senator from Minnesota.

Richard Winger lives in San Francisco and is the editor of *Ballot Access News*.

Aaron Zitner is a staff writer for *The Boston Globe*.

ISBN 0-275-96023-4

90000>

9 780275 960230

HARDCOVER BAR CODE

EAN